From the moment she first stepped ↑
resilience has represented the spirit of
newcomers along their journey in the land of opportunity, *Spared*
delivers a gritty, resourceful road map to help them overcome
obstacles and achieve their dreams. As a fellow alumnus of
the University of Northern Iowa, I'm proud to see Dr. Msengi
continue to blaze trails of hope for those seeking to follow in her
footsteps.

US Senator Chuck Grassley

Having had the opportunity to visit the Kigali Genocide Memorial
in Rwanda, I now realize the absolute horror this must have been
for those who lost loved ones. From the opening pages of her
book, Clementine Msengi thrusts the reader into the suspense in
a manner that leaves no doubt about the fragility of life.

The ensuing events are even more dramatic, illustrating
the power of the human spirit to not only survive, but thrive,
despite the most challenging circumstances. This true story of
the transformation of one courageous human being sets out to
prove how compassion, mental strength, and resilience can open
the doors of opportunity and unite people everywhere.

Spared is an essential read for a world that desperately needs
healing.

Les Hewitt, coauthor of the number one New York Times bestseller
The Power of Focus

If this memoir is difficult to read, imagine living it. It is at
once heartbreaking and inspirational. To survive the Rwandan
genocide where trusted family friends feel no remorse at
disfiguring an infant and viciously murdering entire families is

remarkable. To not only survive but to embrace faith in God's grace, to go on to live a joyful life and to build a loving family—this riveting memoir will take your breath away.

Sue J. Mattison, PhD, Provost, Drake University

Clementine Msengi has a powerful story to tell of survival in a world that can be beyond cruel. But *Spared* is a true story that goes beyond mere survival and instead through the power of resilience and courage becomes a story of hope. Clementine is an ordinary girl who grew up in Rwanda during the genocide. Yet in the midst of horrifying experiences, she tells an extraordinary story of how the human spirit can achieve the seemingly impossible. In *Spared*, Clementine reminds us that one's dreams must not be consumed by tragedy. Instead, she encourages us to fuel our dreams with hard work and courage for the future.

Sandra Harris, PhD, Professor Emerita

Spared is absolutely riveting! As you accompany the author during her harrowing experience in Rwanda during the genocide, you feel as if you are experiencing it firsthand. You will be able to feel her fear as she ran from those who sought to kill her. This book shows how God moved in the author's life to orchestrate her escape from the hands of those that hoped to end her life. This is an emotional read that will leave you admiring her character, as well as her strength.

Linda Tait, Lamar State College, Port Arthur, Texas

I find Dr. Clementine Msengi's memoir, *Spared*, both compelling and insightful. *Spared* illuminates the complexities of cultural conflict within the context of many social constructs as she flees from her home in Rwanda, and ultimately comes to the United States to begin life again. Clementine's life presents a broad spectrum of teaching opportunities: resilience, leadership, how to face conflict, true friendship, the challenges of cultural assimilation, and the role of faith and friends in crisis. I find *Spared* valuable as a teaching tool in high school or college settings, in my role as a caregiving consultant, and also in my work as a consultant on post-traumatic stress disorder. I would also recommend it to social workers and those who work with emigrant and refugee populations.

Shelly Beach, Waterloo, Iowa

I had the privilege of meeting Clementine Msengi soon after she arrived in the United States. Not long afterward, she shared her story with me. I was deeply moved by her tenacity and determination to overcome the horrors she had endured during the Rwandan genocide. And I was equally struck by her lack of bitterness. How could she respond with such grace to injustices committed against her? That question is answered in her book, *Spared,* which is an inspiration to me.

Across our tumultuous cultural landscape, we need voices like Clementine's more than ever before. Her story of resilience will resonate with millions of readers across the world who are struggling with resilience, not only from trauma in their personal lives, but also from the effects of the pandemic, lockdowns, civil strife and their domino effects. Many have encouraged her for years to write her account. Now, she can finally share her story of resilience with a hurting world.

Stephanie Larson, Minneapolis, Minnesota

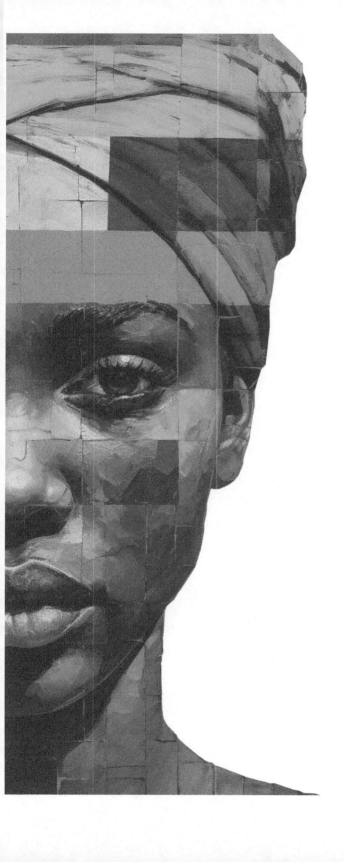

SPARED

Escaping
Genocide in
Rwanda and
Finding a Home
in America

*A True Story
of Hope and
Resilience*

CLEMENTINE M. MSENGI, EdD

credo
house publishers

Published in the United States of America by Credo House Publishers,
a division of Credo Communications LLC, Grand Rapids, Michigan
credohousepublishers.com

ISBN: 978-1-62586-270-9

Unless otherwise indicated, Scriptures are taken from The Holy Bible, New
International Version®, NIV® Copyright © 1973, 1978, 1984, 2011 by Biblica,
Inc.® Used by permission. All rights reserved worldwide.

Cover and interior design by Frank Gutbrod
Editing by Elizabeth Banks

Some names and places have been changed to respect the privacy of people
represented. Not everyone whose story was or is attached to mine chooses to
have his or her identity revealed.

Spared is based upon my best recollection of excruciatingly traumatic events
in my life, followed by years of challenging changes. The book was written to
provide insight and perspective on dealing with suffering and loss and is not
political in nature.

Printed in the United States of America
First Edition

CONTENTS

DEDICATION

*This book is dedicated to my late parents
and siblings.*

To my wonderful mother, who carried me nine months in her womb, gave birth to me, nurtured me, and taught me the valuable lessons that carried me through life, even when she was no longer physically with me. While you are not here with me now, I feel your presence each day, and your courage runs through my veins. Thank you, Mama. Rest in peace, dear Mama.

To my loving father, you left us before you had the opportunity to sit in the honored father's chair and grant permission for your daughter to marry. You fought the system of injustice until your last day. I must admit that I have seriously missed having a protective figure, a person to call me daughter. I missed the opportunity to walk with you and my mother in your old ages because you never had the chance to grow old. Thank you, Papa, and rest in peace, my Papa.

To my lovely older brother, I will never forget your smile and unselfish, protective nature. I saddens me that you never had a chance to get married and have your own family. I detest thinking what you had to endure as a twenty-four-year-old young man. Thank you, my dear brother. Rest in peace.

To my precious little sister, we prayed together, fetched water, harvested beans and potatoes, studied together, and shared secrets. You were my best friend and trusted confidant. I will never forget you. It is too bad that I never had a chance to see you graduate, mentor you, and share laughter and joys with you. I loved you, dear sister. Thank you for the beauty you brought to the world. Thank you, dear sister, and rest in peace.

To my beloved younger brother. You loved to study and dreamed of being a doctor. Your dream was cut short. You were only sixteen. I miss the opportunity to mentor you, dear little brother. Your helpful spirit blessed our family. I will always remember our walks. Your loving spirit inspired me and fed my spirit. Thank you, dear little brother. Rest in peace.

THE ROOTS OF HATRED

I grew up in a tight-knit, loving family in western Rwanda, East Africa. Rwanda's magnificent green rolling terrain is nicknamed "the land of a thousand hills." Here, my parents instilled deep-seated values in their seven children: faith, hard work, compassion, and perseverance. I grew up striving to reach my highest educational potential so I could one day contribute to the well-being of my family, community, and society.

Both my father and mother were protective, involved parents. They taught us to respect all people and hosted guests from all ethnicities and walks of life who were treated like family members. I was raised in a Christian home and the Presbyterian Church, and most of my friends and their families claimed this same Christian faith. It wasn't until I was fourteen and moved away to an all-girl Catholic boarding school managed by nuns in southern Rwanda, that I became closely aware of other religious affiliations.

My primary education was taught in my native language of Kinyarwanda. I was introduced to French—the language of instruction in my secondary school—when I enrolled in fourth grade. I grew up in what appeared to be a fairly homogenous national culture where issues of language, national origin, and even skin color were seldom a problem. However, below the surface, tensions continually simmered—based on ethnic divisions, religious rivalries, regionalism, and social class— threatening to boil over and tear apart our delicate social fabric.

In 1994, Rwanda's population consisted primarily of three tribes: Hutu (85 percent), Tutsi (14 percent), and Twa (1 percent), a native Pygmy group.

The precarious nature of my Tutsi heritage is rooted in tribal rivalry between Tutsi and Hutu that became a perpetual force in Rwanda after World War I. This tension was cemented after 1922, when Rwanda became a Belgian trustee under a League of Nations mandate. The Belgian ruling class favored the minority Tutsi, which spurred resentment among the Hutus. Finally, in 1959, pent-up fury spilled over into a violent Hutu revolution, which forced 330,000 Tutsi to flee the country. My parents were survivors of this first anti-Tutsi violence.

Tumultuous years followed. By early 1961, Hutus had forced Rwanda's Tutsi monarch into exile and declared the country a republic. In 1962, Belgium granted Rwanda independence. In 1973, a military group installed Major General Juvénal Habyarimana, a Hutu, into power. During the course of Habyarimana's rule, tension between the Hutus and Tutsi increased even further. During those days, the national government implemented a policy of discrimination using identity cards, which recorded every citizen's ethnic background.

Little did I know that just two decades later, these identity cards would become tools for extermination.

In early 1994, I had just completed my secondary schooling and was filled with aspirations about launching into adult life and becoming a contributing citizen. Unfortunately, events took a sudden and drastic turn. On April 6, 1994, a plane carrying Habyarimana and Burundi's President Cyprien Ntaryamira was shot down over Rwanda's capital city of Kigali, leaving no survivors. The party responsible for the ambush was never conclusively determined, but the brush fire of revenge had been lit.

Within minutes of the crash, the presidential guard, with members of the Rwandan armed forces (FAR) and Hutu militia groups Interahamwe and Impuzamugambi, set up roadblocks and barricades. As if on a prearranged signal, these groups began slaughtering Tutsis at will. Government-sponsored radio stations began calling on Rwandan civilians to murder their Tutsi neighbors. In fewer than one hundred days, almost one million people (mostly Tutsi) were murdered, chiefly through the gruesome use of machetes. The lush land of a thousand hills became a killing field, soaked in crimson and littered with crumpled bodies.

The wholesale slaughter finally came to an end after the Rwandan Patriotic Front (RPF), a predominantly Tutsi military organization stationed outside Rwanda, took control of the country. Nevertheless, the damage was done. These barbaric acts, deeply rooted in a system of hatred and discrimination, decimated and ended the lives of many—including members of my family.

This memoir is the story of my escape—not only from those who wanted to kill my body, but also from those who wished to destroy my spirit. It is also a story of hope and the power of faith and resilience, describing the human capacity to rise above life's greatest horrors and create positive changes in the world.

Today, as an academic in America, I share how universal human experiences can unite us and encourage us to leverage our individual power and influence to promote compassion, comfort, hope, interdependence, collaboration, and overall goodness in the world.

CHAPTER 1

THROUGH THE DARKNESS

Friendship is the shadow of the evening, which
increases with the setting of the sun.
—Jean de La Fontaine

Darkness crushed my chest, forcing the breath from my lungs as I crouched near the front door of the small, abandoned house where I had hidden. My legs and back cramped, and I bit my lower lip to keep from moaning. I was numb with fear, but I forced myself to remain in control. The slightest noise could mean my life. I'd been hiding inside this house too long, and Hutu forces were coming to search it.

I tried to pull my thoughts away from my parents, brothers, and sisters—where they might be or the bloody death they may have already faced. I forced scenes from my mind, knowing that if I lingered for a second too long, I would lose control.

"We must go," Amaza whispered—one of a handful of courageous Hutu men and women who became my family as

I fled for my life during the Rwandan genocide. He and Jacob, another friend I regarded as a brother, had only minutes to lead me through the early morning darkness to a new temporary hiding place. They would leave me there until they could safely return and guide me to a more secure location.

Please, God, can I just collapse and sleep until this nightmare is over . . . except it will never be over. I am so tired I cannot think, and I do not want to think. I just want to be eating dinner at home, safe with my family again. How could this horror have happened so quickly?

Yet deep down, I knew the genocide had not come upon Rwanda quickly. Generations of anger, frustration, and self-centered struggles for power had ravaged our nation—just as the lust for power had historically fragmented many other nations.

But living in a fragmented society was not a choice I had made for my life. Like other world citizens, I found myself belonging to a club I had not joined, born into a culture and environment not of my choosing and with consequences that outweighed my choices. When Hutu leadership called for violent action against the Tutsi, the reaction had been immediate, visceral, and violent.

I shivered as I envisioned the challenge ahead. Amaza, Joshua, Jacob, and I would need to elude Hutu patrols as my friends led me to my hiding place—an abandoned, unfinished building. I would then silently scale two floors of an exterior brick facade, pull myself over the top of a roofless wall, then drop *silently* to the second story floor.

I had never climbed anything but trees. How was I going to scale a wall? And dropping to a floor from ceiling height without being heard below would require a miracle. While I was not a large young woman, I was pleasantly substantial . . . and had never been known for athleticism.

Silence would be critical. Hutu forces were patrolling the area, and I would have to drop into the building directly *above* the living quarters of my Hutu enemies. My heart pounded at the thought of moving from my hiding place.

Militant Hutu leaders were murdering people by the thousands and had reportedly massacred my friends and family members as part of their genocide against the Tutsi people. They were now searching for me and other potential survivors, and in minutes, they would be upon us. Their mission was to kill and destroy.

While I had always trusted in God, I did not want to die. I was barely out of my teens. Everything I'd worked for was ahead of me, but my dreams and goals were all tied to my parents and my family—making them proud and caring for them. If I survived, would I be an orphan? Would my brothers and sisters be alive? And would I have the strength to live alone in the world, if everyone else had been killed? How was I supposed to think about surviving when my heart was drowning in panic and grief?

My friends were taking me to hide in the open air on a roofless second floor directly above Hutu headquarters.

In the face of fear, we did not have the luxury of quitting. My future depended upon every choice I made. Our desperate plan was the best and only option my friends and I could devise. Searches and executions had escalated and forced us to act quickly. If we did not leave within the next moment or two, my life would end with the blows of a machete. I pushed away images of my parents', brothers', sisters', friends', and neighbors' dying moments as I took shallow breaths of the chill night air.

To my knowledge, I was the only surviving member of my family.

My losses seemed too overwhelming for my mind and emotions to comprehend, as if I was trying to swallow a hippopotamus. How was I supposed to push my way through the struggle of a shattered life on the outside when on the inside I wanted to lie down and curl up in a ball? Every step I took, every word I spoke felt like I was pushing a planet-sized boulder through hardening concrete. Fighting back by fighting for my life seemed too overwhelming for words.

Friends, neighbors, and prayer partners had committed to help me. The Rukundo family, who were our neighbors, hid me from the assassins for as long as they were able. Amaza, who was my prayer partner, kept track of where I was and decided where I should be hidden next. He also monitored the location of the Hutu forces looking for me. My friends responded from a deep well of compassion and sacrifice that flowed from their faith. Their courage and selflessness were bizarrely juxtaposed alongside the hatred that drove fellow Rwandans to kill approximately one million Tutsi in the space of one hundred days between April and June of 1994.

Wherever we find hatred at its worst, we also find sacrifice and love for others at their best. This is the nature of good and evil in our world.

Amaza and I had become good friends and prayer partners soon after he joined a Bible study that I attended. I once saw him walking through our neighborhood looking for work and invited him in for a cup of hot tea and conversation. He was a refugee in Rwanda from Burundi. My parents had taught my siblings and me the importance of hospitality and compassion. He often seemed to be walking through our neighborhood alone, so I welcomed him into our home. Perhaps this simple gesture would help him feel welcome and give him a sense of belonging.

My friends handed me a piece of cloth for protection from the cool, early morning air and to hide my identity, and I quickly wrapped it around me. Then we stepped out of hiding, walking in shadows and behind anything that could provide cover. My friends chose a winding route to help us avoid detection. We walked between a road and a house where a pile of chopped eucalyptus trees shielded us.

When we arrived at the building where I was to be hidden, we spotted a group of Hutu militants gathered near the front door. My heart felt as if it stopped beating as we walked stealthily behind a stand of eucalyptus trees, then slipped behind the house.

My friend Jacob whispered and pointed to a gaping hole in the ground near the rear wall. Gesturing, he warned me not to lose my grip as I climbed, lest I fall into the cavernous cavity—a latrine. Thank heaven it hadn't been used.

I wanted to cry. I did not need *another* obstacle to make the plan more impossible. Certainly, the latrine must have been added for comic effect, but I saw nothing funny about my circumstances. I doubted that I would ever laugh again.

A latrine, God. Really? As if climbing this wall wasn't impossible enough?

My eyes ran up and down the height of the exterior brick wall looking for chinks to cling to as I climbed. I could see none.

God, please send Your angels to help me climb to the top of this wall and catch me when I jump to the other side. And please allow just one angel to stay with me while I wait for Amaza and Jacob to come back. I don't know how long I'll have to lay silent through the heat of the day and the cold of the night without food or water. I cannot do this without Your help!

I pushed away thoughts about the many risks in the plan because nearly every part of it seemed ludicrous. I would be acting in total faith. Only God could protect me. But it was our only option, so we forged ahead in faith.

I shook as a sense of powerlessness gripped me, and for a few paralyzing seconds I felt as if I could not breathe. I tried to pray, but words would not come. God knew my needs and heard my unspoken cries as I stared at the wall in front of me.

My circumstances required immediate, focused action. I didn't have time to grieve the drastic changes in my life, my monumental losses, or bewail what I could or could not do. Crisis required me to live in the moment. In trauma, we fight, flee, or freeze. I could either face danger, flee, or face death like thousands of fellow Rwandans. As I prepared to ascend the wall, my friends Amaza and Jacob encouraged me to be brave and steadfast. They envisioned a goal that would save my life.

Focus on one handhold at a time.

I repeated the sentence over and over as Jacob lifted me onto his shoulders. I struggled to stand and gain my balance, then reached for the wall and searched for gaps and toeholds in the brick.

Dear God, help me. I cannot do this.

I focused on one handhold at a time. Slowly, I pulled myself up several tiers of bricks, clawing for handholds and pressing my feet into the wall to gain a grip. I dared not look down as I fought my way to the top, my arms and legs burning like fire. After what seemed like hours, my fingers curled over the top of the wall of the second floor. My spirit heaved a wordless prayer of thanks. Unseen hands and the prayers of my friends below had lifted me. I was still terrified that I would lose my grip and fall backward into the latrine pit, but I channeled my fear toward my goal.

My friends murmured encouragement for me to be brave. They knew that I sometimes needed a whisper of hope.

I gripped the sharp edges of the bricks and prayed. Then I flung one leg over the top of the wall followed by the other and jumped as lightly as possible to the floor, tumbling into mud and water as I rolled to break my fall. I froze, face down for a moment.

By the grace of God, I had done the impossible! I was dirty, wet, and scraped, but I was alive!

However, reality loomed. I was alone. I had no food or water. I would be lying on concrete in the open air and exposed to the elements—searing sun during the day and chilling cold at night. My only protection during the day would be to position myself near an obstructing wall.

I could not sneeze.

I could not cry.

I could not move.

I could not make a sound. My only protection would be to lie motionless. I did not know how many days I would need to remain silent and still before my friends could safely return. Thinking about the dangers and the unknown made me panic, so I silently sang hymns and quoted Bible verses. They became my weapons of warfare and sustained me for hours as I listened to the sounds of my enemies below. But as time passed, doubt and fear crept back into my mind.

How could I believe I could survive in the same building Hutus used as their home base?

Then, almost in answer, I heard my father's gentle voice in my mind and felt my mother's calming hands stroke my head.

Success is determined one moment at a time, one wise decision at a time. Be patient with yourself and persist, Mukeshimana. You will attain far more than you believe possible.

I repeated my father's wisdom to quiet my pounding heart. After a time, I realized that the conversation below me often erupted into arguments. So, when fighting began again, I slowly pulled myself toward the closest wall and pulled my body into the shade. I could hear my Hutu enemies talking about what they were preparing for their evening meal and praising one another for how many Tutsis each of them had killed. Beyond the house, the voices of adults and children drifted in the breeze on a nearby path.

That night I slumped in a corner against a cold brick wall as my enemies' murderous stories drifted up through the inky blackness. I tried to block the sound of their voices, but their words assaulted my mind like rounds from a gun and stirred images of the carnage of war. My only distraction from my mental torment was to focus my thoughts on Scripture.

Mosquitos swarmed my body. I futilely tried to sweep them away, but they kept coming. They flew up my nose and into my mouth and ears, and I clenched my teeth to keep from crying out and slapping them. I eventually fell asleep, exhausted and shivering.

I awoke the next morning numb with cold and bleeding from bites I'd clawed raw. Hollow with hunger and aching, I was grateful to be breathing. I focused on the sounds of birds and rustling trees, reassuring myself I was not alone. I repeated to myself over and over that Amaza and Jacob had not forgotten me and would never abandon me. They had promised to return as soon as it was safe, and they would come.

Being alone was one of my greatest fears. The thought that my family was dead swept over me in swells like a raging river. More than once I'd been told that everyone had been killed. The thought was too terrifying to think about, but alone on the rooftop, images of their deaths tortured me. In mere hours I'd been ripped from my family and left to fend for myself. I cried out to God over and over again, silently screaming questions that tore my heart.

To live through such instantaneous betrayal left me in shock. Yet Amaza and Jacob and the Rukundo family had never wavered.

The second day dragged by, and I lay as still as possible, tormented by ravenous mosquitos. Although I was miserable and famished, thirst tortured me most. I envisioned every beverage that had ever quenched my thirst. I fixated on the thought of a sip of water and the sweet banana juice our mother made for us as children. I replayed every swallow of the Fanta soda my father had bought for me. I eventually drifted into a daze as I stared at the mud around me.

My mind faded into a fog as I obsessed about mud.

Mud contained water.

My body needed water.

Depleted by exposure, exhaustion, and dehydration, I found the mud strangely appealing. I finally decided that it could make an adequate meal for someone starving and in desperate need of water. Rainwater had puddled in low spots on the floor. As I pondered how to scoop some into my mouth, I fell asleep and dreamed that a friend gave me a glass of clean water. I drank until I finished it and then smiled as I extended the glass for more.

I awoke on the third day and desperately planned my escape. The nights had gotten colder, and it was now excruciating for me to lie still. Every muscle and bone in my body cried out in constant agony. I couldn't moan, shift position, or shield my face from the sun to protect my burning my eyes. A groan or a shift in position could cost me my life.

I still had not swallowed a drop of water. My throat was so dry from dehydration that my only choice was to sip water from a puddle or die. But placing my lips in a puddle only allowed me to suck droplets. Even after multiple attempts, I couldn't get enough to slake my torturous thirst. I finally gave up, more disappointed than I was before I tried. I wondered if my torment was a shadow of the eternal thirst and pain of hell. I knew I was on the edge of delirium, but my only choice was to lie still and trust that Amaza and Jacob would come. If my body had allowed me the luxury of tears, I would have cried. I eventually fell asleep lying in the mud.

During that terrible night, I made a silent promise to God.

My strength is gone, and I am totally helpless. If You save me, God, I will tell the world about Your mighty works for me for the rest of my life.

In the still of the night on the fourth day, a voice quietly called my name.

I thought I was hallucinating or perhaps dying, but when the voice called a third time, I recognized it as Jacob. Relief rushed through me like water overflowing the riverbanks during rainy season. Sobs rose in my chest. I slowly pulled myself toward the sound of Jacob's voice until I saw arms stretched up to help me over the outer wall.

Jacob's eyes widened in fear at his first glimpse of me. For a moment I was afraid he'd spotted an approaching enemy in the distance. Later he told me that he was shocked by how distorted my face and limbs had become from the bites of feasting mosquitos.

But my suffering was over—at least for a time.

I would soon be given food and water to restore my body.

I would sleep in a clean bed.

I would be taken to a welcoming home and be surrounded by friends.

I was no longer alone.

I had survived. As I followed Amaza and Jacob through the darkness back to their home, I realized that no matter how I'd *felt*, God *had been with me* every moment, giving me strength. Yet still, I had suffered greatly.

Days without water, as well as forced silence had taken a toll on my vocal cords. When I arrived at my "hiding" family's home, my voice was so hoarse that I could barely speak. As I rested my vocal cords so they could recover, I devoured my Bible. I had felt abandoned while I was hiding, but God comforted me through His Word and reminded me that He never left my side. He took me to Genesis 16:13: "You are the God who sees." He used this verse to reassure me of His oversight, even in my darkest hours.

Yes, I had felt abandoned, but feelings do not dictate reality. God had attended to every detail of my escape. He had miraculously brought Amaza and Jacob back to safely retrieve me from my dire circumstances. When all seemed lost, He brought me safely through the darkness and remained at my side watching over me.

Although my circumstances had not changed, I was comforted to know that God was working in ways vastly beyond my comprehension. I learned that no matter how I felt, God was with me every moment, giving me strength for the next breath. My parents had instilled this confidence deep within me. Over the following month, I would draw from that strength again and again as I fought to survive.

CHAPTER 2

WATERFALL DAYS

Children are the living messages we send to a time
we will not see.

—John F. Kennedy

The water swirled around me in shimmering ripples of iridescent light. I wiggled my toes and watched the current deflect in sparkling undulations. The water flowed over my feet in soft caresses, and I breathed in a deep sigh of contentment to the backdrop of my friends' laughter.

"Mukeshimana, come play in the water with us!"

In the distance my friends called to me from close to the waterfall. Most of the girls loved to splash in deeper waters where the waterfall unleashed its energy in cascades of tumbling, rushing ribbon that swirled into eddies and whirlpools in the catch basin below. I preferred quieter waters downstream, where I could lie upon large, flat rocks big enough to take naps on with private hordes of wild, freshly picked raspberries and strawberries. Today, the berries had finally ripened to the perfect sour-sweet flavor I loved.

Saturday afternoons were my sacred time. In the morning, I gathered with the girls from our neighborhood at the waterfalls to wash our clothes and clean ourselves in preparation for Sunday.

After eating breakfast with my family on Saturdays, I walked the trail from our home to the nearby stream and waterfall for my weekly sacred time of refreshment with other girls from my community. The stream near our community was one of the bodies of water that fed the Nyabarongo River. Waterfalls are considered sacred spaces to Rwandans, and children often gather near waterfalls at the center of banana plantations or other places of natural beauty, to be mentored by older women in proper conduct, hygiene, character qualities, and home skills. Girls who are fifteen or sixteen typically invite younger girls to join the group. Boys from our community gathered a bit further downstream at a spot that was hidden from view from the girls, around a bend by thicker bushes and trees.

These gatherings were safe spaces where no one felt excluded or looked down upon because of their family, tribe, or social status. My years visiting the waterfall with my girlfriends deeply influenced my life. The focus was on positive nurturing, and everyone was encouraged to develop skills and a mindset that would help them thrive within our culture. We also learned practical skills, like how to weave a floor mat for the home we would have some day. This was an activity that stirred our imaginations in our teens, as we dreamed about the man we might someday marry.

One of the most beautiful aspects of this cultural element of mentoring was the sense of dignity, confidence, and grace it imparted to women. This was a by-product of the positive atmosphere of the meetings and the character-related lessons that flowed naturally from life and the personality of each leader. I met with girls from my community, and our friendships and connection naturally flourished because of our weekly meetings at the waterfall. We also spent time playing games, enjoying the water, and enjoying the Rwandan feminine tradition of smoothing the skin on our feet with stones.

One of my favorite activities was sitting or lying on one of the large rocks in the river and simply watching the water. Sometimes I brought my Bible and prayed. Other times I simply relaxed and allowed the beauty of nature to soothe my soul as I listened to the water. Even if I only had ten minutes to myself, time alone in nature was extremely important to me.

Even as a young child, I had placed very high expectations upon myself for grades. It was very important to me that I rank high because I desperately wanted to achieve an education that would allow me to get a good job that would help me contribute to both my family and community. Above all, I wanted to make high grades to make my parents proud. My Saturday afternoons were one of the few times during my week when I allowed myself the freedom to *not* worry about grades or homework. I watched the flowers and birds, listened to the water, and let my mind wander freely. Sometimes I fell asleep in the sun.

Each Saturday evening as the sun began to dim, our mothers stood outside our houses and called us home. Because we lived in a small community, we could hear the voices of all the mothers calling, their voices as distinct as bird songs. We soon recognized the varied tones of all the mothers, which I found strangely comforting. Over the years, the ritual of listening for the voices of mothers calling their children home became a symbol of the vital role of family and community in Rwandan culture.

Our family worshipped at the Presbyterian church in our town. I enjoyed sitting among my family and listening to the qualities of their voices in harmony. The songs in our hymnal stirred hope, peace, and confidence in God's protection. My hymnal was the second-most important book to me, after my Bible.

After church, our family always ate dinner together. Our Sunday dinners always included animated conversation and laughter—always laughter. Our family was often joined at meals by the many guests who frequented our home—some who remained for a few days of rest after a stay at our regional hospital before beginning the long walk home to their village. Other visitors lived with us for months or even years so they could attend the private secondary school in our town.

Tribal affiliations were not a concern to our parents. People were simply our friends and our guests, and everyone was to be respected. I grew up learning to get comfortable around new people, and I enjoyed it.

When I was a child, I often accompanied my father to the Presbyterian hospital on Sunday afternoons and carried his hymn book when he went to pray with the sick. I always walked extra tall when I "assisted" him. "Helping" my father minister to people was an important responsibility in my eyes, and I waited breathlessly for opportunities to talk to people who were sick.

My siblings and I were taught to help anyone in need. No guest that came to our door was ever turned away. My mother and father never asked anyone to contribute to our household expenses, no matter how long they stayed (sometimes for years) or how little we had. Our parents believed that everything we possessed was entrusted to us by God to be used for His kingdom and to bless His people. I was proud of their generosity and wanted to be like them.

The strong ties of family and community that threaded through my life and strengthened me as a child—a tight-knit family, compassion for all people, forgiveness for personal and social injustice, tribally mixed community practices—were shifting throughout my country. Tensions were rising, based to a great degree on misunderstanding and miscommunication. I have found this pattern to be the same from culture to culture and era to era. Leadership controls who hears what selected information, and people's attitudes shift commensurately.

Every Saturday evening my mother's voice announced that my sacred, personal time had come to an end. It was time to go home and prepare for church and the responsibilities of the following day. My reprieve would come again the following week, but I had homework to finish and chores to tend to. Waterfall days would return every week, the berries would be ripe for the picking, and the stream would still run fresh and sweet.

Except that it would not. In one instant, the beauty and joy would become a memory of a place I once knew that would never be again.

CHAPTER 3

STRENGTH IN THE SCARS

The most beautiful people we have known are those who have known defeat, known suffering, known struggle, known loss, and have found their way out of the depths. . . . Beautiful people do not just happen.

—Elizabeth Kubler-Ross

faced my mother across a rough wood table as I helped her prepare a midday meal of sautéed beans and bananas, with boiled sweet potatoes. I loved helping her cook, but I clasped my hands together tightly to stop them from shaking.

I will ask again today and persist until I learn the truth Mother and Father have been hiding from me.

I chose a sweet potato from a basket beside me. The question had tormented me for as long as I could remember, and although I was a child—old enough go to school soon—I believed I was old enough to know the truth.

Mother and Father would never do anything to harm me, I reassured myself as I chopped. But their many refusals to answer had fed my curiosity.

Why am I different from other children, and why don't Mother and Father answer my questions when I ask?

I carefully sliced through another potato, placed it in the large cooking pot in the center of the table, then looked into my mother's face as I pointed at my wrist.

"Mother, why does this scar circle my right wrist? No one else has a mark like this—not you or Father or any of my siblings. My friends ask me about it, and I do not know what to say."

Mother's knife froze in midair, and for a moment she did not speak. She quickly wiped the corner of one eye with the back of her hand when words finally came.

"Your father and I have told you this before. The mark shows the world that you are a special girl, Mukeshimana," calling me by my last name, as is the custom in Rwanda. Her lips were trembling, and her eyes had pooled with sudden tears.

"This does not answer my question."

She reached for a thin green banana. "We must finish preparing the meal so you can study, my child."

Her eyes darted in the direction of our *umukozi*—our babysitter and house helper, who was washing vegetables on the other side of the kitchen. Delilah's back was turned to us, and she continued washing pots as if she was deaf to our conversation.

Why had mother looked in Delilah's direction? And why did my question always upset her so much?

Delilah had come to live with us before I was born and had helped care for me from the time I was an infant. Her parents had been too poor to take care of her, and my parents had taken her in until she would be old enough to marry. Mother and Father had taught me to respect her and treat her like an older sister, and that is how I had always felt about her.

I continued peeling potatoes, but later that evening, I boldly knocked on my parents' bedroom door. Perhaps my father could answer me and calm my mother's fears. They both answered, and I entered their room.

"May I talk to you?"

My father nodded and invited me to sit beside them. They were seated side by side on the bed, and my father was holding my mother's hand. I repeated the question I'd asked that morning, hoping my mother would not be irritated.

"Where did my scar come from? I do not know how to answer when people ask me what it is."

My mother looked down, and tears dripped into her lap. Father paused, stroked my mother's hand, then began to tell me about my childhood, his deep voice edged with sadness.

I was born in a small western Rwanda town, where Father worked for a Presbyterian parish. Our town lacked a good hospital, so when I was about to be born, he and my mother traveled to a larger hospital in a nearby parish for better health care.

Child naming is a Rwandan tradition called *Kwita Izina*. When a child is born in Rwanda, parents wait seven days and then named their baby at a festive ceremony. During the ceremony, parents give the child a unique and significant first name. When I was young, mothers did not change their name after marriage, and siblings had different *first and last names*. The new baby is named by the father, family members, friends, and well-wishers.

My parents named me Mukeshimana Clementine. In Kinyarwanda, the common language of Rwanda, Mukeshimana means *the child given to me by God*. Clementine is a common name that represents Rwanda's French influence and my parents' enormous gratitude for my life, health, happy disposition, and their desire that I demonstrate gratitude and grace throughout my life.

My father continued talking about the simple life that drew our family together. I was nurtured by love, safety, security, and affirmation that flowed from my parents' words and actions. They often cradled me in their arms as they walked the path to the banana grove. We spent hours outdoors laughing, playing, and relaxing in the warmth of the sun. In the evenings, we gathered in the kitchen to enjoy the fire's warmth, singing, eating, and listening to my father's stories as my mother cooked on a simple wood slab placed atop three stones.

As he'd hoped, my fathers' stories distracted me from my question. I asked about the house we lived in when I was young. Father told me we lived in a modest home with a roof made of metal sheets that clattered when it rained. Skyscraping eucalyptus trees towered in front of our house, and the south side was shaded by a grove of majestic banana trees. On the north side, a path called an *inzira*, similar to a driveway, connected the houses and neighborhoods in our community to one another. Fragrant orange and lemon trees grew on the east side of our house, and I loved to suck on the fruit as a baby.

Fueled by my interest, my father continued and told me about my early love of soft, calming *kubikira* music sung by my father, mother, and grandmother. Kubikira were similar to nursery rhymes. A singer spontaneously makes up lyrics, following their creative leading. Kubikira songs were passed down orally and personally from generation to generation and were often created on the spot at impromptu family gatherings. I often fell asleep in the warmth and security of my mother's lap while listening to family and traditional songs. One popular Rwandan song I recalled with great fondness was titled *Ninde Undirije Umwana Yo Gacaracara, You Gacana Injishi, Ehee,* which means *Tell Me Who Makes My Child Cry So I Can Go After Them.*

We also told tales called *imigani.* My father was an excellent storyteller—skilled in creating fictional stories as well as in the skills required to tell them well. As my father talked, I envisioned family gatherings and the many hours I sat spellbound, listening to my elders tell stories. I loved my grandmother's stories. She seemed infinitely wise, and her lavish white hair gave her a regal presence.

Looking back, I see how my rich childhood experiences seeded security, love, belonging, purpose, and identity into my spirit, and I would carry these gifts with me for a lifetime. My love for family and intergenerational influences were driving forces during my time as a displaced individual and fed my need for connection when I came to the United States. I had not only lost family members in the war, but I'd also lost our life-giving family structure and longed to re-create that womb of nurture and safety.

Still determined to know the answer to my question, I asked my parents again why my right wrist was marked with a scar so deep that my arm was misshapen. This time I pressed further, asking if I had been injured or if someone had hurt me.

My mother's breath came in jagged sobs.

"My daughter, may your tenacity serve you well as you grow. The truth is that someone who hated your father and me hurt *you* to hurt us, Mukeshimana." She drew her hands to her heart as if to soothe the pain. "They poured their hatred on an innocent, helpless, two-month-old child."

Her tears flowed freely, and she pulled me into her arms.

"We kept the answer from you because the truth is very, very hard, but you *are* a special child, Mukeshimana, and older than your years. You will someday learn that you cannot always protect those you love from evil. People who allow hate to rule their hearts will justify any action—even harming an innocent infant."

I murmured agreement, disturbed by my mother's emotion.

My father solemnly explained that when I was born, tension and hatred caused conflict between people of differing ethnic groups and creeds, not only in our nation, but in our community. When I was two months old, a neighbor lady visited our home. When the neighbor picked me up, she embraced me, pleasantly congratulated my mother on my birth, handed me back, then left.

"She seemed truly happy about your birth. Her actions and words gave me no reason to mistrust her," my mother sobbed, and I nestled closer, hoping my hugs would reassure her.

"But several days later she returned when your father and I were not at home, Mukeshimana. If we had known the evil in her heart, we never would have left you that day—you were still a newborn. Our babysitter was tending you. Your father and I did not know that the neighbor woman had befriended your babysitter and convinced her to assist in amputating your right hand in return for financial reward."

I pulled away from my mother. What was she telling me? The same babysitter had taken care of me since I was born and *still* lived with us. Delilah helped care for me, cooking and helping with household tasks. My parents had taken her into our home when her parents were unable to care for her. This was a common practice in Rwanda—friends and neighbors often provided homes for children who otherwise would become homeless. Without my parents' kindness, this would have been Delilah's fate.

I began to shake inside as a fireball of emotion surged through me. *Delilah? Attempted to amputate my right hand? The girl who cooks my food and helps care for our household? She would be living in the streets without my parents' kindness!*

And they allowed her to stay! Why?

I felt as if I was going to be sick. My father slid his arm around mother's shoulder and pulled her close then spoke. "You asked us to tell you the truth, so we will tell you. The women devised an evil plan, Mukeshimana. The neighbor returned the next day, and she and Delilah attempted to sever your hand. Their goal was to disfigure you and leave you unable to write, attend school, or enjoy life. They wanted to make you an outcast. Jealousy and bitterness ate away the goodness and kindness in this neighbor's heart, and she wanted to do evil—to the point that she was happy to maim a newborn child and persuaded someone to help her. Asking other people to join in evil acts makes the people who do them feel right about their actions. Your mother and I saw this during the war between Hutu and Tutsi when we were first married. This neighbor wanted to destroy your mother's and my happiness by hurting you, our baby."

I stared at my scar, speechless.

My mother took my shaking hands. "Hatred, Mukeshimana, is like murder because we take joy in the suffering of others. I asked God to protect me from hating the woman who disfigured my child, and I asked Him to help me forgive Delilah. This is why she still lives with us, and we will provide for her as we promised her father, until she finds a home with a husband one day."

My mother wiped the tears from her face, then from mine.

"When your father and I left the house that evening, Delilah notified the neighbor, who came to our house and brought a zip tie, as she and Delilah had prearranged. They bound it tightly around your right wrist to block the flow of blood, which they believed would result in the loss of your hand."

I wanted to place my hands over my ears, but I willed myself not to move.

"Several hours passed before your father and I returned and discovered your right hand had swollen so much that the zipper was no longer visible. We were shocked and tried to figure out what could have caused this to happen. We searched for answers.

An animal bite? A venomous insect? I was so frightened for you that I could barely think.

"Delilah assured us that nothing bad had happened and suggested that perhaps you had made your way to hot water or a snake had bitten you."

I looked at my mother and shook my head. Even as a child, I knew that such an explanation was impossible.

She nodded. "Yes, we found her answer highly suspicious. Your father and I had never heard of a child being bitten by a snake in our community. And at only two months of age, you were unable to crawl, scoot, or make your way to a hot water source."

She stroked the scar on my wrist.

"Your father and I frantically tried various remedies to stop the swelling, but nothing worked. Several days passed, and the swelling engulfed your entire arm. We knew you needed medical treatment. Terrified, we took you to a dispensary where a doctor prescribed medication.

"The medicine did not work, Mukeshimana." My mother's eyes had grown dark, and she looked away from me. "We despaired of your life. We begged God to spare you.

"After a week of useless treatments, we took you to a regional hospital. I carried you on my back as your father and I walked for hours over our 'Land of a Thousand Hills.' But that was only the beginning. Once we arrived, we waited in long lines and couldn't be seen until the next day. We were fortunate—often a doctor with the right training is not available, and patients must walk even further to a larger hospital.

"The new doctor took an X-ray that revealed a zipper embedded in your arm. He decided you needed an operation."

I wiped a tear from my mother's cheek. In another room, I heard Delilah cleaning.

"We did not know the operation would be the beginning of your treatment. When the surgery was over, you were hospitalized for an extensive time to monitor your healing. Your father and I were in agony as we watched you struggle in pain. The doctors had dug deeply into your flesh in one area of the wound, and it would not heal. The surgeon had cut many nerves to get to the zipper, since it had become embedded so deeply.

"Exasperated, we were forced to take you to yet another hospital in a Catholic parish hours from our home. A nurse at this hospital poured powdered medicine into the wound. Two months later, praise God, your injury healed."

As my mother finished the story, she wiped the final tears from her face, then mine.

"Your father and I sought the best care we could for you, Mukeshimana. We thank God that He spared your life and your hand and has a purpose for you. But we will never understand how a heart could become so twisted by hatred that someone would harm an infant."

My mother's lips trembled, and my father pulled her head to his shoulder.

"God overruled evil, and the scar is His mark of protection and purpose," my father added. "It is also a reminder of our love and commitment to you. Remember, someone else's hatred is never justification for our hate. There is no middle ground with forgiveness—it is all or nothing, and God asks us for all."

I could still hear Delilah cleaning. The anger that had boiled up inside me had calmed to a simmer. I was a child, and I fought the urge to run from the room and scratch Delilah's eyes out as my mother held me tightly in her arms.

In one sense, I received my answer that day. My parents told me the facts regarding my scar, but the mysteries of hatred, spite, and forgiveness mystified me. In the years ahead, I would learn to forgive. As I matured, my anger at Delilah faded and was replaced by forgiveness. She had been an impressionable teenager at the time and had been persuaded by the twisted logic of an older woman. Certainly, I could see the power of such ruses throughout world history and the history of my own nation. But my heart ached for people who chose the poison of hatred and did not see its insidious and inevitable corrosive influences.

As I grew older, I learned that everyone bears scars. We can choose to look at them with shame, or we can view them as evidence of our resilience, inner strength, and courage. I realize now that who I am—my core identity—is rooted in something and someone greater than myself. Scars can show the world that we draw our greatest strength from a Source greater than the conflicting, subjective opinions of humanity. Through His grace, God would also give me strength to forgive the seemingly unforgivable—again and again.

CHAPTER 4

LESSONS FROM THE STICK

Education is not the filling of a pail,
but the lighting of a fire.

—William Butler Yeats

I sat high in an orange tree, my legs dangling as I drank in the pungent fragrance. The branches below me shielded my body from view. If I remained still, I might evade my older brother Zacharie's searching eyes. I loved when my brothers and sisters all played together, teasing, laughing, and always watchful of one another, like a flock of hens.

"Children! Come into the house for a talk."

My father's voice drifted into the orange grove, and I reluctantly climbed down the tree I secretly claimed as my own.

A talk. Whatever it's about, it can't be good.

Family "talks" were reserved for sad news, big changes, discipline, or unexpected announcements.

When we gathered in the kitchen, my father soon put my fears to rest.

"I have been offered a new job." His voice was reassuring.

I glanced at my brothers and sisters, and they all looked pleased. No one was in trouble.

"We will be moving to a different Presbyterian parish." Life would change, and our responsibility as children was to adjust. The decision had been made.

I was six and about to begin school in a new place. I would not see my friends after we moved, but moving would be an adventure, and new friends and a new house sounded like fun. Our parents had taught us to face challenges as opportunities to grow. Even at six, I'd learned I must choose my attitude, so I anticipated the changes with excitement.

One morning soon after our move, my mother told me she was taking me to a tailor who made school uniforms. I became so excited I could barely finish eating my sorghum meal. Girls at my school were required to wear dresses, and we could choose the design. My school color was blue.

As we walked to the tailor shop, my mother and I discussed options for the style of my dress . . . the collar, sleeves, buttons, and other details.

"My daughter, you must tell me what you want *your* dress to look like."

I had never been asked about my clothing preferences. I felt like an adult as I expressed my desire for feminine puffed sleeves and a neckline accented with white fabric.

Along the way, we came to a small bridge shaded by bamboo trees. The bridge consisted of two logs laid side by side over a narrow stream. My mother paused.

"You will cross this bridge often, Mukeshimana. Your father will be proud of you when we tell him tonight that you crossed it by yourself. I will show you how."

My mother and father taught us by placing a vision for success in our minds, then guiding us to help us achieve our goals. Learning always felt safe and exciting for me because my parents and my older siblings who helped me with my homework were positive. They were willing to show me or explain a concept several ways until I understood. My family members were my first teachers, and they instilled confidence in me. That day my mother walked with her arms outstretched to catch me as she gently encouraged me. I still remember the feeling of exhilaration as I crossed successfully to the other side.

We continued our walk to the dressmaker, climbing a hill, passing banana fields, venturing through a eucalyptus grove, and eventually arriving at the market where we found the tailor's shop on the front porch of a local pharmacy. Wooden tables were pushed against the railings and piled high with fabrics of assorted colors, prints, and fabric types. A long table against a wall held a sewing machine, scissors, measuring tapes, thread, and assorted buttons, zippers, laces, and other sewing needs. The sight of the colorful sewing supplies filled my thoughts with visions of beautiful dresses.

I sat on a wooden chair and waited as my mother told the dressmaker the details of our design. The man smiled pleasantly at me as Mother talked.

He waved his arm, inviting me to stand by his sewing machine. He was tall and wore a white shirt. Measuring tapes hung around his neck.

"You are a beautiful girl, and your dress will look beautiful on you," he reassured me as he took my measurements. His eyes smiled as he spoke.

I smiled back.

"Return in two days for the fitting."

We thanked him as we walked out the door.

My dress would be beautiful, and I sang as we walked home.

As we approached the bridge, my mother told me I would need to do one more thing to prepare for school.

"When we get home, I must shave your head."

All primary school children were required to shave their heads. A shaved head would identify me as a primary school student. I beamed with pride.

When we arrived home, my mother washed my hair, leaving soap in it to make it easier to run the razor over my head. When I went to bed, I ran my fingers over my freshly shaved head over and over. I was now prepared for school. Life in a new world was about to begin. The moon crept far across the sky before I finally fell asleep.

I sat in the kitchen gulping down my favorite breakfast dish—cooked meal mixed with sorghum flour. I'd gotten up early, worried that I might be late for school.

"Mukeshimana, give it time to cool so it does not burn your mouth." My mother peered at me with concern as she stirred a pot over our wood stove. But I shoveled in another cheek-puffing spoonful, barely noticing if the sorghum meal was hot or cold.

This was my first day of school. I needed to be on time. My dress had to look perfect. I needed to show my teacher I would be a *good* student.

You must make your parents proud, Mukeshimana.

I swallowed my last bite and raced to my room to get ready. After washing my hands and face, I slipped my uniform over my head like a wedding dress, then gathered my things, hugged my mother, and raced out of the house, certain that I would be wearing the prettiest dress in my class. Since it was the first day and I was a bit anxious, my father accompanied me. Our walk passed in a blur.

My school was housed on the Presbyterian Church property near our home. The church also offered a school for accountants, a theology department, and residence housing for pastors, evangelists, and missionaries. My father filled various roles in these ministries, and his presence comforted me as he walked me to my classroom. I didn't want anyone to know, but I was happy that my father worked in a building so close to my classroom.

He smiled and squeezed my shoulder, then turned and left me to walk into my room on my own. My heart pounded as I stepped into my first-grade class and smoothed my dress. I was a student now.

My first-grade teacher, Mr. Mugisha, had greeted my father and me at the door with a solemn nod. Our small classroom was stark: a blackboard and teacher's desk at the front and benches in rows for students. I chose a seat on a front bench close to the teacher's desk because I was short, and I wanted a clear view of the blackboard and Mr. Mugisha.

First-year students were not given desks. We were expected to hold our slates in our laps during our lessons. Desks, small tables for two students sitting side by side, were only given to upper-level students. I sat with my *urubaho* and *itushi* ready as my classmates filed in and filled the benches around me. A girl named Shushu sat on the bench next to me. We were good friends. Her father was a doctor, and I often played at her house, which sat behind a protective gate near the hospital.

Our first task was learning to greet our teacher when he came into the room. When Mr. Mugisha entered, we stood erect and said in unison, "Good morning, Mr. Mugisha." We were not allowed to speak or move until he greeted us in return and gave us permissions to sit. If Mr. Mugisha did not tell us to sit down, we were to silently remain standing until he told us to sit.

A few moments after class began, Mr. Mugisha asked all the Hutu students in our class to stand. As everyone looked around, most of the students in my class stood, while a few of us remained seated.

I was curious. What was the purpose of this lesson?

"Sit down now," Mr. Mugisha stated matter-of-factly, "and all Tutsi stand up."

The sprinkling of students who had remained sitting stood.

"Mukeshimana," my teacher said to me, "when I called Hutu students to stand, you did not, and when I called Tutsi students to stand, you did not. Why?" His voice was kind, not scolding, but I was confused. Mr. Mugisha knew my parents and my family. Why was he asking me this question?

I looked down out of respect for my teacher and softly replied. "I did not stand because I do not know which one I am."

I heard a quiet intake of breath around me and glanced up. Mr. Mugisha was looking at me with a look that unsettled me.

"Mukeshimana, your father's office is only a minute away. Run quickly to him, ask him which ethnic group you are, then come back to class and tell us."

I could not imagine how such a minor detail could be so important, but I quickly stood up and respectfully walked out of the classroom door. In my bare feet and with my blue uniform dress billowing as I ran, I raced to the Presbyterian department of theology in the church next to my school. My father spotted me from his office window and came to meet me by the door, concerned about what would send me running to him on the first day of school.

"Daughter, what is the matter?" he asked.

With my head lowered in respect, I told him that Mr. Mugisha had sent me to ask if I was Hutu or Tutsi. My father reached out and took my hand. I saw both pain and pride in his eyes. "We are Tutsi, Mukeshimana." Then he promised to explain what this meant when we got home. "But now you must run quickly back to class and tell Mr. Mugisha. Then listen very carefully to your lessons."

Eager to please my father, I did what I was told. When Mr. Mugisha asked my tribal identity, I answered that I was Tutsi as the rest of the class listened quietly.

"Now everyone knows 'who is who' in our class! Let's continue," Mr. Mugisha stated with a smile.

I was confused. I did not understand how knowing a tribal label helped us know "who was who," or what that even meant.

I did not understand how tribal ethnicity told me anything important about who my classmates were. I wondered what they had been thinking as we all announced our tribal labels. Did they feel awkward, as I did?

Looking back, I see that we were being taught to look at our classmates, not as other first graders, equal and the same, but instead, as students divided into separate ethnic groups: Hutu, Tutsi, and Twa. I have always assumed that Mr. Mugisha was required to conduct this exercise, along with every other teacher in the school. He was a friend of my father's and probably knew we were Tutsi. Mr. Mugisha must have been required by the school to have each child identify their tribe. But what purpose did this fulfill but to divide us and to point out that more Hutu than Tutsi were in our class?

These questions and others came to me later in life. But in that moment of my first forced tribal identification when I was young, I innately sensed a divisive, power-driven purpose. In that instant, I was publicly identified as a minority. It was a lesson so important to authorities at some level that my teacher halted the class and sent me to my father to bring back an answer about whether I was Hutu or Tutsi.

I also learned that students were required to obey many rules, which worried me. Before lunch the first day, Mr. Mugisha brandished a stick as he spoke to us with an intimidating tone and narrowed eyes as he stressed the importance of obedience. Students who did not follow the rules would be spanked. He flourished his eucalyptus branch for emphasis, and I shook.

Older siblings and friends had told me about school spankings. The thought of being spanked as classmates watched horrified me. I had heard that when Mr. Mugisha gave spankings, he sharply struck students across their legs again and again. The thought made me cringe, and a negative association between fear and learning, over time, became deeply engrained in my mind.

Mr. Mugisha read and explained the classroom rules to us:

1. Hair must be shaved.
2. No shoes allowed.
3. Uniforms must be worn for all school activities.
4. No bathroom breaks before recess.
5. Be clean.
6. Be obedient and respectful to the teacher.

As I listened, I sighed in relief that my mother had shaved my head the night before. I had always tried to respect my parents, so I did not think it would be difficult to respect Mr. Mugisha. But at lunchtime, he was still scowling and glancing frequently at his stick. I felt like a fist was pressed into my stomach, and I felt it frequently as the days passed. The thought of going to school now made me fearful of Mr. Mugisha's stick.

As an adult, I understand that Mr. Mugisha's mode of discipline was the norm in Rwandan schools at this time. He was responsible for upholding school rules and classroom order in a manner that was believed to be effective and appropriate in that culture. Mr. Mugisha taught me how to read, write, and learn basic math. Despite his severe disciplinary methods, I am thankful for the foundational educational skills he taught me.

Despite my fears, I became a student who excelled, made many friends, and enjoyed learning. One of my best friends was

Mila, the daughter of a Dutch missionary. She was the only white girl in our school, but color did not separate us. Our friendship stood not only the test of time, but of distance and differences, and we are still friends today. I learned that friendship bonded in respect, loyalty, and selfless commitment will stand the test of time.

Students who performed at an unsatisfactory level repeated the entire academic year. This meant some students repeated several grades, which caused shame that predisposed them to even greater risk of failure that can devastate a child. These students were typically the oldest, tallest, or most physically mature in a class. Fear of failing remained with me through my college years and drove me toward excellence, but I also struggled to find balance.

At the end of each semester, students and teachers gathered for grade promotion announcements. I would sit with my classmates, smiling, yet quaking with fear. Teachers also announced students' percentages on academic work for the semester, from highest to lowest. I struggled to breathe as teachers started with the highest grades and worked their way down. By the time the third-grade teacher stood to read class results, my anxiety was so high that I felt as if I might pass out.

When Mr. Mugisha stood, I was so terrified that I could not look at him and stared at the neck of the girl sitting in front of me.

The first name he spoke was not mine.

I held my breath.

"Mukeshimana."

I do not remember what he said after that, only that relief coursed through my body like a mountain stream in rainy season.

Although I did not know it in first grade, my name would be read among the top students for the remainder of my childhood education. Fear motivated me to remain at the top of the list, and pressure to succeed academically followed me into my adult studies. No matter my age, I studied incessantly—goaded by fear of failure. More than anything, I wanted to make my parents proud. Academic success brought me joy because it honored them. Anything less than success was never an option for me.

While my devotion to produce excellent work was one of my strongest character qualities, it was also a passion I would need to learn to balance with other aspects of my life to maintain positive, physical, mental, and spiritual health. This balance would come slowly, over the course of many years.

CHAPTER 5

COMPASSION'S PLEDGE

Love and compassion are necessities, not luxuries.
Without them humanity cannot survive.

—Dalai Lama

I hoped I would find glimmers of kindness in my new second-grade teacher.

I did not.

Mr. Sinkina was a tall, slim man whose razor-sharp authoritarian demeanor could slice through a student with a word or a glance. Of course, this terrified me.

His classroom was arranged in a similar manner to Mr. Mugisha's, but large windows along the east and west walls flooded the room with light. Our classroom also boasted desks with two students assigned to each table. Unfortunately, the positive differences ended there.

At recess, students would bolt for the bathroom, then run to the playground, bare feet slapping. We would jump rope, enjoy games with balls, socialize, play soccer, or watch other students engage in games for thirty minutes or so before the bell ended our reprieve. I enjoyed jumping rope the most.

The girls often enjoyed playing *akadenesi*, bouncing a tennis ball between our legs, then catching it. The girl who bounced the ball the most times without dropping it was the winner. This game was one of my favorites, and I often won, which made me feel happy, but my parents had taught us not to be proud and boast or make other people feel uncomfortable.

As I grew older, recess lost its appeal. Achieving high grades controlled my priorities, and any free moment became study time. I took notes in class and hid them in my dress pockets so I could read and memorize them during recess. Studying occupied my focus almost every waking minute.

Although my parents did not place pressure on me, I became obsessed with getting high grades and making my mother and father proud of me. I was also driven by my terror of being spanked. I used every minute of my school day and free time at home to master course content.

In the middle of the first semester of second grade, an opportunity finally came to prove myself. Our principal regularly assessed teachers' and students' performance. During these evaluations, teachers called on their strongest students to make a good impression so the teacher could earn the highest possible evaluation. However, students never knew if the principal would observe a single lesson or remain in the classroom and ask students random questions to test their skills. This put even more pressure on top pupils, who could make their teacher look like a success or a failure with a correct or incorrect answer.

Teachers often chose who should volunteer to answer questions during the principal's evaluation and who should remain silent. Mr. Sinkina informed us that on the day the principal visited, he would be teaching a mathematics lesson, so we should refresh our skills. He also told us that only students who were highly skilled in mathematics were to raise their hands during the lesson—especially if the principal asked a question.

I was one of the top students in our class. However, I also lived in mortal fear of failure. All I could think about was the stick leaning against the wall behind Mr. Sinkina's desk. I doubted I could give him a coherent answer under pressure, no matter how much I knew.

I dragged my feet and formulated a plan as I walked home from school. Mr. Sinkina would expect me to raise my hand and answer questions, but I decided I would not raise my hand and give the other smart students in the class an opportunity to be recognized for their correct answers. I wanted to avoid the risk of embarrassment, failure, and a dreaded spanking at any cost. I would not respond and, therefore, not risk the possibility of failure.

My mind was at rest with my plan until the day of the evaluation. When the principal walked through our classroom door, a tsunami of powerlessness overwhelmed me. A voice inside me yelled, *You are only in second grade, Mukeshimana.. Everyone is watching, and you will fail. Mr. Sinkina does not believe in you. He is waiting for you to fail.*

Our principal looked like a police officer. He wore a khaki suit with a pen tucked primly in his jacket pocket, and he was carrying a black briefcase. The students froze when they saw him, then stood at attention and greeted him in unison.

My heart pounded as we awaited his response and permission to sit.

With lips drawn tightly, he assessed us, then, in clipped tones, told us to be seated.

The principal began a stroll around the classroom while Mr. Sinkina taught the lesson. He periodically walked to the teacher's desk and made notes in his notebook, and my stomach knotted. Was something wrong with my dress? Was I slouching? Was my expression disrespectful?

I held my breath as the principal walked away from the desk. Mr. Sinkina moved to the blackboard, wrote a mathematics problem, then turned toward the class.

"Mukeshimana, come solve the problem."

I froze. My worst fear had come true—I'd been asked to answer a question, and I could not refuse and disrespect my teacher.

Mr. Sinkina's smile told me he was confident I knew the answer. I probably did. But I was quaking, my brain was jumbled, and my stomach was churning. My doom was sealed.

I could feel the principal's eyes boring into my back as he waited for me to move. Trembling, I stood and walked to the blackboard as nonsense whirled through my head. In that moment, I could not have answered that one plus one equaled two.

My mind froze as I stared at the numbers. The harder I tried to focus, the more confused I became. My hand shook as I wrote out an answer I was certain was wrong.

Dejected, humiliated, and petrified, I returned to my desk and stared at my feet, praying that I would melt into a puddle on the floor and seep out of sight. Mr. Sinkina quickly selected another student, who correctly solved the problem.

For the remainder of class I pleaded with God that Mr. Sinkina would forget I had given a wrong answer. He looked at everyone except me, and I begged God to erase my name from my teacher's memory.

At the sound of the bell, the principal left, and the class was excused for recess. I breathed a sigh of relief as I bolted for the door on shaking legs. Mr. Sinkina had not even glanced in my direction for the rest of the mathematics class. Unfortunately, I was too smart to remain hopeful and spent my recess time counting down the minutes until I had to return to class, like a kid waiting for a shot.

Just as I thought, when we returned from recess, my teacher was waiting for me at the door with a thick stick newly cut from a nearby eucalyptus tree.

I went cold as Mr. Sinkina called me to the front of the classroom.

"How dare you disrespect me?" he yelled. "You made me look like a fool. The principal will think I am not a good teacher. Lie on your stomach!" he screamed.

I was terrified, but I willed myself not to cry. I had no choice but to obey and laid down.

I can still remember the pain as the stick lashed my flesh. Mr. Sinkina struck me with full force several times across both my legs, so fiercely I feared my bones might break. Cries erupted from me with such force at the fierceness of the pain that I continued to sob on and off for the remainder of the day.

Even more wounding were my classmates' responses. A few winced to see the pain I was enduring, and I saw compassion in their eyes. Others remained impassive. We all knew that a show of sympathetic emotion would have further infuriated Mr. Sinkina. But other students smiled in morbid joy at the sight of my humiliation and pain.

I can still see the faces of those classmates as I lay writhing on the floor in pain. Years later I learned that when pain stirs pleasure in others, their response indicates the heart of a sadist. This is true in all cultures, and the reaction is often instilled in children by adults who justify hatred rooted in pride or ignorance.

How tragic that the cold pride that drove men and women to massacre fellow Rwandans was already alive in the hearts of second graders. Where had this animosity come from? Had my classmates learned to enjoy watching others suffer from adults? Was it possible that schools and governments and parents and institutions and even faith communities participated in perpetuating hatred, both overtly and implicitly?

In that moment my spirit tore, and I scorned those who observed my pain with pleasure. My spirit pledged to do all I could to instill compassion and empathy in the world, although I was too young to know the words for those things. As I lay on the floor humiliated and throbbing in pain, I resolved to never coldheartedly look away from the pain of others.

By the time I left school, my legs were badly swollen. I was beaten so badly that I missed several days of school because of the intense pain. But more importantly, I was emotionally debilitated and developed a fear for school, refused to return, and contemplated dropping out altogether. My experience that day greatly influenced the positive learning experiences I eventually pledged to create for all students in my classes.

My parents met with the principal and explained what had happened in class. He determined that I would never again be struck in punishment by a teacher. Instead, I would be given chores, such as cleaning the classroom.

I do not blame my teachers for applying corporal discipline. They were complying with school policies during an era when discipline was administered harshly in Rwanda and other areas of the world. Many educators believed that corporal punishment was an effective form of discipline and, therefore, to be carried out in the best interests of their students. The practice was standard for that era.

However, harsh corporal policies come with long-term consequences for children—not just in the classroom, but in life. I have done my best to transform experiences by creating positive outcomes, not just in my life, but in the lives of others. Respect for my students is one of my primary goals as an educator, as well as providing learning environments that stimulate personal success.

Painful experiences in early childhood taught me that life brings challenges. I could face them or be defeated by them. My parents wisely did not allow me to drop out of school because of my fear. My principal responded astutely to my disciplinary situation. My parents supportively taught me to overcome and move forward. This was one of many challenges that gave me an opportunity to build resilience that would serve me, not only during the Rwandan civil war, but for starting over in America and, eventually, in creating my own classroom culture.

Little did I know in second grade that the lessons I was learning would not only serve me for life—they would help save my life.

CHAPTER 6

THE TEST

If your determination is fixed, I do not counsel
you to despair. Few things are impossible to
diligence and skill. Great works are performed
not by strength, but perseverance.

—Samuel Johnson

I leaned against my favorite avocado tree as a breeze rifled the papers in my hands and scanned the view from my special study spot in front of our home. Our house sat atop a gentle hill, and sweet potato fields blanketed the valley below. Hills dotted with fragrant cedar and banana trees embraced our house, and I drank in the aroma as I lifted my face toward the sun.

My brain cannot absorb another minute of study.

A tear rolled down my cheek, and I brushed it away, fearful my parents or one of my brothers or sisters might see me crying and ask what was wrong. I rubbed my aching eyes.

I was fourteen, and eighth grade was ending—the final grade of primary school. My friends and I were seniors who were facing a life-determining decision: continue our education, seek employment, get married, start a business, or choose alternative education.

From my earliest memory, I'd desired one goal: attending a government-sponsored secondary school, then graduating from college. But only a small percentage of Rwandan students (at that time) passed the mandatory national examination required for entrance to prestigious government-sponsored secondary schools.

Anxiety hung over me like a November thundercloud. Passing or failing this grueling test would determine my life path and whether I would be allowed to step through the door to higher education, better career options, and the opportunity to fulfill my dreams. Years of tedious study had been invested in preparing for this examination. Every day I'd studied, sacrificed, and driven myself to excel, I'd envisioned passing the national exam.

My years of effort would be in vain if I failed. Passing was a daunting task for even the brightest students. I had never experienced such intense pressure, and the thought of dishonoring my parents by failing made me physically ill.

God, You know I have done all I can do. Please help me. I am making myself sick with worry.

I looked at the beauty surrounding me and reassured myself that if God cared about every detail in creation, He cared about every detail about me. My school was located beside a private secondary school. If I failed the national test, I would easily be admitted to this school, but I desperately hoped I would not face this choice.

Most government secondary schools were boarding schools, and officials assigned students to facilities across the country, regardless of the distance from their homes. Tuition was affordable, and being accepted at a government school was prestigious. I desperately wanted to earn this opportunity to honor my parents and place myself in a position where I could help care for them and my brothers and sisters. This was one of the driving passions of my heart.

In the days following graduation, I did little else than study. I reviewed lessons all day and into the night, praying that God would bless my efforts. My parents had taught me to rely on God in everything, and I believed He cared about every detail of my life.

However, I still found it difficult to fully trust Him sometimes. I'd always placed pressure on myself to try harder to honor my parents. My intense fear was rooted in negative school experiences when I was young, combined with an intense desire to please my parents because of my love, respect, and appreciation for them. Sometimes I struggled to trust God with problems and to stop trying to control my world.

Another factor heightened my anxiety. When students passed the national exam, their names were posted on the exterior wall of our city hall building for the community to read.

The absence of a student's name on the list was a public announcement of failure. Only a small percentage of students passed the test, which was considered an enormous honor.

For years I'd watched older students agonize for weeks and sometimes months as they waited for test results to be posted. The stress was excruciating. I dreaded the time when I would be subjected to this torturous wait. Thinking that my name might not be posted and that I might publicly disgrace my parents would bring me to the brink of tears. But, again, I was fearful about something I could not control. The Spirit of God nudged me. What should I be doing to control that fear?

The time had come, and the national exam was just days away.

I sought comfort in music that reflected my faith. I often sang a song titled *Standing on the Promises of God* to myself as I studied. And when I felt fear overwhelming me, I turned to God in prayer.

One day as I sang, I decided it was time for me to claim the words of the song for myself. The promises of God never expire. He was waiting for me to exchange my anxiety and fear for trust. I shifted my thinking and told myself that I could count on His loving promises and direction to help me pass the examination.

Mukeshimana, do not waste your strength fighting battles that are God's.

I knew the thought wasn't my own, and this simple truth was the essence of faith. God had given me His answer.

The day of the exam came and went, and I felt as if the weight of a crushing rock had been lifted from my shoulders. I could do nothing more than wait for the results and pray.

My friend Lydia and I sat in the backyard of my house washing our feet and rubbing them with a stone to remove dirt and dead skin. I enjoyed the simple ceremony, much like a pedicure, called *gukuba* that women shared before going out in public, ensuring their feet would appear clean and healthy. Then we applied lotion to help our feet look smooth and soft. I was enjoying this simple time of relaxation before Lydia and I walked to the market together. I de-stressed in the quiet pleasure of conversation and good company. I was blessed with good friends.

Inside the house, I heard voices. My mother was talking to a woman, and I caught fragments of conversation. The woman had been carrying potatoes to market to sell and had stopped by our house with news. In Rwandan culture people often visit one another's homes spontaneously. My mother and father were speaking with her, so I continued my conversation with Lydia.

Moments later my mother called me into the house.

"Mukeshimana, our friend Iragena has just walked from the city hall to bring us news."

The woman's beaming face stirred hope in me, but I was afraid to ask.

"Your name is posted among the students who have passed the national examination. I have come to offer you congratulations." Iragena's hands waved in the air with excitement as she spoke.

My parents and siblings cheered as they turned to embrace me. For a moment I felt nothing, as if Iragena had repeated a bit of local news. Then an instant later, I felt as if I might faint.

My life had changed the blink of an eye! God had answered my prayer. I had achieved my first goal for my education and been granted entrance to a government secondary school! Elation flooded through me, and I wanted to run and tell everyone.

I forced myself to temper my joy, even though I wanted to run to city hall and see the posting. Lydia was with me, and she had dropped out of school for a year and not taken the test. Showing my enthusiasm in front of her would be unkind. Passing the test opened possibilities for me that would never be available to her.

A second reality hit me full force. Passing also meant that I'd soon be leaving my community, family, and friends. The examination was a line of demarcation in our culture. Those who passed were given the keys to careers in medicine, education, business, technology, science, and politics. Those who did not pass worked as farmers, laborers, tradesmen, and in other lower-paying jobs. The results of this test determined our access to higher levels of education and elevated social status.

I had always felt extremely grateful that God had blessed me with the ability to learn, parents who valued education, and siblings who graciously tutored one another. Some of my most precious memories were, and still are, of older brothers and sisters leaning over younger ones, including me, explaining mathematics and history, or helping us learn to read.

My family and I humbly accepted the message and thanked Iragena for bringing us such welcomed news. Out of respect for Lydia, my family members minimized their enthusiasm. But inside, I could not wait for my friend to leave so our family could fully celebrate and thank God.

My parents felt they needed to confirm the news, so they decided to send my two older brothers to city hall. The following morning, the boys took the bus to town and returned in the evening.

I spent that day helping my mother cook, then sat under an avocado tree watching for my brothers' return. I felt suspended between worlds. I knew that if Iragena's report was wrong, I would be devastated, and my life dreams would be shattered.

When I finally spotted my brothers in the distance, my heart froze, fearing to hope. But as they drew closer, I saw their proud smiles. The moment they reached me, they lifted me off the ground, crushed me with hugs, and showered me with praise. They had told no one—not boasting but practicing humility as our parents had taught us.

Even now, I remember the gratitude that flooded my heart the moment my brothers confirmed the news. I leaped into the air, beside myself with joy. My parents and siblings hugged me, acknowledging the honor of my accomplishment and the opportunities it would bring me. Emotion soon overcame me as I tried to grasp that all I'd labored for had been granted to me, by God's grace. When I found an appropriate moment, I slipped away to a favorite prayer refuge outside.

I wept freely in those moments of intimacy between God and me. Early in life, I'd discovered that words often cannot express the sentiments in our hearts.

That night I rested in God's arms, overwhelmed by His deep, personal, unfathomable love for me. I poured out my gratitude until my thoughts faded, and I slipped quietly into deep sleep.

Today as a parent, I see how desperately I feared dishonoring my parents, which was caused in great part by the extreme discipline I received from my teachers in my early school years. I carried a near obsession for studying into my college and my graduate study years. I still wanted to make my parents proud— even more so after their passing. I love them and miss them so deeply that my academic success became, in part, a memorial of love to them—a tribute to *their* dreams for their children.

When I became a parent, my perspective began to shift as I experienced unconditional love, and I began to see how much more this is true of God. We have nothing to prove to the world or to Him. Knowing God loves us unconditionally unburdens us to do our best and be our best, fully and *freely*.

CHAPTER 7

FINDING A NEW COMMUNITY

When you come from a big family, you see that,
growing up, you're learning how to share.
Your sisters have got your back; you're not alone
in this—"We all support you!" Your family
provides that; it gives you a sense of safety,
and it's a very grounding feeling.

—Gisele Bundschen

Three students from my school passed the national exam: two boys and me. Friends, extended family, teachers, neighbors, and people from our community congratulated us. For a brief time, we were treated like celebrities, which I found uncomfortable. I did not enjoy being the center of attention, so I focused my time on a Bible study I'd been attending.

After several weeks, I was informed that I'd been placed at a Catholic boarding school in southern Rwanda. Nuns managed the school, and I'd only seen a nun once or twice in my life. Naturally, I was curious and a bit anxious about what school life would be like and how I would adjust to being separated from my family. I tried not to think about life without my family.

I told myself I would need to be brave. I could not bring shame upon my parents or cause problems at school. Over the next days, I focused on positive thoughts.

Set your mind to be content and invest your best efforts to succeed.

I refused to think about my fears and, instead, focused on my remaining time with my family, trying to soak every detail into my memory.

On my last Saturday at home, my family woke early and ate breakfast together. Everyone tried to act as if it was just another Saturday morning, but I could see emotion on everyone's face— even my father's. He quietly busied himself filling our plates.

When we finished eating, we gathered in our living room and sang *Guide Me, O Thou Great Jehovah* to commemorate the importance of my leaving. I cried through the entire hymn as I looked at the faces of my family members crowded around me. Singing as a family was one of our traditions, and singing to commemorate important events was especially significant. After all my years of study and waiting, I was leaving for boarding school . . . and now I felt uncertain and afraid to go.

After we finished singing, my family comforted me, hugged me, and gave me their best wishes. Soon everyone was in tears except my father. His smiled stiffly as he tried to control his emotions.

My parents had arranged transportation for me to school via a neighbor, who was a businessman and family friend. Shortly after we finished the hymn, he knocked on our door. My brothers picked up my luggage as my mother, sisters, and house helpers, who were like brothers to me, accompanied me to the car. My brother placed my bags in the rear of the car, and my father and I slid into the back seat.

At that moment, reality hit me in a clash of emotions—

. . . euphoric joy about beginning school

. . . wrenching sorrow about leaving my family and friends

. . . fear and questions about a new life at school.

I was fourteen and in shock at the thought of leaving my family. I'd never experienced summer camps away from them or even a vacation with relatives or friends. My mother and father had been with me day and night and anchored me to safety and security. Now my father was taking me to live among strangers far from our home and community.

My life would be different from this moment on, and I was afraid.

As the car pulled away from our house, sobs rose in my chest. A sorrow I'd never felt before crushed my heart. I suddenly longed to be a child again and lifted into my mother's arms. I was transitioning into a new phase of my life. *Will all changes be this painful as I grow up?* I wondered as my home and family disappeared in the distance behind me. I knew so little about the pain life can bring.

The school was four hours away. We drove south, passing eucalyptus and cedar trees, then through thick vegetation as we headed toward Gitarama. I caught sight of my primary school as we reached the Nyabarongo River, which separates the prefectures of Kibuye and Gitarama, and memories flashed through my mind. Just before we crossed the river, I caught a final glimpse of my community. My spirit shifted as I began to absorb new scenery and unfamiliar territory. I was fascinated by everything new and different.

We soon came to the Kubuhanda market, and my father stopped in front of a small store. He ordered a Fanta orange and a loaf of bread for me, and I thanked him as he handed me the drink. I understand today that he was marking this distinct transition in my life with special memories and treats. Beneath the gestures he was speaking a subtext of love.

About thirty minutes later, we continued the drive. I soon read a sign that told me we were entering the historic prefecture of Butare, which was near my new school. I leaned back and imagined what my new world would be like.

Few children in my primary school had ever been granted the opportunity I'd been given. My blessings surpassed my limited understanding, and again, I was overwhelmed with gratitude. I prayed that my sense of thankfulness would never fade.

Nevertheless, I was also gripped by anxiety at the thought of being separated from my parents, far beyond their reach, practically speaking. Neither they nor I had cell phones, and they did not own a car. How would I communicate with them if a crisis occurred?

When the rough roads smoothed, then became paved, I knew we were nearing the city. As we crested a hill, the school gates came into view. Several nuns stood at the gate with a man. The nuns' clothing fascinated me: light blue dresses and starched white full-length aprons. Their clothes looked so intriguing that I wondered if they spoke a different language, but as I exited the car, they greeted me warmly in Kinyarwanda. Their smiles and warmth set my heart at ease. Their demeanor was different from what I'd experienced in previous schools, where authority was accompanied by an air of fear and intimidation. While I felt a clear sense of authority from the nuns, I also felt a reassuring sense of peace, calm, and nurture.

My father introduced me to the man, Pastor Kalinga, who lived near the theology school. Father had planned for me to stay with Pastor Kalinga and his wife that Saturday and Sunday. Pastor Kalinga joined us back in the car and gave my father directions to his home. When we arrived, Father told me he would be returning home with our driver Eugene. I would remain with Pastor Kalinga and his wife for two days until school started on Monday.

I was stunned and terrified. I had assumed my father would stay with me until classes started. I was inconsolable. Pastor Kalinga's wife warmed food for me, but I could not eat. I cried all night, trying to quiet my sobs beneath my pillow. I could think only one thought: my parents could no longer protect me. They would not even know what was happening in my life.

On Monday, I awoke to another surprise. My father had arranged for Pastor Kalinga to take me to school on his bicycle.

I was hesitant, but I bravely climbed on the seat and soon relaxed as I learned that Pastor Kalinga managed a bicycle quite skillfully. I clung to the frame beneath my seat as we rode from the seminary toward the school, passing people working in the fields and scooting to the side of the road to make room for passing school buses. By the time we arrived, I was enjoying my excursion.

Several nuns, accompanied by two girls from my home region, stood at the front gate to greet me as I dismounted the bicycle. Before the day was over, they introduced me to other girls who treated me like an old friend, which helped me feel accepted and took my mind off my homesickness. This system of introducing new students to returning students from their home area created strong family-like bonds.

The tall, brick gate surrounding the school was edged on the inside by velvety roses and lush green grass. The gate encircled the school like a protective embrace and gave me a sense of security and sanctuary.

The modest campus included classrooms, a kitchen, and a dining room, two dormitories, a small health clinic, and an office for the Director of Discipline. The headquarters building housed showers, bathrooms, a kitchen, and a laundry facility. The grounds also included a playground, basketball and volleyball courts, and a separate area for sports such as handball. The center of campus housed a beautiful chapel, faculty office, a meeting hall, and more classrooms.

Banana trees towered over the campus behind the west gate. Housing for the sisters in charge of the school was located on the north side. The complex resembled a village, and I focused on trying to remember what building was used for what purposes.

By the end of the tour, I was feeling as if I had entered an entirely new world, and I wanted to sit down next to my mother to talk. But, of course, I could not talk to her. So, I focused, instead, on practicalities.

My parents had prepared me well for this new phase of life, both spiritually and emotionally. They also bought me everything I needed: comfortable bed sheets, school uniforms, and supplies. Secondary students were expected to wear khaki skirts and a white blouse and to keep our hair short, but not shaved, as we had done in primary school. We were not allowed to braid our hair or apply a relaxer. I assume the theory was that if we did not focus on our hair or clothing, we would pay better attention to our studies. Students from poor families also did not have to worry about "keeping up" with better-funded peers. Instead, resources could be spent on educational supplies, which made sense to me. One item we were expected to purchase was a bucket, which we were to label with our name and use for showering and doing our laundry. I was happy to be in a different uniform and have the distinction of short hair.

Students were assigned a major; I wanted to be placed as a teaching major but was assigned to the literature major. Opportunities occasionally arose for students to change their major, but the vast majority remained in the major they were assigned. Rather than waste my energy being disappointed, I accepted the decision and decided to be grateful that I was in a good secondary school and make the best of my opportunities.

I followed a sister across the grounds and into my dormitory. Students greeted me with smiles, and by the time I walked into my room, my spirit was joyful. The sister showed me my room, and I unpacked, then made my bed. Then I labeled my bucket, sheets, bags, and other belongings. My room was close to the discipline coordinator's room, but more importantly, it was close to a classroom. I wasn't sure why I was so excited about having my room next to a classroom, but something about it made me feel special, as if I had won a prize.

My heart leaped in joy at my first glimpse of bunk beds. I'd never slept in a bunk bed, and I was assigned a bottom bunk. After making my bed, I laid down to discover what this new sleeping experience would feel like. I felt encapsulated in my own private space as voices buzzed around me. The tiny area comforted me; it was *my* space.

Girls' voices swirled around me. Excited. Scared. Soft sobs and words of assurance. Bursts of laughter and babbling conversation. The chaos felt somehow comforting, as I lay cocooned in the privacy of my bunk—embraced by my new community and my new home.

As a mother now all these decades later, how many times have I been forced to walk away from my heartbroken child—as their hospital bed was being wheeled away, as they walked into a classroom, as I pulled away from their first overnight at sleep-away camp? How difficult was it for my father that day to leave his daughter, knowing he would not see her again for months, and knowing that she would shed tears and not understand why he left her that day, perhaps for a very long time?

How grateful I am for the perspective that comes with time—time that allows me to see my most painful moments in life as the most transformational moments in my life. This allows me to both acknowledge the pain and the loss, and yet move forward into the new.

CHAPTER 8

FRIENDS AND ENEMIES

Enemies are often former friends or potential friends who have been denied or think that they have been denied.

—Idries Shah

I huddled in my bunk and stared at a brick in the wall behind my bed, obsessing about what might happen tomorrow.

Will students be kind? What if they know more than I know? What will my teachers expect, and what if I don't understand what I'm taught? Will the nuns have rigid rules? What are the punishments? What kind of friends will I make, and will I ever stop missing home?

My thoughts were a jumble of joy about new opportunities mixed with grief from missing my family and fear of the unknown. Tears saturated my soggy pillow.

The sound of footsteps interrupted my thoughts. Suddenly everything plunged into darkness. The nun in charge of discipline had turned off the lights.

As the darkness swallowed me, I sobbed quietly. An ache throbbed in my chest. I couldn't imagine how I could live for weeks and months without seeing my family. Tears soaked my sheets, as well as my pillow. I sobbed into the night and cried out to God for comfort.

The bell that would punctuate the segments of my life over the next six years woke me in the morning. I prayed as I mechanically cleaned up, ate breakfast, and headed to class. As I walked across campus, I saw a statue of Mary in the distance. My hometown was populated by Presbyterians, so I was unfamiliar with Catholicism. I'd never seen a statue and was fascinated by Mary's lifelike details. I walked closer, touched the statue's feet and looked into her eyes, imagining what her life may have been like.

Mary had also left her family to follow God's plan—a plan that must have seemed irrational to everyone except Joseph. I pondered how lonely she must have felt leaving her family. I silently poured out my heart to God and thought more about Mary's loneliness and my own. Deep in thought, I lost track of time. Words formed in my mind faster than ants on honey, and I silently poured out my heart to God, unaware that I was missing my first lecture.

Across campus, the nun in charge of discipline spotted me. As she approached, I panicked as I realized I was missing my class. Would I be expelled? I hadn't skipped intentionally, but would anyone believe me? My primary school teachers had never allowed students to explain their actions before they doled out disciple.

I inwardly cringed as she stopped in front of me. "What is your name and major, child?"

My legs trembled as I answered, explaining that I'd lost track of time as I'd gazed at the statue.

The corners of the nun's eyes crinkled as she listened, although her face remained stoic.

"Go to class immediately and explain to your teacher."

Faint with relief, I ran toward the building where my class was nearing conclusion. When I arrived, I was so shaken that I was unable to think straight. I decided I was doomed to fail all my classes and needed to return home immediately. I was homesick anyway and wanted to see my family.

Two girls who lived near my hometown approached me after class and told me they would help me adjust to campus life. My heart flooded with relief and gratitude. Over the following weeks, we became close friends, and my confidence in my abilities soared as my homesickness subsided. They taught me that simple kindness can transform the lives of people struggling through unfamiliar or overwhelming circumstances. Simple acts of friendship can change the life of a newcomer fighting to find their place in an unfamiliar community.

As the year progressed, these girls and others consistently invested their time supporting me and other new students. The nuns had organized a system that encouraged veteran students to reach out to incoming girls. My new friends' compassion gave me hope hemmed in by friendship during those first few critical months. They were God's angels, loving and protecting me, and they inspired me to do the same for other people in new or unfamiliar situations. I'm grateful that my school taught this spirit of responsibility and compassion for those who felt displaced and alone. Their system inspired me to reach out to others and, ultimately, to create a nonprofit for refugees and immigrants in my future community.

The campus provided comfort and security, and I spent as much time as possible studying. I also participated in group chores, which helped me mature socially, as well as emotionally, and to better cope with my new environment. I also honed my study skills and learned to study more efficiently.

The dormitories, like everything in my school, had been thoughtfully organized. Eight to ten students of different majors and varying grade levels from different areas of the country were assigned to a group. Groups helped students gain a sense of belonging and "family." We sat together in the cafeteria, and each group was assigned a leader and assistant leader. This system gave me a sense of security and belonging.

My school also encouraged students to participate in activities to foster team building and personal responsibility. For instance, students were responsible for cleaning, including washing the windows of the dormitories. I enjoyed these activities because they offered us a chance to bond, socialize, and created a sense of family.

Students also bonded through our various religious affiliations. The school was Catholic but allowed religious choice among both faculty and students. Protestant students joined other Protestants in worship. No one was forced to worship as a Catholic; however, corporate morning and evening prayers were required. I was grateful for times of unified prayer because I believe God hears the prayers of His people, regardless of denominational affiliations. I quickly found friends when I attended worship services and prayer groups.

I began to learn that prayer is a crucial source of strength that helps us overcome challenges as we turn to God. As a result, my coping skills improved, and I became a stronger person.

I also joined a group of close friends that prayed together. We regularly gathered at three alternating locations at three in the morning. As a safety precaution, students were forbidden to go outside in the middle of the night. We did not want to break rules, but we took the risk so we could spend time in corporate prayer. Maintaining our prayer time was stressful, but it was a high priority for us because we were all relying on God's help to overcome academic pressure and graduate. I felt a close bond of friendship with my prayer partners, especially because we shared our deepest concerns with one another.

One of our locations was the campus chapel. After waking, we dressed in traditional African fabrics called *ibitenge* and silently crept to the chapel. As we crossed the grassy courtyard each night, we tried to elude the nun who was the discipline coordinator and patrolled the dormitories. Once we arrived at the chapel, we opened the door slowly, always fearful that a sister might be inside. We dropped to our knees at the altar as quietly as possible. Then after praying, we exited and stealthily returned to our beds. Now years later as I look back, I wonder if the nuns ever spotted us but left us alone.

We also prayed in an area behind the reception room. A brick wall separated the reception room from several rabbit houses. We would identify a vacant rabbit house and squeeze in one by one. However, this location proved to be unaccommodating, since it was difficult for everyone to squeeze inside a tiny rabbit house. Once we were in, we didn't have room to kneel or extend our legs. But while we may have felt uncomfortable, we always felt safe, since we doubted anyone would look for a group of praying students inside a rabbit house. However, out of caution, we did not sing when we were in the rabbit houses. When we were done praying, we awkwardly exited one at a time.

Before 1993, I boasted that the only thing I feared was academic failure. But after 1993, I could no longer say this.

Days before my graduation in the summer of 1993, a group of Hutu students, teachers, and community members devised a plot to massacre all Tutsi students at our school. This kind of activity was also going on in other schools across Rwanda. Word of this plot shattered my sense of safety. I later learned that several of my prayer partners, as well as people I considered my close friends, were among those who had plotted to execute us.

How does a person absorb the unthinkable reality that their closest friends and faith partners plotted their execution?

And not only my execution—*all* Tutsi students in our school.

Some Hutu students from my school—including some of my prayer partners—had collaborated with hateful Hutu community members led by a local teacher—to plot the murder of *all Tutsi students* in our school. The students were acting in allegiance with Hutus who were plotting national genocide against Tutsi. A group of select Hutus in our school and community had met and formed a plan to sneak into the school dormitories at night and stab Tutsi students while they slept. As part of the plan, these (not all) Hutu students and teachers from our school, led by a group of Hutu adults from the community, had created a map identifying the bunk of every Tutsi in our school to streamline the executions. Again, this activity was not unique to our school.

Tribal infighting was not new to Rwanda, but self-avowed Christians—some who had been my trusted prayer partners—had plotted the executions. I did not have words for this level of betrayal. Who could I ever trust again? Later, during the genocide, many church leaders and members acted upon their political ideologies and emotions. They abandoned their faith and participated in the execution of opposing tribal members.

My memory of these days is sparse. Like many students who were targeted, I went into shock.

How could I move forward?

Would the world ever feel safe again?

Were those of our genetic makeup hated so vehemently that our friends justified abandoning their faith and coldheartedly massacring friends in their sleep?

My world had turned inside out, and for weeks I walked through life in a fog.

Through God's grace, the plot was discovered days before we were scheduled to be killed. Perhaps if I had not been contemplating my future since I was about to graduate, I would have foreseen the coming terror.

A Tutsi friend had heard stories about a possible massacre but did not believe they could be true, so she did not pass the report on to anyone. However, some Tutsi students heard the rumors and joined Hutu friends in their rooms at night, hoping to escape possible tragedy. Not every Hutu was involved in the plot, in the same way that not every Hutu committed acts of violence against Tutsi.

The most heartbreaking reality for me was learning that some of the saboteurs were among my inner circle of friends— people with whom I'd shared my greatest burdens and joys. We'd praised God together, worshipped and studied together, and supported one another. Hatred had overtaken their hearts as they justified their hatred and perverted God's Word. People betrayed friends, confidants, and brothers and sisters in Christ, based on tribal affiliation.

In the days following the failed massacre, I faced unanswered questions and anger at the injustice of this betrayal. Releasing my will to God was not easy, but I determined to live moment by moment, leaning on God's grace. I resolved that those who attempted to kill me would not poison my spirit with bitterness. I determined to forgive them with the understanding that forgiveness does not release people from the consequences of their actions. Nor does it condone or justify the evil. As Christians, we forgive because we have been forgiven by Jesus and extend His mercy to others. Forgiveness frees us from the chains of hatred and bitterness.

Evil can destroy us or teach us. People we trust can turn against us. We're all born with the capacity to do good or evil, and we all fall short. God's greatest gift to us is the gift of change. Even those guilty of genocide can change through the power of God, and through the power of God's grace, we can forgive. Forgiveness does not release those who have done evil from consequences, but we have the power to release our anger and bitterness toward them.

We can change, but we cannot eradicate the consequences of past choices. I lost much to the genocide. I cannot eradicate the painful consequences of others' choices, but I can choose my responses to pain. I can refuse to allow bitterness and hatred to rule my heart. The work of forgiveness was and is a daily choice.

I achieved my education. I trusted again. I faced my fears and turned to God for answers bigger than myself. I promoted peace and reached out to help others.

God heard my prayers for comfort, wisdom, and grace to forgive and move forward. I am eternally grateful that my life was spared in 1993—the year I was initiated into the racial tensions brewing in Rwanda. I had no idea that the genocide of my people lay ahead, as well as the darkest hours of my life.

CHAPTER 9

NEXT STEPS

A bridge can still be built, while the bitter waters
are flowing beneath.

—Anthony Liccione

In the summer of 1993, I fell to my knees during chapel and thanked God for helping me graduate from secondary level at my Catholic school. I was overjoyed that I'd achieved this monumental milestone. Primary school was eight years, then six years of secondary education was comparable to high school before students got a job or went to university. Graduating from secondary school was highly respected in my culture, and I was now qualified for a secure job that could provide a good living. I had attained my goal!

But a thought still pulled at my heart . . . another dream.

A friend and I headed to Nyanza to be measured for graduation dresses. Praise songs echoed through my thoughts as I looked out the taxi window and saw workers in the fields. I could now support myself and build for my future, but I wasn't sure I wanted to begin work right away. I still dreamed of completing a college degree.

The countryside slipped past in a blur. How had time passed so quickly? Graduating with my secondary degree was one of the greatest joys of my life, and I felt as if I was floating on air. My friend asked me about the style and color of my dress, and my heart raced with excitement as I envisioned my parents watching me receive my certificate at the ceremony. But after that . . . did I want a job or to continue to college?

After arriving in Nyanza, my friend and I visited several shops and found a tailor who displayed stylish samples of his work. We went in and I explained I needed a graduation dress by Thursday for a Saturday ceremony. He reassured me he would be able to complete a dress within that time, then measured me.

For the next few days, I focused on how proud I would feel on graduation day with my parents and siblings in attendance. I also thought about options for my next steps in life, but I refused to obsess over making a "right" decision for my future. I was learning that we can only live in the now, trusting that every good decision will lead us to a better future.

That night, I slept better than I had in a long time.

The next day, my friend and I returned to the tailor's shop to pick up my skirt and blouse ensemble—a yellow skirt and top with decorative green trim. I laughed in delight when I saw it. I felt indulged to own a dress designed and created just for me. As I tried it on and my friend nodded in approval, I fought back tears. After years of wearing loose khaki skirts and white shirts,

I felt like a beautiful young woman marking her entry into the adult world.

Before my friend and I left Nyanza, we stopped by a local store for *mandazi*, (African fried doughnuts) and *ikivuguto* (cultured milk) for our celebratory snack.

I awoke on graduating day giddy with anticipation. My father, sister, brother, and father's cousins had made the long journey to witness the ceremony. My mother and two brothers stayed home to prepare for the graduation party, which I understood was necessary but saddened me. My celebration would not feel complete without them. Their love and encouragement had been an enormous part of my educational success.

I put on my new dress and prepared my hair. I'd worked hard every day of my primary and secondary school years to make my parents proud. I hoped I would see pride reflected in their eyes.

As I left my dorm, I spotted my father across campus, gracefully striding toward the reception hall ahead of my other family members, slim and stately, his right hand decorously placed in the pants pocket of his brown suit. Even my father's polished shoes reflected his pride. His clipped beard and curly hair added to his look of distinction. He was smiling, but the corners of his eyes told me what I wanted to know: he was proud of me.

My beautiful, elegant, younger sister Vestine walked behind him. She was dressed in her finest green and white polka-dot skirt with a green top, black shoes, and matching bag. Her bulging purse held presents she would give me later, including avocados and a songbook. My brother Zacharie followed next, his brilliant white teeth flashing. He carried a new camera. He spotted me, and his smile grew. He broke into a run and grabbed me, his hug lifting me off the ground. In that moment I knew that the loving smiles and embraces of family are the true meaning of home, especially when loved ones have been separated. I melted into his hug.

My father's cousins, Reba and Rugira, had also come and brought bags filled with presents, including a delicious appetizer called *sambusa*. Rugira owned a clothing business and brought me a fine jacket from his store. Their attendance was an honor as they'd sacrificed significant time to travel a long distance. This alone was a gift to me, and I thanked each of them for coming to help me celebrate.

I fell against my father's chest and hugged him. Something inside of me did not want to let go. He was a loving man but expressed few emotions. He chose to show his children strength so we would trust him to take care of us. And we did. My father and mother were my safe place.

At the time I graduated, my younger sister Vestine was in her fourth year of secondary school, studying accounting. She loved mathematics and business, undauntedly enrolling in difficult subjects. We were two years apart, and she was inspired that I had achieved graduation. I was inspired by everything about her.

I admired my sister's grace. Vestine had a sweet spirit and approached every task without complaining. She styled her soft hair beautifully and dressed fashionably. She had a beautiful singing voice and was a choir member. The last song I heard

Vestine sing expressed that life comes and goes like flowers that quickly bloom and wither. I did not know the words would be prophetic. I cherish my graduation memories and all memories of her.

My ceremony was held inside the school compound on a beautiful patch of grass marked by a long path that led from the dormitories to the classrooms. Red roses and the statue of Mary that captured my heart my first day of class highlighted the reception area.

Seating was located between the dormitories and classrooms. Teachers came forward, read the graduates' names, then placed our highly prized diplomas in our hands. I listened as students' names were called, and my heart pounded as I anticipated hearing mine. I smoothed imaginary wrinkles from my skirt to calm my nerves.

"Mukeshimana Clementine."

I rose and made my way forward, as a deluge of joy and gratitude washed over me.

I had achieved a lifelong dream. How could all my years of study be in the past? I glanced back in time and saw thousands of decisions to study, to memorize, to give up social time, to work harder, to stay home, to ask my older brothers for help, to review one more time during recess and on weekends and when I was tired . . . and now I was *here*, with my diploma in hand.

Within what seemed like moments, the ceremony was over, and we headed back to my home to celebrate. I closed a door on a crucial period of my life as I anticipated a new world of work and adulthood, independence, and possibly even marriage.

Life awaited me. Dreams flew through my head as my school life receded in the distance. I did not know my dreams would soon be replaced by nightmares more horrific than anything I could imagine.

I arrived home to the rich aroma of *ikigage*, a traditional beer made from sorghum and yeast). *Urwagwa*, traditional banana beer, was also being served to guests in an *ikibindi*, a large clay pot. The aroma of *urwagwa* drifted through the neighborhood. As we approached the house, I could also smell delicacies being cooked in our kitchen, and my spirit embraced the aromas of home and the sounds of friends laughing.

We entered the house through the back door. I lovingly hugged my siblings, Dave, Josiah, Honorine and Mirelle then walked into the living room where I met our guests, who were already drinking and celebrating. When my mother saw me, her gaze rested on my face and held me.

She did not have to speak. I saw the love and pride in her eyes.

I have always believed my mother was beautiful. She was tall and bore herself with elegance. Her skin was the color of honey, and her long hair felt like silk. She hurried to me and hugged me, her grace enhanced by her regal, traditional Rwandan clothing. "You did a good job, my child," she whispered in my ear.

I treasured her words and still do. My mother's words carried great power and integrity, and she never spoke lightly. Her opinion meant everything to me because I knew no one with more beauty of character and spirit than she. Her words—and my father's—had always been wisdom and light to me.

She took me by the hand and showed me where she had placed the food in the kitchen, pointing out all my favorites. My siblings and extended family had crowded into the kitchen to gather around the fire, talk, and eat. This included Beata and Hiana, who we considered our sisters because Mother was their godmother. Beata was the same age as my mother and was overseeing the food while my mother entertained the guests. Hiana was a year older than I and, like many girls in Rwanda, never had the opportunity to attend secondary school.

Beata enjoyed being the kitchen boss. Deciding I must be tired, she ordered two children to get off a stool so I could sit down. People were feasting on plates of warm beans and cassava. The ladies were eating, and the men were enjoying beer.

I sat and dutifully ate, then returned to the living room where more people had gathered, so I gave more hugs and politely responded to the many congratulations. My father announced my accomplishments as I stood at his side, and everyone clapped. As I glanced around the crowded room, I fought back tears of gratitude for the support of loving family and friends.

According to our family tradition, my father sang a prayer song that thanked God for using us for His purposes. I laughed silently as we sang because several people who had drunk too much were singing louder than the rest of us. Laughing out loud would have been disrespectful to our guests, but I wondered how many people in the room were secretly laughing inside.

After the song, we offered prayers of thanksgiving and continued the lavish party. I continued to roam from room to room, chatting, eating, laughing, and occasionally helping in the kitchen. But my mind was stuck in slow motion, as if the people and the party were not real. I had dreamed of my graduation all my life, and now I had attained it. What was I to do next? I no longer had a schedule, classes, or assignments to do. How would I transition to the next place—and *what was* the next place? My stomach churned at the questions looming before me.

The party was a celebration of God's grace, lasting late into the evening, when most of the guests left. Those who had come from out-of-town stayed overnight. I enjoyed this opportunity to spend extra time with loved ones. A week later, our company had left, and life returned to a new normal.

Memories of my graduation are among my most precious possessions. My family was together and as happy as I can remember them to be, indulging in the simple joys of life and love. Every moment of preparation, recognition, celebration, and simply *being* that day sent ripples of contentment through me that would last my lifetime. As I stepped across the platform, I crossed a threshold from a world with few choices to a world of breathtaking possibilities. But I did not do it alone, which was and is my greatest graduation gift. I crossed the threshold empowered by love and cheered on by the confidence of family and friends, and most importantly, the power of God.

But again, the time had come for me to step into a new beginning. But what would it hold?

Although I'd arrived early, the small living room was crowded. Men and women from their late teens into their forties and fifties were scattered around the room, some on chairs, and some sitting on the floor.

Our Bible study had grown since the time I'd last visited. The group included a mix of men and women seeking God's direction about their future, as well as people who'd come to our area to find work. We prayed about personal direction, employment, and peace in our nation, which was experiencing escalating racial tension. We met in the homes of several of the attendees who lived in a popular commercial area of the city on a beautiful hill close to the hospital, nursing school, and market.

My eyes scanned the room for my two closest friends, and I soon spotted Amaza, who had come from Burundi to our area to find work in construction. He was staying with a neighbor who had recommended him to our prayer group, and he and I quickly became friends. Amaza was a foreigner in a strange land, and to some people he appeared to be without purpose. During the time he lived in Rwanda, he never found a job, eventually became a refugee in the Congo, and ultimately returned to Burundi.

But God had brought Amaza to Rwanda, to our Bible study, and to me as a friend for a unique purpose. I did not know this, however, as we shared stories, laughed, sipped banana juice, or ate hot sorghum meal, prayed, and encouraged one another, I began to understand the significance of his presence.

When Amaza was not searching for work, he often walked through the community talking to people about God. On other occasions, he and I hiked into the mountains to join friends for prayer.

I greatly enjoyed the transitional weeks between graduation and the next stage of my life. My father soon informed me that he had secured a job for me at a local secondary school. I was excited about establishing myself in a vocation, but even though I accepted the job, Father and I discussed whether I should pursue college instead. I also wondered if I should consider marriage.

Except, I had no idea who I might marry. I had never even dated anyone.

At that time in my local culture, women did not go on dates or refer to male friends as "boyfriends." Male-female relationships were often hidden from public. Most people did not outwardly show interest toward the opposite sex, especially in some conservative Christian circles. In fact, some Christians considered it sin for young girls to even talk to boys. Oddly, however, after high school, young men and women were considered old enough to get married.

During our prayer meetings, it was common for girls to publicly repent of their sins because guys had talked to them. The girls would rebuke the devil, and people would join in and rebuke the devil on their behalf. Looking back at this "norm" now, the practice seems quite strange. However, the motivation behind these mores was a desire to honor God when someone was with the opposite sex—a worthy and timeless goal for Christian men and women.

These transitional months were a confusing time in my life, so I focused on God. I needed His help to discern what to do in the next stage of my life. I believed He'd He would give me peace and wisdom to make wise, sound decisions.

During this period, I attended a revival in the city of Remera, one of the primary locations of the Presbyterian Church at that time. I went to the conference with a friend, and went to Remera by bus and joined Christians who'd come from other regions of the country. While there, I asked God to speak to me about the direction I should take with my life.

I journaled while I was at the Remera conference, believing it would help me discern God's will. The speaker preached on a theme from Nehemiah: "Let us start building." At the time, I was uncertain about how the speaker's message related to my life, and I left disappointed.

However, not many days later, I understood. The conference message was intended to give me strength and help me maintain my faith during the next unexpected, devastating phase of my life.

Genocide and loss.

CHAPTER 10

NEVER SAID GOODBYE

In their hearts humans plan their course,
but the LORD establishes their steps.

—Proverbs 16:9

Early in April, soon after returning home from the Remera conference, I dreamed about a preacher who was teaching a message on Proverbs 16:9: "In their hearts humans plan their course, but the LORD establishes their steps." He spoke about the wisdom of following God's path and that those who are not wise will follow the wrong path.

When I awoke, I underlined Proverbs 16:9 in my Bible. I felt strongly that God had given this verse to me for a purpose.

A few days later, on April 6, 1994, the airplane carrying the president of Rwanda, Juvénal Habyarimana, crashed. This event triggered national chaos and ignited immediate hostility. The Hutu majority claimed that the Tutsi (my tribe), were responsible for the president's death and decreed that all Tutsi should be killed in retaliation.

This rash proclamation constituted a national order for the execution of 14 percent of Rwanda's seven million people. My parents optimistically believed the political fallout of the conflict would remain isolated in Kigali, where the crash occurred and that the conflict would not extend to our small rural town. However, the verse I had dreamed about haunted my thoughts.

We would soon discover my parents were wrong.

My family had gathered in the kitchen around the comfort of the fire. A day or two had passed since we'd heard about the president's death. News about President Habyarimana's death and the Hutu decree had unsettled our community, but my father remained calm and reassuring. I had taken a seat next to my mother that morning.

As we talked, a slamming sound came from the front of the house, and my father went to check. Moments later he returned. His face was drawn into an expression I had never seen before, and my body went cold. I steeled myself for tragic news, but nothing could have prepared me for his words.

"Hutu militants have targeted Clementine and Vestine to be killed. I do not know why they have been singled out, but we must all leave immediately and find somewhere else to sleep tonight."

I was too shocked to speak.

Targeted to be killed—Vestine and me? What had we done that could threaten the Hutus—or anyone? We had never been involved in politics or spoken out about national affairs—we were young students with no interest in such things!

My mind raced, and I could feel my heart pounding. The rumor did not make sense.

Fortunately, Vestine was traveling in the southern prefecture of Butare and would remain there for several days.

If the rumor about us is true, she will be safe, but what should I do?

I repeated the words over and over.

My father told me I needed to run to the house of my friend Shushu. Her father was a medical doctor, and her mother was a midwife. Our mothers were close friends and trusted confidants. The family lived in a large home surrounded by a high gate close to our local hospital.

"You must leave immediately, Mukeshimana. You will spend the night there."

His tone was urgent, and his eyes darkened as he gestured for me to gather my things. The look on his face frightened me out of my state of shock.

I ran to my room. I grabbed a red and gray sweater that I pulled on over the dress I was wearing and slipped into black wool-lined rain boots. I did not put on socks and eventually regretted that decision. I also took my *indangamuntu*, my identity card, and placed it inside my Bible. Rwandans were required to carry their identity cards at *all times*. The first item listed on the ID card was our tribe, not our name. Tribal affiliation had become

Rwanda's primary form of identification, and ID cards would soon become not only tools used for discrimination, but also instruments of death. A single glance at an identity card marked every Rwandan for favor or hatred. How ironic that I nestled my ID card within the pages of my Bible, which I slipped inside my dress with my hymnbook so I would not arouse suspicion by carrying anything. Something in my spirit told me that I would need spiritual resources in the coming maelstrom of hatred and death. I also grabbed my notebook, which was filled with sermon notes and songs of consolation.

I was afraid to take my cherished photo album. If I was spotted carrying it, Hutus would assume I was fleeing, and I would become an instant target. Later, I would deeply mourn the loss of my precious photos.

My parents comforted me as best they could and instructed me to return in the morning. They reassured me that the rumor was probably untrue but that we needed to take precautions. I numbly agreed, still in shock that I was being separated from my family under such emotional circumstances. With false confidence, I told my brothers, sisters, and parents I would see them the next day, but I was cold with fear that I might never see any of my family again.

I turned and stumbled from our home as I cut off my emotions and willed my legs to run. I fled northeast through a stand of chopped eucalyptus trees that provided cover, then melted into a mass of people headed toward the market, hoping I would be less conspicuous in a crowd. But before I had traveled half the distance, two muscular men spotted me and blocked my path. I was shocked, because both were neighbors who our family considered friends.

"Where are you going?" the taller man challenged me.

"To visit someone, then to the business center."

"Give me your money," he demanded, stepping toward me.

"I don't have any," I said firmly, which was true. I prayed that my false bravado would persuade them to leave me alone.

"It doesn't matter anyway." The man leaned forward and leered in my face. "You'll be dead in a few hours. You and your people will soon be wiped from the face of the earth."

I forced myself to look straight into his eyes, but I did not speak. I felt like I'd been kicked in the stomach. I knew this man. Our families had been friends—meaning that my parents had treated them with kindness, generosity, and hospitality.

Can what he is saying be true? Are Tutsi in our neighborhood being killed—simply for being Tutsi? This man is our neighbor. The wife of one of the other men is my mother's friend! They often spend time fellowshipping together. How can this man speak to me with such rage? How can friendship turn to hatred? My family and I have done nothing. Who have they been listening to that has poisoned their minds? Government officials? Hutu tribal leaders?

"Wherever you're going, they will find you."

Raging hatred spilled from his eyes. I will never forget look on his face. The two men beside him laughed, as if they were envisioning my death. Then as suddenly as they'd accosted me, the three staggered off.

I inhaled slowly. *I do not have the luxury of panicking, I must hurry. They could come back or send someone for me. How many people in my town had been infected by this evil? When and how did it happen? Where hatred is planted, murderous hearts seek death.*

My heart pounded like a drum as I fled. The reality of death had suddenly become palpable. I could not think clearly. My thoughts raced: fear for my family, calculating routes to elude my pursuers, pushing away thirst, envisioning ambush possibilities, and a tangle of other thoughts. I'd left my house without food or water and only the few items of clothing on my back. I had no resources. I did not know which way to turn—right, left, or to head north or back south. I wanted to cry, give in to terror, and run back home.

My brain was muddled, and although I did not know it, I was in shock.

Confused, I took the wrong route. Instead of heading north toward Shushu's house, I turned west toward the home of my friend Adele, who had been my longtime prayer partner. I changed direction out of fear for my life. It was still a ten-minute walk to Shushu's, and I was terrified I would meet people on the road who would recognize me. So, I changed my plan and ran to the home of Adele, who lived nearby.

Fortunately, Adele was home when I arrived and was distraught about my safety. Her husband was traveling, and she was home alone with her preschool-age son and the house helper.

We struggled not to panic about the erupting violence in our community, and I told Adele the Lord would protect me. I believed this was true, but it was important for me to say the words out loud to affirm that truth does not rely on what we see or feel. Truth rests in God's hands. We only see glimmers and shadows from our limited perspective.

I'd always been a prayerful person, but my prayers now carried a new intensity and poured out of me with every breath. Despite my fears, I trusted God. Focusing on God instead of chaos, rumors, and threats comforted me. My hope rested in Him, not in what I was seeing and hearing.

In just a few short hours, my perspective on life had shifted. I did not care about getting married, pursuing school or a career. My only desire was to survive and be with my family again. Everything else seemed irrelevant.

Darkness soon set in, and Adele prepared a meal of cornmeal and vegetable sauce. We sat in the dark sipping soothing hot tea as we tried to formulate a survival plan. I was acutely aware that God had protected me from hate-filled neighbors, directed me to a safe house, and provided food, shelter, and a wise counselor. I possessed only the clothes on my back, my Bible, and a hymnal, yet I had all I needed. Although I was overwhelmed with grief, I was also grateful for God's miraculous protection. But it didn't feel right to be grateful about my survival when I did not know if my family members were dead or alive. My emotions were so conflicted that my stomach felt as if it had been tied in knots.

After we ate, Adele went outside to assess the danger while I prayed. When she returned, she ordered me to hide.

"The men who threatened you on the road are looking for you so they can kill you," she hissed as she shoved me into a closet. "Be quiet. I need to get more information."

I heard the front door close as she crept into the darkness a second time. A few minutes later, footsteps entered the house, and the closet door opened.

Adele was trembling, and tears were streaming down her face.

"What's wrong? What did you find out?" I searched her face. She was terrified and refused to look at me.

"I . . . I am not sure I can protect you. You are not safe here."

She sobbed as she told me she'd overheard people gathered in the streets talking about who had been killed. She cried as she listed the names of our friends and coworkers, as well as the family where I had planned to spend the night when I fled.

"They are dead? Everyone?" My voice went weak. I could not believe my good friends had been executed with machetes. If I'd not become confused and mistakenly come to Adele's, I would have been killed.

"Do you understand, Adele? God led me here. He used my fear to redirect me to safety."

I was overwhelmed but at the same time grief-stricken by the news Adele continued to tell me between jagged sobs.

Every Tutsi I knew who worked at the hospital and local church was dead. The killers were now searching for those who had escaped and were in hiding, and my name had been listed among them. Hutu leaders believed I was likely hiding somewhere between my home and the city center.

I was numb with fear, wondering if my family was still alive. Going home to look for them would put them . . . and me at even greater risk. But how could I flee, not knowing if they were . . .

I could barely give thought to the words "still alive." I wanted to go to sleep and wake up back in my house again, surrounded by my family. Hopelessness suffocated me. I felt as if I would never breathe again.

Adele had started crying inconsolably. Wiping tears from her eyes, she told me she could not continue to hide me.

"The two men who stopped you earlier are back searching for you. If you stay here, they will eventually find you."

Of course I had to leave. My pursuers would not stop until they slaughtered me.

We sat on the bed and brainstormed a list of families I trusted who could possibly hide me. We evaluated my neighbors first. One close friend I trusted was a mother of four children who had been my primary school teacher.

Adele said no. I offered other names, but she had overheard the name of each person I suggested listed among those who had vowed allegiance to the Hutu cause. All of them would be searching for me to kill me, no matter how close our friendship had been before.

I could feel the death grip tightening.

I hid again in the closet while Adele walked to another neighbor's house, our good friend Amaza, whom I'd met a few months previously at my prayer group. As I sat in the closet praying, he and Adele discussed people who might hide me.

I heard noises of war outside—threats and screams for mercy, clamor, as well as victory songs. The manhunts had intensified, and the killing was now widespread. I cried until my eyes became painful and swollen. No matter how hard I pressed my hands to my ears, I could not drown out the sounds of the screams.

When Adele returned, I gathered courage and asked her the question I had been dreading. But I had to know, I had to face the truth, no matter how brutal.

"Have you heard anything about my family?" I spoke the words into the darkness as we huddled on the floor. She inched closer to me.

"I do not know. I have not heard them named among the dead, but I doubt they could have escaped. *All* Tutsi are being executed. Killings have been reported everywhere in this neighborhood," she whispered. "The Hutu militants do not want a single Tutsi to escape."

. . . *do not want a single Tutsi to escape.* The words echoed through my head.

Have they all been killed? Is it possible that I am the sole survivor?

A picture flashed through my mind of my family happily gathered in the kitchen. Now, just a few hours later, hate-driven Rwandans were ravaging our nation like frenzied piranha. Despite what I knew to be true, I could not absorb the horror. But I also could not stop thanking God for protecting me.

But why me? I could not think of a single reason that I should be spared among the many remarkable people I knew. And why me from among others in my beautiful, life-giving family?

I did not know, conclusively, that my family had been killed. In desperation, I clung to threads of hope that they were alive. Adele and Amaza had decided where I should be taken to hide next, so I placed myself in God's hands and trusted their leading.

Suddenly, God helped me to snap out of it and to focus on surviving, taking the next step. If I could focus on helping others, it would help me cope with the unthinkable. Little did I know that I was developing and applying survival and resiliency skills. From my frame of mind, I was simply persisting as best I could with God's help.

I did not know until years later that God would take my daily acts of persistence, tenacity, and focus on achieving goals beyond my abilities and multiply those things for His glory. I believe He blessed my tenacious faith because I was part of a bigger story. My day-to-day tenacity to choose faith and keep taking wobbling steps would one day lead me to a place where I could show others the way to hope and healing.

CHAPTER 11

THE GOD WHO SEES

Don't worry. God is never blind to your tears,
never deaf to your prayers, and never silent to
your pains. He sees, He hears, and He will deliver.

—Author Unknown

needed to be relocated, but we couldn't think of a way to leave the premises without being spotted—and killed.

Hutus were patrolling neighborhoods day and night, searching for survivors. They knew where all my friends lived and had identified Adele's house as a target. Soldiers could already be lying in wait in the bushes or watching from a nearby home. One step outside could end my life. But no matter the risk, I could not remain with Adele.

I had to go. Somewhere.

I awoke on a rainy morning soon after a conversation with Adele The bad weather would discourage patrols. The time had come to leave. Fields surrounding the house had grown high with corn, sorghum, poison ivy, and thorny green plants called *ibitovu*. The thick foliage would provide coverage and protection while discouraging Hutus from pursuing us. Rain, mud, and thorny plants were only inconveniences to me. I was desperate and saw God's hand in anything that enhanced my odds of staying alive.

My friend and I agreed that I could not try to find my way through the fields alone. Amaza came to the house, and at a moment when the area looked clear, he and I raced into the covering of the crops. As we pushed through the tall plants, Amaza scanned the field ahead as he listened for the sound of rustling corn and cracking branches.

I fought back tears with each step as my feet sank into deep mud. I tried to calm my heavy breathing and told myself not to panic. Several times I feared we had been spotted. We were moving slowly so not to alert potential pursuers—perhaps too slowly.

Thorns tore at my arms and legs as we pushed through the field. It felt as if we were moving at a snail's pace to avoid disturbing the foliage and giving away our location. My feet sunk deep into mud, and my legs ached from pulling my feet out of the muck. Plants slapped my face, and *ibitovu* sliced my hands, but I focused on moving forward, despite the pain.

I focused on keeping my balance to keep my thoughts from racing out of control. No matter how quietly I tried to step, twigs and plant debris snapped beneath my feet. The sounds echoed in my imagination like a percussion band, and I inwardly cringed as I waited for our enemies to barrel at us out of the darkness.

After what seemed like endless slogging, we arrived at the back gate of my new host family's home. Amaza shoved me inside the fence, then disappeared back into the dense foliage. I hadn't expected such an unceremonious departure, and I felt strangely abandoned. Two members of the Rukundo family hurried me into their house. I drew in a huge breath, and my muscles relaxed as I collapsed onto a bed in the room where I would be hidden. The entire family crowded into the room to greet me, which was comforting.

I didn't know how long I could safely remain in the Rukundo's home, but as I lay on the bed, I did not care. I was simply grateful to be resting inside a house where people cared about me, plants were not tearing at my skin, and mud was not pulling at my feet every step. I'd survived the perilous trip through the fields with my friend Amaza, and I was alive.

The reality of my grief crushed me like a falling boulder.

I could rest—at least for the moment—and grieve my many losses. If only I knew what they all were.

For the remainder of the day I gave myself permission to cry and mourn the mind-numbing losses I'd suffered and the tragedy that had consumed my nation. In one day, I'd transitioned from life with a beloved family to unverified orphan, running for my life to escape my own slaughter. From the minute I said goodbye to my family, I'd been engaged in a fight for survival. My parents and siblings had reportedly been executed, as well as many of my closest friends. Friends I once trusted were now hunting me like an animal.

My grief felt insurmountable. Hopeless, I could not envision a future. I had no home, no family, no possessions. Assassins sworn to kill me continued their search. I wondered if it might be better to die after all. My life had been rooted in family, school, church, and loved ones. How could I survive this new reality? I did not even want to think about what life would be like without my family. I could not envision a world without them.

I was desperate to know if any of my loved ones had survived and asked the people who were hiding me if they had heard reports. They evaded, and I asked repeatedly. I learned later that they were trying to spare me the painful truth. I questioned mercilessly, and after repeatedly asking Jacob about my father, he relented.

"I am so sorry. He died."

I could see Jacob's sorrow, but he had answered me truthfully. While the truth was terrible, I was persistent because I wanted to know. Now that I knew the truth, I wanted it to be a lie. Or a mistake. However, I knew it was not.

I tried to absorb the blow by telling myself my mother and I could struggle through our grief together when we were reunited. But that dream only lasted a few seconds. Impulsively, I asked if my mother had survived.

"She is also dead," Jacob mumbled, staring at the floor.

Everything in the room went into slow motion as his words pounded through my head.

Mother. Father. Dead!

For a moment I wasn't sure if my legs would hold me. *Why did I ask?* Emotions tore through my heart. Without thinking and desperate for any good news, I sobbed out the same question about my brothers and sisters. Instinctively, I braced myself for the worst—and the worst slammed into my soul with the force of a bomb. One of my brothers and one of my sisters had died—no names were known. Jacob was unsure what had happened to my other two sisters and brother. Most likely, they were also dead.

My thoughts disintegrated. I could not speak. I could not feel. I did not want to feel.

I felt physically sick. Two of my siblings had been killed. I fought not to envision how. Could any of them have possibly survived? Jacob did not know who had been killed and whose status was unconfirmed. How could I grieve, not knowing *who* to grieve?

I'd asked too many questions to turn back, so I asked about our house helpers.

"One left with Hutu militants who were killing Tutsi."

I dropped to my knees. We had treated them like family. Had our friendship meant nothing? My sobs became guttural moans.

Where are You, God? Are You not the God of love, the God of power? Why didn't You protect my family?

Anger flamed in me. Why had I been protected, spared, and cared for? Why was I left with nothing but grief? Odds for my survival were stacked against me. Many had been savagely executed without regard for guilt or innocence.

Pregnant mothers were cut open and their infants butchered. The handicapped and elderly were mercilessly tortured. Children were torn from their parents' arms and executed. The cruelty of the militant Hutus mimicked the acts of mongrel dogs and rabid animals. Sadly, I knew many people who carried out the massacres: neighbors, colleagues, church friends, and acquaintances. How tragic that they had been so easily persuaded to commit such heinous evil against friends and neighbors. Against my mother and father? My brothers and sisters? How—against people who had lived their lives loving and serving others? How, God? Why?

I turned to my faith. I read my Bible and highlighted Scripture. I silently sang hymns and gospel songs as I languished in hiding. With each new day, I realized anew that I would never again see my parents or siblings, and I struggled with fresh grief.

Even as I reached out to God, I wondered if He had deserted me. He seemed distant and silent. I cried incessantly. My pain was so intense I knew only God could heal it, and somehow that simple truth affirmed His presence with me, no matter how I felt.

Weeks passed. Because of the danger outside, I rarely saw sunlight, which tortured me physically and emotionally. I longed to feel sunshine or watch the birds. Why had I taken these things for granted? I tried to imagine what grass and trees and water looked like and envision how vegetation changed with the seasons. I promised God that if I ever saw sunshine and nature again, I would never, never take them for granted again.

But even though sorrow and loneliness burdened me, I was grateful for many things.

I was safe.

God had provided a comfortable, secure home where I could hide.

Kind people cared for me.

My friends fed me every day.

My health was stable.

But on most days my grief consumed my gratitude. I cycled through changing and conflicting emotions: fear, rage, relief, gratitude, panic, grief, and abandonment. My mind raced continually with an avalanche of questions, fears, and sorrow. Although I participated in little physical activity, I was constantly exhausted.

Day after day passed in a fog. One afternoon my friend Amaza came to talk to me and asked, "What will you do and where will you go if you survive? Who will take care of you since your parents are dead?"

I had not considered these questions. In fact, my mind typically bolted like a horse from thoughts of the future. Visions of days to come were overshadowed by hopelessness. I'd been too busy staving off despair to think beyond the next breath. I finally answered.

"I will go home and start my life over again."

Amaza shook his head. "Your home does not exist anymore. Everything was destroyed. Nothing is left." I was shocked by his boldness, but he was right.

He went on to tell me he had stood outside our home and watched people take our chairs, tables, bookshelves, pots, and even cooked food that was uneaten on the table. Hutu enemies even stole the bricks from the walls of our house. Our home had been leveled, as if consumed by a plague of locusts.

A feeling of intense violation washed over me.

How dare these vulgar animals kill my family and ravage my home?

I forced myself to control my anger so I could respond.

"I will live with my uncle in Nyanza."

Amaza managed a faint smile.

"The Tutsi massacre was nationwide. It is likely your uncle is also dead, but we will inquire. If he is alive, we will find him. Your only choice now is to depend upon God. The Lord has protected you this far, and He will see you through."

I nodded silently, unable to speak.

I had no home, no family, no possessions. I had nothing but God. But what plan could God possibly have for me?

I'd been taught that when we cannot change our circumstances, we can choose our attitude. If Amaza was hopeful, I could somehow be hopeful. He saw God's hand in my life, and deep inside, I knew he was right. But I was overcome by sorrow. My heart felt dead.

Amaza opened a hymnal to a song that included words from Isaiah 6. He told me that no matter what happened, to praise God, never stop worshipping Him, and to recognize His holiness.

I thanked my friend for his words—true words, but words I could not hear in that moment. Somewhere deep inside of me, I knew I would never stop worshipping God, but I also knew that, in my profound grief, worship would be as simple as getting up or eating that day.

I thought about Amaza's words over the next few days as I sat in hiding crying. If I was going to survive, I would need to look beyond my grief, change my focus, and find reasons to be grateful. I determined to change my attitude and began to look for things to be thankful for. Feelings could come later.

I was alive. I had not been found by my enemies. As I meditated on the miracle behind this truth, I saw God's handprints all over my life: delicious food, sweet-smelling soap, safe water for drinking and showering, and even the luxury of lotion. All these good gifts were from God. I only needed the heart to see them.

I spent the next several weeks focusing on God's goodness and love for me, and ever so slowly, my heart began to heal.

The genocide continued for weeks, and I had been hiding with the Rukundo family for approximately a month. One day, the family announced that danger had escalated, and I needed to move once again. Hutus militia had started house searches in our area, and they could show up at the Rukundo's home at any time, day or night.

Terrified and hypervigilant, I was now too afraid to sleep. I listened for the slightest noises and remained inside in hiding day and night. I prayed incessantly that I would not be found. At times I felt like fear was eating me alive.

After several days, the Rukundo family gathered to discuss alternate safe locations where I could be moved. They had heard that a man named Pig had been asking people if they had seen me. Pig claimed I was his fiancée and said he wanted to save my life. The truth was that he was lying and was searching for me so he could kill me.

Pig was not my fiancé. We had never dated, and hearing that he was using the ruse of trying to protect me was infuriating.

But the Rukundo family believed Pig's story and wanted to take me to him, believing he could protect me.

I refused to go and suggested another family that might help me, but the Rukundo family thought this option was too risky. So, I suggested that I hide at the home of a distant relative in a mountainous village two hours away. She was married to a Hutu man, so Hutu assassins would be less likely to search her home. We agreed that this was a reasonable option. The only danger was how to get me there. Hutu militants were patrolling streets everywhere.

A two-hour trip would be risky. I suggested having my friends carry me in a wood carrier called ingobyi that was used to transport sick people in Rwanda. Four men typically carried it. This method of travel might be deceptive enough to avoid suspicion. We agreed this would be our best option.

The family contacted my friends, but the plan did not work for them.

Their answer felt like a death sentence. Without their help, we could not carry out our plan. Hutus militants were searching homes everywhere. Their raids had intensified, and even an hour delay could mean my life. I was devastated.

Agonizing, we searched for another answer. My host mother, Miriam, announced that she would be greatly disappointed if I died after God had protected me for so long.

I almost gasped. Was she expecting God to desert me? Had she given up hope?

Their son Joshua added his opinion, adding that if I died, at least I would know they had done their best to help and that they would see me in heaven. I'm sure he meant to be encouraging, but I was devastated. Had he given up too? Was he admitting he believed God had turned His back on me?

My friend Amaza added that if I was caught and killed, he would never trust God again. Then he added that God, who gives promises of life and in whose name we had gathered in prayer, would surely save me. As I listened to him, I thought of the verse, "I do believe; help me overcome my unbelief!" (Mark 9:24).

Amaza's words resonated with my heart. He struggled with doubt, yet he chose to believe. His words spurred my hope, and I clung to them.

A vision flashed through my mind. God had given me wings and the power to fly away from the Hutu militants trying to kill me. A moment later I returned to reality. A new vision replaced my dream—I was dying, and I could feel the pain.

The story of Daniel flooded my memory. Daniel was thrown into a lion's den but was unharmed because of his faith in God. I wondered what he thought about while he was face-to-face with the lions. Was he afraid to move, for fear that his motion might stir the lions? Or did he sleep peacefully, with total trust in God? Did he experience hunger, fear, or worries about personal needs, like going to the bathroom? What was it like to watch deadly lions prowl in his presence, leap, growl, or stare into his face? I *chose* to believe that the same power that saved Daniel could save me as well. I would choose to be a Daniel.

I put my faith to the test. Faith is confidence in things we hope for and assurance in what we do not see (Hebrews 11:1). I placed my confidence in God's plan for my life. I chose to believe

I would live, and I acted on that belief. I focused on remaining positive.

June arrived, and one afternoon the Rukundo family and Amaza announced that militants were coming to search the house that evening. Fortunately, they had found a place for me to hide. Material or monetary wealth could never repay all they had selflessly done for me. Words cannot describe my gratitude for their gracious generosity. I was sad to leave them, but I could not think about it.

Amaza and Jacob had found a partially constructed abandoned house nearby. A group of displaced Hutu families had taken up residence in the basement, but upstairs an unfinished room remained empty. The room had no roof or entrance. Amaza, Jacob, and Joshua would take me to the house and leave me in the upstairs room until they could return to move me back to the house after the search.

At first, I thought the plan was a joke, but no one was smiling. The idea seemed outrageous—but that seemed to be the point. No one would suspect a Tutsi would be bold enough to hide in the same building as Hutus. Every cell in my body cried out to refuse to go.

As the family explained the plan, my mind raced to the absurdities and risks. But we did not have an alternative plan, and within hours Hutu militants would be at the door.

Faith is confidence in things we hope for and assurance in what we do not see. I certainly could not see how I could survive this plan.

I would be taken to the house under cover of darkness. Around two o'clock in the morning, I was told it was time to go.

Based on faith alone, I forced my feet to move. Someone gave me a cloth to cover myself.

Logic told me a certain, painful death awaited me, but faith told me to look into the eyes of God as I walked the path into the darkness ahead.

CHAPTER 12

VEILED

I pray because the need flows out of me
all of the time, waking and sleeping.
It doesn't change God, it changes me.

—C. S. Lewis

never felt more alone in my life than I did during those three days and nights hiding on a rooftop above Hutu militants who were trying to kill me. But God knew. Yet, I could not envision a future without my family or friends or living in a country hemorrhaging with hate.

God *had* seen me. He *had* been with me—at my side every moment. "[I am] the God who sees" (Genesis 16:13). My human inability to see Him did not mean He was not there. Faith trusts when we cannot see. The concept of God assumes He supersedes our limited understanding. I must allow Him to be God and trust Him when my human understanding is confounded.

God had directed my steps from the moment I said goodbye to my parents and fled my home. I determined to cling to the God who *sees*—not only my circumstances and my needs, but *every corner of my heart*. The sovereign God of the universe who loves me is my only hope when the world looks hopeless.

My Bible had suffered damage from the rain, and most of the pages were stained and ruined. The battle scars made it even more precious to me. When I returned to the Rukundo's home, I turned to the Bible verses God had whispered in my ear on the rooftop.

He had blessed me with a family that surrounded me with comforts. For several weeks, I bathed, ate, relaxed behind the protection of a roof and walls, and slept in a bed. My gratitude was heightened by the fact that I had no way of knowing how long I would enjoy these comforts. The rising sun each morning told me I was one day older, but I never knew if each new dawn would be my last.

I could not listen to the radio or read newspapers. I had absorbed too much death and bloodshed, and hearing updates about the continued slaughter was unbearable. But occasional conversations slipped through the thin walls of the house to the room where I was hidden—especially when my new family entertained visitors, which they often did. My hosts had open hearts and welcomed people of all tribes into their home. Conversation sometimes centered on killings and the war.

The Rukundo family often gave me conflicting reports about the deaths of my loved ones—reports that came by word of mouth from family members, trusted neighbors, or acquaintances. People were circulating rumors about my death, reporting they had seen my body floating in the river of Nyabarongo located near my town. Some were quite convinced of their reports, although the search for me continued, since Hutu authorities could not confirm that I was dead. Something inside me cringed at the thought of my lifeless body floating in the river while people casually speculated about my death as if they were discussing the weather. The power of groupthink stunned me, and I have since seen its power to distort the heart again and again.

I was horrified that people were so interested in my alleged murder. But genocide had shown me that hatred often includes a form of irrationality that erases humanity, compassion, and reason.

I was later told that members of the Hutu military were uncertain of my death and wanted confirmation. No one could confirm my death, and reported sightings of my corpse varied, so military officials ordered that the search for me be continued, along with other potential survivors.

Tutsi forces were drawing closer, and the Rukundo family needed to escape. They had protected me as long as they could, and now Tutsi forces were closing in. The family had been packing for days and preparing to flee. I understood, knowing they had no other choice. One day as I sat praying, family members came to me one by one and said their emotional goodbyes. Joshua told me not to worry because the Lord had saved me thus far and would save me all the way to the end.

I clung to his words.

The family had prepared food for me. They could not take me with them and left me at the house to save their lives. I understood their choice. They had graciously helped me, but they needed to go. I forced my tears away.

They said their final goodbyes, gave me food for several days, and left. They locked the door behind them and began the long walk to the Congo where they became refugees, along with thousands of other Rwandans.

As I sat alone in their house, my mind ran wild with images of what would happen to me if Hutu militants found me. The harder I tried to control my thoughts, the harder the struggle became. The silence overwhelmed me, and loneliness devoured my spirit. For weeks, I had basked in the presence of friends, companionship, and comfort. Once again, I was alone, and my food supply was limited. Once my food was gone, I would slowly starve unless God miraculously provided for me.

Every second of my isolation was agony. Nights terrified me, and I listened for the slightest sound. When I heard people passing by the house, I imagined Hutus patrolling the neighborhood looking for Tutsi to kill. I seldom slept, and when I did, I awoke with my face saturated with tears.

Two days passed and no one entered the house.

The evening of the third day I fell into a fitful sleep. I was awakened by the sound of someone coming through the front door. Terrified, I stopped breathing.

Had Hutu killers entered the house? Was this the night I would die?

I thought about crawling under the bed, but it was too low, and I would not fit. I resigned myself to a bloody death, thanked

God for sparing my life this long, and asked Him to welcome me to His kingdom quickly.

The door to my room burst open. Jacob and Joshua stumbled into the bedroom. My friends had come back. I threw my arms around them.

They told me they hadn't felt peace about leaving me behind. They had returned for me so they could take me to French peacekeepers stationed four hours away. The peacekeepers helped survivors and turned them over to the Tutsi military.

My heart leaped in relief, but the plan would once again put me in danger. However, I had no other option for survival, and God had once again brought me help. How could I not accompany my friends and trust that He would protect us again?

My friends and I discussed how we could safely leave the cover of the house. Searches and murders were intensifying as Hutus routed out the last Tutsi survivors. Hutus, who felt justified in their killing, opposed all defense. They believed their violence was justifiable.

As we discussed our plan to make our way to the French peacekeepers, I became light-headed. One more escape was more than I could bear. Jacob suggested I take deep breaths and promised me that he and Joshua would deliver me safely. I argued that we would be spotted, and I would be killed. They calmly told me there were no other options and we needed to try. My legs went weak.

I begrudgingly consented, hoping they were right.

I covered my face with white fabric that looked like a veil. It was important to conceal my identity since many people in the area knew who I was. Joshua gave me a small jar to carry on my head and told me to pretend I was a Hutu fleeing from the Tutsi. If I carried belongings, I would look more like a Hutu headed for the Congo. I brought my plastic bag, which carried my Bible, songbook, and dress. I was wearing the nightgown my host sister Sarah had given me. The boys wedged me between themselves as if I was a sister, and we walked out of the house.

I was trembling. I had not been in public for almost three months, and even then, I had only ventured out at night when I was being taken to new hiding places. My parents had never allowed us to go outside at night as children, so I was afraid of the dark.

However, this night I welcomed darkness. I took comfort from the book of Genesis, where God created day and said darkness was good too. I suddenly realized that God could use even the things we fear to protect us. I kept silently repeating that the dark was my protection.

My world had changed. People crowded the roads, and homes and businesses had been destroyed. Hollow-eyed people stared at the ground as they walked. Conversations focused on bloodshed, terror, hate, despair, and hopelessness.

We headed south toward my home. This would be the last time I would see it, and I wanted to drink in every detail. When we arrived, my eyes searched the debris, but I recognized nothing. My home had been utterly destroyed—the kitchen where my family had gathered for meals, the bedroom where I'd safely slept. The house was gone—the place where I had known love, enjoyed childhood memories, and learned lessons from my parents. I had thought that I had nothing left to lose, but the sight of our ransacked, decimated home filled me with rage. That day, the last vestiges of childhood were torn from my heart. I learned the important role of compartmentalization in survival. Inside, a child was shrieking in grief for her mother, father, and beloved siblings; outside, a determined young woman pressed forward, inwardly grieving in the moans and silent sobs that tragedy allows. Although I was angry, I could not understand what drove people to acts of violence. How do we come to the point of reveling in hating people we do not know? How do people one day pick up a machete and kill friends and relatives?

I stared at the ruins. I didn't want to tear myself away, but I did not have time to mourn. My chances of making it to the French were slim. I had no choice but to move on and force my grief to be silent.

My friends led me through my backyard, past our banana trees, then continued through nearby sweet potato farms. We waded through small streams and scaled a small hill covered in cedar trees. At one point I stumbled and fell, but Joshua pulled me to my feet and encouraged me to be strong.

I could not see in the darkness, and my heart was pounding. The presence of my friends comforted me. Futility tugged at my mind. I felt the urge to drop to the ground and wait to die, but another voice deep inside me told me to push my fears away and press on.

We soon found a road that led to a nearby town where a military checkpoint would be our best option as refuge. I felt this route was too dangerous because people walking the road might know me. Panicked, I tried to dissuade my friends, but they insisted the route was the best.

"Keep quiet and let us do the talking."

I forced myself to do what I was told. We continued, and I kept my face downcast, my heart pounding with every step. Before long, a Hutu checkpoint came into sight.

I staggered as my legs went weak.

Dear God, I cannot do this. I will certainly be identified as Tutsi and be killed!

My friends walked steadily forward. What were they thinking?

As we steadily made our way down the crowded road, I overheard people boasting about the number of Tutsi they'd killed and their plans to kill remaining survivors. In a surreal moment of divine protection, someone walking near me asked another person about the fate of my father and whether his daughter (referring specifically to me) had survived the massacres.

I was certain my heart stopped beating, and I forced myself not to run. *You will not cry, Clementine. Keep walking and do not even blink.*

A man answered, saying that I had *not* been killed. However, others in the crowd quickly chimed in and disagreed, saying they had heard I died in a pastor's home as I was walking to a nearby city for prayer. Then another person joined the conversation, boasting about killing four hundred Tutsi and his hope to kill more. A person walking near me admitted shame for having killed only two hundred people.

Hearing these conversations and more like them escalated my panic to a new level. I was walking among my enemies, so close they could touch me. A voice inside me told me I was walking to my death.

I forced my feet to keep moving. I had no other choice. We passed a forest of eucalyptus and coffee trees, then returned to the main road. About fifty meters from the checkpoint, I stopped.

An opportunity for escape lay before me.

Not far from the road, a ravine ran beside a field.

"I will run into the ditch and die there. We will never pass the checkpoint. I have only Tutsi identification papers—it is impossible."

"If you run, you will be seen and killed. We need to keep walking and trust God," Joshua encouraged me.

I walked two more feet and stopped, fearing I would burst into tears and make the guards suspicious.

"Clementine, today we will know the power of God, if you can pass this checkpoint," Joshua whispered. However, he could no longer contain his fear and whispered, "Although I think you may die."

My heart plummeted. Even Joshua did not believe my life would be spared. He had seen God's hand at work in sparing my life to this point. But he had also seen senseless death and bloodshed so overwhelming that hope crumbled in its wake.

I did not blame my friend. While circumstances seemed impossible, his actions still demonstrated his faith. Together, we walked forward.

When we arrived at the checkpoint, Jacob stepped in front of me, and Joshua walked behind me, surrounding me. The guards asked us to present our identity cards. Presenting my Tutsi identification card would mean certain death. Two guards examined my friends' cards.

"Let these kids go. We know them," one stated. He pointed at me. "But who is this?"

"My sister," Jacob replied with false confidence.

One of the guards shone a flashlight in my face. My legs trembled as I waited for them to ask me to uncover my face or present my card. What seemed like hours ticked by as I held my breath. The guard with the flashlight waved us through.

I stepped forward in a daze. What had happened? I had safely passed through a Hutu checkpoint carrying a Tutsi identity card. The purpose of the checkpoint was to identify Tutsi survivors for execution. The guards had looked at my face but not asked me to lift my veil. They'd not asked me for my card, which would have meant my death. God had miraculously intervened!

Confident of God's protection, we pressed forward in the darkness, following a road bordered by trees. We walked until we neared another Hutu checkpoint and discerned that we should go around it. This would require us to climb a steep mountain. I refused to see the mountain as insurmountable, and in gratitude and praise, I named it the "Mountain of Hope."

Since that day, I have climbed many mountains that appeared insurmountable. Every faith-filled footstep in my life has strengthened me for my next challenge. Our mountains bring us closer to God and teach us that our success is not limited to what we can see and understand. I've learned that reality does not lie in what I see but in the God who sees everything—from the beginning of time into eternity. I can push ahead today because when everything I thought I could see told me "impossible," God proved His faithfulness again and again.

CHAPTER 13

OPERATION TURQUOISE

Friends show their love in times of trouble,
not in happiness.

—Euripides

The first glittering rays of dawn splayed over the mountain as we arrived at its rocky base. The incline rose, steep and foreboding. I forced my bare feet forward, despite fear that I would tumble backward down the mountain and toward my enemies.

I stepped carefully between jagged rocks as stones poked my feet. I'd removed my shoes, which made it easier for my feet to grip dirt and small stones while I pulled myself up. I clung to fistfuls of *ishinge* to help inch my way forward, praying the roots would hold.

I gingerly moved from handhold to handhold. Progress was tedious, which magnified my tension. Jacob carried my belongings and stretched out his hand to me when I needed help. I wasn't physically weak, but mental exhaustion had so overwhelmed me that every impediment felt devastating. Because I'd remained inside in the darkness for so long, my vision had degraded, and it was hard for me to distinguish the features of the ground in front of me. The color of the rocks blended into the brown earth, and I could not distinguish a firm handhold from an unanchored grip. The terrain was steep, and my unexercised legs, arms, hands felt the burn of each step. When we reached the halfway point, I allowed myself to feel a sliver of hope. Perhaps conquering the top of the mountain would be another miracle on my journey. Perhaps my life *would* be spared.

By the time we reached the summit, morning had broken in blinding brilliance that shouted of God's power. The sunlight at the summit was a personal message to me from God: He was continually with me and heard every prayer.

I have been with you every step, and I will never leave you. Trust Me.

My fears lifted as we walked the mountain ridge, as if weight was falling from my shoulders. People in this part of Rwanda did not know me. My friends and I could talk freely, laugh, and hug each other. I thanked them over and over for guiding me on my journey. No matter how many times I said it, my words were not enough. I owed them my life.

Jacob and Joshua led me toward the home of a couple who were their relatives. Immediately, I wondered about their Hutu identity and whether they would report me, but I did not mention my fears. I needed to trust my friends.

For the first time since we'd set out, I traveled without threat of imminent death. Our typical silence was replaced by laughter, conversation, and singing as we reflected on our experiences, marveled at God's protection, and praised Him.

We soon arrived at a pleasant home surrounded by banana trees and were welcomed by a husband and wife whose warm smiles immediately eased my concerns. I felt embraced like family as we feasted on cooked plantains, beans, and tea while we poured out the details of my escape.

The husband and wife were aghast when we told them Jacob and Joshua had boldly walked me through a Hutu checkpoint. They lifted their hands in praise to God.

Although our escape had been miraculous, we could not linger. Our hosts did not know how long they could keep me. Tutsi forces were approaching, and they needed to flee soon for the Congo with other Hutus. But they assured me that I could stay in their house as long as necessary.

Their grace warmed my heart. No matter our tribe or color, like my parents, they believed that everyone shares the same need for compassion in times of suffering. They did not see me as Tutsi to be killed—they saw me as a sister in need.

In the morning, we ate a breakfast of sorghum meal. For lunch, the couple served potatoes, beans, and fresh spinach. They also fed us *kamaramesenge*, which are small, sweet bananas. They spent the greater portion of their day packing and choosing the few things they could take with them when they left for the Congo. As I watched, my mind went back to the day I left our family's home. I did not have time to pack. I had fled my home in less than five minutes with the clothes on my back. If I'd had just a few minutes more to think, I would have taken a handful of cherished pictures from my photo album and placed them between the pages of my hymnal. My hosts were blessed to be leaving for the Congo together. It was hard for me not to see the world in terms of what I no longer had. Everything I did or saw was a reminder of what no longer was. I slipped away and quietly went outside.

Later that day, Jacob and Joshua approached me.

"We must leave you for a short time, Clementine. We must explore the surroundings to see if it is safe for you to leave the house, or if you must hide here until you are rescued by the Tutsi army."

I was shocked. I had only just met the couple we were staying with. I did not want my friends to leave me, but their words also touched me.

I immediately thought of Joshua in the Bible. Twelve men were sent to survey enemy territory. Ten spies came back with discouraging news. Only Caleb and Joshua believed that, despite the enemy's strength, God would guide them safely into the promised land. Jacob and Joshua had served as my Caleb and Joshua.

Solemnly, we said our goodbyes, and Jacob and Joshua set out on their scouting task.

Within hours, the couple who lived in the house fled for their lives, hoping to outdistance approaching Tutsi forces.

Suddenly, I was alone. And I was terrified.

I tried to calm my fears, telling myself that survivor searches were not as intense in this area, and no one in this region knew me.

I could hear gunfire exchanges between Tutsi and Hutu fighters in the distance. The insurgence of Tutsi fighters was forcing many Hutus to evacuate and quickly flee to the Congo. I could not blame the couple that had helped us for leaving so quickly.

My food supply was sparse, and I had no idea how long my friends would be gone scouting. I rationed my food and water. As morning dawned the next day, I remembered anew that I was alone. The day dragged by endlessly as I listened to sounds of war echo on the horizon and hid in the house.

The morning of the second day, I woke up and ate some yams our hosts had left for me. Then I gathered my courage, walked a short distance outside, and sat by the cow house, where cows typically slept. I was protected from view by a wood gate, banana trees, and a nearby kitchen building. I'd strategically chosen a place where I could not be seen but could feel the sunshine warming my face and back. Most of the homes in the area were vacant, so the neighborhood was eerily quiet. It felt comforting to sit in the sun and breathe fresh air. I always feel closer to God when I am outdoors.

The sounds of gunshots rang out, but I could not see anyone. I wondered if Hutus or Tutsi had fired the shots and thought about climbing the gate to look, hoping I would see Tutsi forces coming to my rescue. But there was danger that Hutu fighters were firing the shots. It would be too risky for me to climb the gate, so I stayed where I was and returned to my yams.

I could not identify the shooters as enemies or possible rescuers, so I tucked my head between my legs and began to sob. In desperation, I prayed like Daniel had prayed.

Dear God. I've fought a good battle, and You know I can't fight any more. I give this battle to You.

I could not see how I could survive another day. I was too exhausted in body and spirit to move. I do not remember how long I slumped in the shadows of the cow house. Eventually, I made my way back to the house and closed the door behind me.

As the sun set, my fears intensified. I sought refuge on a bed, crawled under a blanket, and cried until my tears saturated the mattress, and I could not find a dry place to lay my head. Gunshots rang out through the night, and I slept very little.

The next day dawned hot and bright. I cautiously stepped outside and sat again behind the gate by the cow house. Around mid-afternoon, I heard footsteps near the fence by the banana trees. They stopped, then moved in my direction—toward the gate.

I held my breath. Fearing I would be seen, I squeezed into the narrow space between the cow house and the gate. Footsteps came through the gate, entered the structure, then walked behind the cow house.

Someone was obviously searching the premises. I forced myself to peer around the corner, praying I wouldn't be seen. My body was shaking, but I could do nothing to stop it.

Then I saw them. Just feet from me stood my friends. They spotted my movement and erupted in joy as they ran toward me. My eyes burned from crying, and my mouth was dry from thirst. I had run out of food and water, and I was ravenous.

Jacob gently pulled me from my hiding place.

"We have good news, Clementine. The French have launched an operation to create safe humanitarian areas and agreed to accept you as soon as we can deliver you to their location."

I could scarcely absorb their words, and chills rolled through my body. Was it possible that safety was within reach? The thought seemed impossible. My friends added that the journey forward would be safer. Displaced Hutus were too occupied saving their own lives and would likely not bother or recognize me. They instructed me to gather my belongings so we could leave as quickly as possible.

My explosion of joy was tinged with fear. Walking to the French station that had been set up under Operation Turquoise would require me to again walk openly among Hutus. Everything within me shouted that I could not take that risk. But Jacob was insistent. It was the only way to get me to safety.

Once again, God was asking me to put my life in His hands. Despite my reservations, I told my friends I would follow them and do what they asked.

My agreement, however, did not erase my fears.

To reach the French, we first needed to descend the Mountain of Hope. By this time daylight had faded, and darkness encroached. Still, we forged ahead and hiked down the mountainside and through the banana and *ishinge* fields. We saw no one as we walked the mountainous terrain, and my anxiety eased. Eventually, we reached the foot of the mountain and stepped into the road.

Immediately, I began to perspire, and my heart began to race. I had survived checkpoints before, but we did not know how many lay ahead and what dangers they would present. Daylight was once again dawning, and Hutu crowds were passing us on the road. Jacob suggested I hide my face with my arms and walk with confidence. I tried to project courage, and I reminded myself that the Lord was with us and had protected us before.

When we approached Hutu camps, I barely glanced at people's faces, fearing someone might recognize me. But in my peripheral vision I saw families displaced by war milling about temporary housing trying to survive their ravaged lives like I was. Even in my exhaustion, compassion surged through me as I simultaneously wondered if any of the people surrounding me had participated in the deaths of my loved ones. My emotions ebbed and surged like a raging sea as I walked through throngs of Hutu and past clusters of homeless, hollow-eyed people shuffling toward the Congo.

Automobiles occasionally passed us as we drew close to the checkpoint. A blue truck packed in the back with Hutu people heading to the Congo slowed as they passed us. I recognized the driver, Eugene, my father's close friend who had driven us to my secondary boarding school. He was Hutu but married to a Tutsi wife. As he drove by, our eyes met, and I immediately recognized him as a familiar family friend. The truck stopped and Jacob approached Eugene, whose expression told me he was obviously shocked to see me.

I could overhear Eugene as he spoke. He had heard many reports that I had died. He knew with certainty that both of my parents had been killed, and he wasn't sure if he was looking at me or was seeing someone else.

His confusion worried me, and I wondered if he might want to kill me. After all, he was transporting people who had possibly participated in the genocide in the area where I had lived.

He looked at me again, more carefully this time. I fought the urge to panic, but instead, I smiled. Eugene had often visited my father and been a guest in our home. The affinity I felt for him was real.

I strained to listen as Jacob spoke to Eugene, but I could not hear their conversation. After talking to him briefly, Jacob and Joshua turned and told me I was safe. They told me to get into Eugene's truck with the other passengers and he would take me to the French station.

I was apprehensive and uncertain if Eugene was truly my ally, but I trusted Jacob and Joshua like brothers, and they reassured me I would be safe. Skeptically, I climbed into the crowded bed of the truck, and my friends accompanied me. I remained tight-lipped and stared straight ahead. In my peripheral vision, I saw people staring at me, but I had no idea what they were thinking. I silently prayed that no one would pull out a machete to kill me as we rode.

I silently pleaded with God for my life as I watched the war-ravaged landscape slip by. Much to my relief, Eugene did exactly what he promised and dropped us in front of the French station. My friends stood at my side as officers opened the gate.

In the middle of the genocide, God delivered me to safety by putting me in a truck beside men who were supposedly my pledged enemies. But God delights in delivering His children in ways we would never imagine.

My friends and I embraced each other, and they reassured me that the French peacekeepers would take care of me and transport me to the Tutsi army.

"God brought you this far, our friend, and He will take care of you wherever you go from here. Be strong," Jacob encouraged me.

"Your journey has encouraged our faith," Joshua added as he hugged me.

Profound sadness flooded my heart. These two courageous men had chosen love and compassion instead of hate, and now it was time for them to find their way to safety.

Before we separated, I thanked them for all they had done for me. We shared Bible verses from Isaiah 43:1–3: "Do not fear, for I have redeemed you; I have called you by name, you are mine. When you pass through the waters, I will be with you, and through the rivers, they shall not overwhelm you; when you walk through fire you shall not be burned, and the flame shall not consume you. For I am the LORD your God, the Holy One of Israel, your Savior."

I hugged them, then ran toward the French peacekeepers, afraid I would burst into tears. Before I passed through the door, I called back, "Will I see you ever again?"

"We will stay in town a while. If the war continues, we will flee to the Congo. Please pray for us."

I watched as they turned to go, and my heart cried out for their safety. They had become family. I had depended on them for survival. Separating felt like losing family once again, but it was necessary, and God comforted me with His Word: "Do not be afraid. Stand firm and you will see the deliverance the LORD will bring you today. . . . The LORD will fight for you; you need only to be still" (Exodus 14:13–14).

Many times in the years ahead I faced circumstances where I was tempted to fight.

My challenges taught me that growth does not come without hard work. I learned that compassion is the best weapon against despair. I learned to work hard, to be humble, and to trust God to fight for me.

He has never failed me. And He never will because it is impossible for God to fail or to not love His children.

CHAPTER 14

SOAP AND A SWEATER

A kind gesture can reach a wound
that only compassion can heal.

—Steve Maraboli, author of *Life, the Truth, and Being Free*

R elief engulfed me. I was finally safe from the horrors that had overshadowed me for more than three months. By the grace of God, I'd narrowly escaped the blood-drenched hands of the "human animals" who had killed thousands of Tutsi. Because brave people had altruistically protected me, I avoided the deathblows of the machete, but fear and sorrow still gripped my heart.

At last I could rest, think, and sleep peacefully.

For the first time since fleeing my home, I would have time to think about my losses and the atrocities my native nation had experienced. My grieving—our grieving—had only begun. The magnitude of what had happened to me and around me would set in, and I would begin to absorb the many ways genocide had changed me and my nation.

French guards escorted me into a large hall where survivors were gathered in scattered groups. I clutched the small plastic bag that contained all my possessions: my Bible, hymnbook, a brown skirt, a blue long-sleeved shirt, a dress, green Palmolive bar of soap, and a bottle of body lotion. The bag that had seemed a burden when I was fleeing suddenly seemed meager, and my possessions felt like treasures. One small bag held my few earthly possessions, yet I knew I was blessed simply to be alive. The juxtaposition of grief and gratitude felt unsettling and strangely wrong.

I glanced down, suddenly aware of my appearance, mismatched layers of practical clothing often seen on those who were fleeing. I felt no embarrassment, knowing I was in a community of people who shared my story. I was wearing the nightgown my host sister Sarah—whose brothers Jacob and Joshua had guided me—had given me, as well as a sweater I'd brought from home. I was also wearing my sturdy black boots that had protected my feet over long distances and rough, treacherous terrain. Without them, my journey would have been torturous, if not impossible. Once again, I was grateful for God's protection in what seemed to be obscure choices and gifts.

People were sitting and talking in small groups. I had not enjoyed the simple pleasure of leisurely conversation since the day I left my family. I surmised that this was true for others in the room. Many wore expressions of grief and some looked dazed and confused, as if they did not know where they were or could not stop searching for someone they could not find. Several people smiled when they saw me, as though they were surprised to see me and were happy I had survived. I found their smiles welcoming and, in a surprising way, healing.

I approached a group and suddenly recognized my friend Shushu, the girl whose home I had planned to flee to when I first left my parents. Her nose had been sliced and a tooth badly broken. As she turned to greet me, I noticed she walked with a limp.

She had obviously experienced a beating or other violence that had robbed her of her natural physical beauty. I wanted to weep for her pain, but at the same moment my heart rejoiced that she was alive. My friend and I had both survived and found each other. We fell into each other's arms as I thanked God for reuniting us.

There are no rules of etiquette for responding to sorrow and pain—only to love others as you desire to be loved. Out of respect, I did not draw attention to her disfigurement, nor did we talk about our painful journeys or how we had both come to be with the French peacekeepers. Instead, we talked about the future and moving forward. Our hope rested in looking beyond our shared sorrows, but my heart was heavy for my friend.

I continued to hug and greet other survivors. I felt drawn to a woman in her early forties who was carrying a Bible. She was dressed in traditional Rwandan clothing called *ibitenge*, and her hair was neatly wrapped in colorful fabric. We hugged, and I asked her how long she and those with her had been at the camp.

"Two days, but we have been promised transportation to another location protected by the Tutsi army."

I was uncertain how to respond and hesitated. She showed me a large cut on her neck.

"It causes me great pain. Hutu militants sliced my neck, hoping to kill me, but I survived."

I hugged her, but I could find few words of comfort. I didn't feel comfortable asking her questions, but later we developed a strong friendship and formed a prayer and Bible study group. In those first moments meeting her, the words of comfort I offered, while true, seemed shallow and trite.

Later, I spotted a child of about three wandering through the hall. Her dress was tattered and stained, and her stick-thin limbs and sunken eyes told me she was malnourished. She obviously had no parents. She reminded me of my younger brothers, sisters, and cousins. I took her to a corner, stripped off her dress, took off my sweater, and slipped it on her thin frame. Then I washed her dress with my Palmolive soap, trying to hold back my tears as I scrubbed. I could not imagine what it would feel like for a three-year-old to lose her parents and be swallowed by a sea of strangers fleeing for their lives.

I could not offer her much—only what I had—comfort and the dignity of soap and a sweater. Over the coming weeks, I observed everyone in the camp offering this child what they had each day.

As I washed her dress and tended to her, my spirit shifted. When I finished bathing and dressing the child, she found her way to a small group that pulled her beside them. I made my way back to my friend Shushu passing old and young people with medical needs who were rummaging through belongings, staring into space, and caring for one another. I struggled to digest the gravity of all that had happened to my loved ones, those around me, my nation, and to me. A voice deep inside me told me my parents and siblings were alive and near, and we would go home soon. I clung to that thought.

Looking back, I believe part of me identified with the three-year-old child. I was alone in the world. I had been wrenched away from everyone I loved and thrown into a maelstrom.

No closure.

No goodbyes.

No time for grief.

Over the next few days, I sank into a semi-delusional state, thinking—perhaps hoping—I would wake up one morning and see my family again. I often dreamed I saw them in the crowds of displaced Tutsi at the French headquarters. My family and I would spot each other, race to meet, hug and cry, then return home and rebuild our lives.

But eventually my mind returned to reality.

My parents were dead.

I was an orphan, totally dependent upon God to restore my hope and give me a future.

I soon fell into a routine at the French station. Personnel provided us with nourishment that included unfamiliar canned food and bottled water. I was content and grateful to be alive.

About a week after I arrived, we were told to gather our belongings and board a truck to be transferred to a local boarding school, where we would be housed.

I was excited. A boarding school sounded like it might be more comfortable, but I tried not to get my hopes up. I was now transitioning into a new stage of life as a displaced person living among other displaced individuals. I was no longer struggling for survival, but I was fighting to find a new sense of "normal" in this new, temporary world of strangers. Authorities determined where I would live and for how long, what I would eat, and the types of accommodations I would share. Although I was now technically "free," I did not have freedom or choice—and if I had been given choice, I don't know how I would have used it. Or if I yet had the capacity to choose.

People talked eagerly as we crowded into the truck and expressed hopes for better accommodations and privacy. When the truck pulled into the entrance, I spotted a building that looked like the dorm at my boarding school. Memories triggered, and my mind flooded with images of Hutus creeping into the dorm rooms to murder Tutsi students in their beds. My vision was from a dream that had plagued me for weeks after students at my school had been told about the insidious execution plot to murder Tutsi students.

I told myself the plot had been discovered, and I had been spared, but the feeling of doom returned as a guard led us into our new dorm facility. It was a large building where we could comfortably shower, eat, and sleep. Other survivors had moved into the school several days before we arrived. Like us, most of them had been isolated from the outside world and had no idea what had happened to their families. The only things we were certain were true were our own survival stories, which became our bond as we comforted one another.

Several of us sat on the grass outside our dormitory talking about the rhythms of our life, but a pall of grief hovered over our conversation. The monotonous routine of camp life locked us inside a prison of desperate grief. We could not change the past, and we could not move past our sorrow and heal.

A man named John leaned forward, preparing to speak. I liked him. He reminded me of my father's friends, and he made me laugh. John was dark-skinned, in his early fifties, and had the big belly of a man who had probably been wealthy before the war.

John loved to tell humorous stories. It was his way of lifting the sorrow that crushed our souls. John told us about his long walk from his business in the city of Nyanza to the city where his home was located. To make us laugh, he exaggerated his gait to illustrate his journey.

Because of his short stature and big belly, his walk appeared silly, and we all laughed, which felt awkward because I had not truly laughed since before I fled my parents' home. But in this moment, I allowed myself to forget my grief, and I was grateful for John's sensitivity. He had purposefully showed his belly to give us a moment of happiness and ease our sorrow.

A twinge of guilt and sadness settled over me again like a shroud, but as I glanced around, I saw others in our group still laughing. I knew I had no reason to feel guilty and the scars on my heart needed time to heal, but being entertained somehow felt disloyal to my family. A voice inside my head whispered that enjoying myself meant I was forgetting them.

John showed kindness in other ways. He had brought a supply of new clothes with him to the camp. On his journey, he distributed shirts, pants, and sweaters, pretending to sell them so Hutus would not suspect he was a Tutsi.

One day John asked me if I had enough clothes. He'd noticed that I wore the same dress almost every day. I told him I had one dress, one skirt, and one shirt. I reassured him that I was content with what I had, but I'd exhausted my supply of soap and was using only water to launder my clothing.

Although John did not have skirts or dresses to share, he did have new T-shirts. He was a businessman selling his shirts, but he gave me one, suggesting that when I washed my blue shirt, which was my only shirt, I could wear the new one, and vice versa. He also gave me a bar of soap to launder my clothes. I smiled, gratefully accepted the treasured gifts from him, and thanked him. His generosity touched my heart. I believed it was important to share my meager belongings as well.

Resources were scarce in the camp, and John's generosity inspired me because he had more to give than most of us. Sensing my overwhelming gratitude, he told me he wasn't concerned about owning the clothing so his needs would be met. He could start a new business later. John believed that if he was kind to people when they were in need, they would return the kindness when he started his new business. He gave as much as he could to those in the camp who were less fortunate, knowing that many would never have the means to help him in return. He simply wanted to give to bless others.

I came to look up to John like a father. Everyone in the camp longed for family connections. We called people we met *sister, brother, cousin, aunt, father,* and *mother* to forge a sense of belonging with others. We possessed little and had suffered much, and our connections helped us cope with the enormity of our individual and corporate losses. Creating new temporary family units helped us heal and establish a semblance of normalcy.

I'd finished washing my clothes when I spotted a woman from the camp walking toward me across the grass. She was smiling broadly.

"You have a visitor—a young man."

I was puzzled. How could I possibly have a visitor? No one knew where I was.

I raced toward the gate. As I approached, I recognized a friend, a young man I'd prayed with when I was in secondary school.

He grinned at me, like a child who'd been given a new toy.

"I'm surprised you survived, Clementine. Many of our friends have been killed. I almost did not come because I was afraid I'd discover you were not really here. I heard a rumor that you were alive and living at this camp, and I needed to know if the rumor was true."

I smiled as I nodded and told him what I knew about my family members. We chatted for a while about his family and other friends. After a time, he asked if he could do anything for me.

"It would be a great favor to me if you could give a message to a friend who lives near the camp. Please tell her, 'Clementine is alive and is living at the school camp near you. She is well, but she is cold. She is asking that you please bring her some soap and a sweater."'

My friend promised he would deliver the message, then he left.

As I watched him walk away, I pictured my girlfriend's joy when she learned of my survival. I played the scene over in my head in the days that followed.

Two weeks passed, but no one came.

I wondered if my girlfriend had received my message. I'd counted on my prayer partner to deliver my message, and his promise had seemed sincere.

Another week passed. And another.

I eventually learned that when my girlfriend received my message, she'd laughed. "These are difficult times," she'd said, "and giving away my resources is not possible."

Her answer surprised me because my girlfriend was well-to-do and had enough to share. Our families were friends, and she had stayed at our home. Her sister had also lived with us while she attended the private school where my father worked.

This girlfriend chose not to share the most basic needs with me—the warmth of a sweater and the dignity of soap—perhaps because we did not share the same ethnic affiliation, but I was not to judge. I freely shared my soap and sweater with an orphaned child the first day I arrived at the French headquarters. No matter how little we have, we always have something to give those who have less—without judgment.

My friend never responded. Although I was disappointed, I determined to be happy and content, and I refused to be angry or bitter. Gratitude engenders contentment, and generosity feeds purpose. We must fight feelings of entitlement when we feel we have little and, instead, cultivate generous and compassionate hearts by reframing our thinking.

I chose to be content with what God gave me and to trust that He, who had kept me safe on my journey to a new life, would provide all I needed—even soap and a sweater.

I learned that people do not owe me kindness. When it is offered, I receive it as grace. My outlook became this: Receive kindness gratefully and multiply it by passing it on to those God places in your path. These attitudes foster our empowerment.

CHAPTER 15

OASIS OF HOPE

What makes the desert beautiful
is that somewhere it hides a well.

—Antoine de Saint Exupery

E ventually the Tutsi army came to the camp, packed us into trucks, and transported us into the mountains to a school located in a forest. Many young Tutsi had stood against Hutu forces and saved the lives of many of us who were in hiding by pushing back against the Hutu onslaught. Although the Tutsi had secured the area, the other side of the mountain was still up for grabs to either the Hutu or Tutsi military, which made me extremely nervous.

People in this camp took care of one other. We were given soap and clothing, and we helped the sick and wounded and cooked and ate together. I found this ethos wonderfully healing after the ravages of loss and suffering that had torn us apart.

Although all people at the camp were not physically injured, everyone I met was spiritually and emotionally scarred and uncertain about their future. So I formed a prayer group where we found common ground in our suffering, prayed for healing, and thanked God for keeping us alive and for His many graces. This was one positive contribution I was able to make to our camp community, and it lifted my spirits. My friend with the neck injury helped me organize the group. Prayer was crucial to us as we leaned upon one another and God's power in our shared sorrow.

One day, I walked through the camp asking new friends to meet with our group to pray and sing praise songs. Not surprisingly, an angry, grieving survivor lashed out at me.

"Why are you wasting your time praying?" he challenged as he shook his head. "Where was your God when your parents were killed? Where was God when your family, neighbors, and friends were killed? And where was God when your home and your possessions were destroyed?" His voice shook with rage. "You are a homeless orphan, with nothing but the clothes on your back, praying to a god who took everything from you. You are a fool!"

I forced myself not to recoil. This man was not the first survivor I'd met to show such anger. His words and angry response made sense in light of what he had suffered.

Although I trusted God, I pondered what he'd said after I walked away. When I went to prayer group with my friends later, his questions still nagged at my heart. It wasn't as if I hadn't asked some of the same questions myself, but they had always passed, and I'd returned to the foundations of my faith.

In the days that followed, however, I began to frequently ask God why He had not spared my family and why people in my country had suffered so much, physically, economically, and psychologically, and in ways that we would not see for decades. Doubts about God's goodness often overwhelmed me at night.

God, if You love me, why didn't You save my father and mother and my other family members? Why did so many children lose their parents? Why did You allow so much suffering? Why have I been left alone and an orphan, God?

Night after night I wept and asked God why He'd forsaken me. At times I felt as if I'd been a fool to even trust Him.

Yet in spite of my anger, questions, and doubt, I read the Bible, constantly searching for answers. One passage was John 6:68, where Peter asked Jesus, "Lord, to whom shall we go?" As I read these words, God spoke to me. I instantly realized my answers could never be sufficient. I had not created the world or designed the intricacies of my body and mind. Instead of being angry with an all-knowing, infinitely loving God, I decided to be wise and lean on Him in faith, instead of relying on my limited reason.

I chose faith. I also acknowledged I didn't have easy answers.

From that point on, my time at this camp was marked by gratitude. I was blessed to be in a place where I was safe and cared for, and I was grateful to be among caring survivors and under the protection of people I trusted. The world was full of horrifying ugliness, and it was also filled with indescribable beauty. I believed that life held purpose as we firmly stood on the unwavering and loving truth found only in God.

One afternoon as I was cooking with friends, one of them turned to me.

"Clementine, I have heard a rumor. I've hesitated to tell you in case it is false, but I've heard the same report from several people and must let you decide what to do."

I searched my friend's face. Her eyes were drawn in concern, and my stomach knotted.

"I've been told that during the massacres, one of your younger sisters became separated from your mother, and a family friend found her. Your friend took her to another friend in a safe rural area, hoping that hiding her in a remote mountain location would keep her safe from Hutu militants. If the story is true, God has also spared one of your sisters, and you are not alone."

I struggled to believe what I'd been told and could scarcely speak. Tears flowed down my cheeks as the words sunk in.

Had I attempted to flee to that area of the country, Hutus who knew me would have recognized me as a Tutsi and killed me. But amazingly, no one in that area knew who Mirelle was. God had miraculously protected her. An unknown friend of a friend had known right where to take her . . . because God had given her direction.

I told Tutsi military personnel at the camp about the rumor and asked for their help in locating Mirelle and bringing her back to our camp. They said they would investigate and take the situation into consideration. Later that day military authorities informed me they believed it was worth the effort to search the area to look for my sister.

I could barely contain my joy! My heart immediately fixed on the belief that God had answered my prayers and gifted me with a sibling to love again. I could barely think of anything else the remainder of that day.

I gave military personnel Mirelle's name and description and as much information as I could about her likely location. The search would require many hours walking through mountainous terrain. Two tall, handsome Tutsi soldiers agreed to take on the difficult task, and I was flooded with immense gratitude that these two men would volunteer to sacrifice such effort to find my sister. Perhaps they, too, had young sisters or had lost family in the conflict.

Early one morning, the soldiers slung their guns over their shoulders and set out to find Mirelle. I prayed for their success as they disappeared in the distance, then I turned and went about my chores as I awaited their return, trying to distract my anxious mind. But I couldn't help turning and looking down the road where they'd disappeared as I jabbered excitedly and waited.

Around four o'clock that afternoon as I was talking with friends, I spotted two military men with guns over their shoulders leading a little girl by the hand down the road. She was wearing a blue primary (elementary) school uniform and a red sweater. Although they were still a good distance away, Mirelle broke into a run, her arms flailing as she called my name.

For a moment I felt I might collapse. They had found her!

My precious sister Mirelle was alive!

I was not alone in the world, and she was no longer alone.

As she approached me, I could see that she did not appear malnourished or abused, and my heart sighed in relief. Her smile refreshed my soul like a mountain stream.

We raced toward each other and embraced—a long, soul-quenching hug. I held Mirelle to my heart and sobbed, not wanting to let her go. My heart kept repeating "Thank You, God, thank You. Thank You, God, thank You," in rapid-fire succession. I felt as if I could not say it enough.

Emotions washed over me—protection, nurture, and a deep maternal love. I suddenly felt like a mother more than a sister. Awareness of my new responsibilities to my sister gripped me. I had never been fully responsible for the welfare of any of my siblings and wondered how I would explain to her what had happened to our family members. I had no idea how much she had been told about the fate of our family.

I took time to clean her up, then I introduced Mirelle to other camp residents. She was carrying a plastic bag that held an orange sweater and a letter from the friend who had hidden her. In her letter, my friend wished us well and said she had done her best to take care of my sister. She told me she knew we had many needs and expressed remorse that she could send Mirelle with only an old skirt and sweater. Her grace and generosity humbled me.

As I made a bed for Mirelle later that night, doubt engulfed my heart.

How will I care for her without an income, home, or family support, God? We live in a camp—how will I give my sister a life beyond a mere existence? Please, I need Your help!

I rose the next morning joyful to have my sister with me, and I have never forgotten the miracle of our reunion. But questions about how to care for her haunted me.

Mirelle quickly adjusted to camp life. I found it ironic that she did not seem to be burdened by anxiety. She soon became a source of inexpressible joy and hope to me. Mirelle quickly made friends, enjoyed kicking soccer balls made of banana leaves, and discovered the delights of the playground.

She taught me the value of a carefree spirit and letting life unfold without worry.

The evening of the first day Mirelle arrived, I began a bonding ritual with her. I used water, soap, and a stone to exfoliate the rough skin from our feet, then applied soothing lotion. I repeated the process morning and evening. The simple ritual of maternal touch, routine, and pampering drew us together. I drew upon simple experiences like this to strengthen our bond, build a sense of security within Mirelle, and reestablish a sense of familial ties. We were a family again, and my most important role had now shifted to loving, nurturing, and protecting my sister.

Two widows at the camp reached out to Mirelle and me. Madame Jeanne and Madame Rose had decided not to let their losses destroy them. They were two young widows whose circumstances had forced them to face their grief, then use it to rise again. They helped us create a new normal, by creating an "artificial family" with new bonds of trust, routine, structure, safety, and belonging. We provided strength for one other as we discussed how to move on and establish new lives. Mirelle and I felt honored by their kindness and love, and we highly respected Madame Jeanne and Madame Rose.

Many people within our camp created similar family groupings. We found that by re-creating a family structure, we were able to once again feel emotions that had been blocked during the deep trauma of the war. This helped us transition into stages of healing and dealing with the emotions of our losses. We were not trying to replace lost family members but to find functioning roles for ourselves again within a family structure. I struggled with knowing how I could go on without the support of my parents. Madame Jeanne and Madame Rose provided comfort for me and helped me envision life without my parents in positive ways.

Despite our efforts to build new "families" and reestablish connections with surviving relatives, life in the camp was not "normal" and could not give me the life I desired for Mirelle or myself. However, each day I did things our parents taught us were vital to honor and integrity: to be grateful and giving, to be content, and to refuse to complain and whine. But we could not move forward. There were no educational opportunities for either of us—not even training of any sort. Without daily activities to stimulate us, it was difficult to look toward the future and not fall into despair.

Although I tried to remain positive, life was difficult. My attitude dictated my focus, but it did not change my circumstances. I still faced loss, grief, questions, and sparse living conditions. Sometimes I sat in a solitary spot and imagined how life would be if I was living back at home again. I also thought about how blessed people were who still had living parents.

One day, I was in a reflective state and found myself feeling especially sad. As I sat under a tree and looked at the camp around me, I was gripped afresh by the realization that my parents and some siblings had been taken from me. As I contemplated the atrocities committed against my family and people, I was engulfed by sorrow, and my spirit crumbled.

I sank into an abyss of grief and despair. Time drifted by unnoticed as I stared blindly at the hills, mountains, military personnel, camp survivors, and children surrounding me. Eventually, I rose and wandered through the camp and passed a group of children that included my sister. They were kicking a ball made of rags tied tightly together and laughing joyfully.

My heart ached as I watched them. They did not seem to understand what they'd experienced and lost, and I wondered if this was true of my sister. For an instant I envied their seeming youthful ignorance of the horror that had inverted their lives. Yet, I believed the losses in their spirits and souls were greater than mine. Mirelle's mother and father had been taken from her at a much earlier age than I'd experienced. I had many more memories imprinted on my life. The pain of her loss would be much different in nature than mine.

I walked on and observed several young men who had been engaged and had lost their brides to the genocide. Not far from them, young, middle-aged, and elderly sat together, their makeshift canes lying beside them. Several orphaned children wandered among the groups. Childless women mourned the loss of their sons and daughters. Even the Tutsi soldiers assigned to protect us had lost family members. Everyone had lost people we held dear. Grief marked all our lives, and we all bore it uniquely: anger, apathy, silence, grit, grace, questions, doubt, confusion, and every variation of emotional state and grief.

I wondered how many other young women in the camp wondered if they would grow up to be mothers. Did they worry about how they could care for their children and families without the guidance of their mothers who had been killed? This thought overshadowed my thoughts. My mother had been integral in my life, as was commonly the case in Rwandan culture. I had always envisioned her near me to help raise my children. Every aspect of survivors' lives had been touched, and we were all connected in the layers of our losses—past, present, and future.

I began praying for everyone in the camp. Whether or not I knew their name or their story, I felt as if I was grieving with them. The outpouring of grief in our midst was so immense that we could not sustain a vision for ourselves. Perhaps this is one reason why God's tears alone can heal our suffering.

God's grace helps us move from despair to contentment, but I was struggling to do this. I often chose to focus on God's creation and splendor in the trees, mountains, valley, and the beauty of His image in people in the camp. This shifted my thoughts, and my gratitude would return. I decided that as much as it was possible, I would create normalcy and a plan for Mirelle's future and mine.

I knew I was powerless to do this. Other people had control of my life, and I'd become acclimated to the thought that I no longer controlled my destiny. Although this was a negative way of looking at the world, my sense of powerlessness taught me that life was fragile and precious. Powerlessness and pain taught me to value life and to gratefully live each day to the fullest. I wanted control over my destiny, and I decided to work toward that goal through every positive means available to me.

I would no longer wait for other people to intervene in our fate. I spoke to a member of the Tutsi army and told him I wanted to take positive steps for our future. I was powerless to control my future, but I could use what I had—the influence of a simple conversation. Sincere, honest words often become the pivot that directs our future. Soon after my conversation, I was thrilled to learn we were being moved to a better facility where we would receive improved care. As soon as arrangements could be made, we would be transported there with the other residents of our camp.

I was astounded and ecstatic that one simple conversation had brought about such positive news. But more than that, I was overcome with gratitude. Once again, God had answered my prayers. Our heavenly Father was caring for our needs in ways I would not have imagined. All I had to do was bring God my request and do my part, and He answered me.

On a bright sunny day around midmorning, my sister and I were washing and drying our cooking pots atop a green hill beneath a grove of eucalyptus trees. From the corner of my eye, I glimpsed a middle-aged lady dressed in a green and white sarong-like kitenge, a white hair wrap, and white slippers frantically rushing toward us.

I immediately panicked, thinking that perhaps war had broken out again, and Hutus were attacking our camp. The woman must have seen my fear because she instantly called out to me. I will never forget the words she uttered in Kinyarwanda.

"Ntimuhangayike, nfite ubutumwa bwiza!"

My heart calmed because this meant, "Don't worry, I have good news! Gather your belongings! They are taking us to another camp . . . a much nicer camp."

I grabbed my sister and hugged her. The soldiers had done what they'd promised and arranged for our transfer! I grabbed Mirelle by the hand and ran toward our sleeping quarters. As we gathered our few possessions, I thanked God repeatedly and prayed that the truck would not leave without us. We grabbed our bags, raced back outside, and clambered into the back of the truck.

Every bump in the road took us closer to beginning a new life. We were being taken to another camp, the beginning of our journey toward the future. I chose to believe that God was unfolding His plan for Mirelle and me as the Bible promises (Jeremiah 29:11).

When I was a child, our parents gifted all their children with vision for their future and taught us never to lose sight of our goals. So in the middle of chaos and tragedy, I never lost sight of my next objective. My eyes were always fixed on the next obstacle, the next step. I trusted in a power bigger than myself and a divine plan for my life. I found my motivation then, as I do now, in the purpose God promises for my life. This is a commitment and life skill I owe to my parents, who instilled this concept in all their children before they were old enough to go to school. I have always been convinced that I was created for a purpose to partner with God to accomplish His work in the world. This truth gives me strength to press through tough times.

We were driven to a secondary school founded and managed by the Anglican Church. Tutsi military welcomed us at the gates and helped us step out of the truck. We carried our bags and followed single file into the school with other exhausted and bereft survivors who were walking away from their past and toward hope and the promise of a new beginning.

Through God's grace, Mirelle and I had made it one step closer to home.

CHAPTER 16

REUNION

Family means no one gets left behind or forgotten.

—David Ogden Stiers

A s Mirelle and I settled into the Anglican Church camp, officials announced that local employment openings might become available. Those with an education would be given opportunities to work for nongovernment organizations (NGOs).

The thought of possible employment excited me. But until jobs opened, I was assigned with other older survivors to care for children who had been separated from their parents. I assisted in bathing, dressing, and feeding the smaller children. As I worked, I often pondered the overwhelming number of minute details that had aligned to bring about my rescue, Mirelle's rescue, and our reunion.

As people flowed in and out, they brought news of survivors and fatalities. One day as I sat on the grass talking to friends, a woman told me she'd heard that another one of my sisters had survived and was living in our former neighborhood in Kibuye, a long distance from our camp. More than anything, I wanted to believe her, and I only had one way of confirming whether the story was true.

I ran through the camp asking if anyone had heard news about my sister. I eventually found a man I knew from my old neighborhood. When I asked if he knew if my sister Honorine had survived, he sighed, as if I was wasting his time.

"I know nothing, and I'm surprised to see you alive," he said as he rolled his eyes in annoyance.

His answer confused me, then angered me. He was indifferent to my losses, and his lack of compassion was obvious. But I could not waste time on useless anger. I needed to find my sister, and bitterness would only get in my way.

Unwilling to give the man's intrusive and rude comments another second of my time, I turned and walked away. I needed to figure out a plan to take steps to find her—but how? She was reportedly very far away. I continued to question newcomers to the camp while I tried to formulate a plan to reunite Honorine with Mirelle and me.

I found growing comfort in my newfound "family." One day a group of us were walking to a nearby neighborhood, we found ourselves in a grove of majestic eucalyptus trees. We slowed our pace to enjoy the beauty, as well as the shade.

Pounding footsteps interrupted the serenity. A tall young man from our camp named Yohana was running toward us, his eyes wide with fear. We immediately surmised that he'd spotted a threat and was racing to camp to warn everyone. We called out to him as scenes of a potential attack flashed through our minds.

When he reached us, he stopped and gasped out his story.

As he was walking through the forest, he discovered an abandoned church and went inside to pray.

"Masses of dead bodies. . . blood. . . so many bodies," he gasped.

His demeanor had shifted from fear to sorrow.

"Missing family members may be inside. You will only ever know if you go in and search through the dead, but what you see may be more than you can bear. Be sure you can live with the horror if you choose to enter."

Then he raced off as quickly as he'd appeared.

We were stunned and discussed Yohana's warning. Some of us felt confident our family members were not inside the church, since we had already been told of their fate. Others, who did not know their family's whereabouts, considered going inside so they could bury their loved ones' remains if they were among the dead. Some people felt they would not be able to bear what they would see if they went inside.

I was among this group. I knew that looking at what was inside the church would affect me forever. I would never be able to erase the images from my mind. I did not want to carry this scene in my memory for the rest of my life.

I remained outside while others went into the church. Some people reasoned that viewing the dead would give them better understanding of what our people had experienced. I respected their courage. I sat on the stairs near the door and prayed as people entered.

A few minutes later, men and women emerged one by one. Some were shaking. Many were sobbing. Some were struggling to stand, but all came out profoundly troubled and deeply changed. Some people had collapsed inside and had to be assisted out of the church.

As people exited, we gathered in small groups to comfort those who had gone in. Words seemed inadequate, and we grasped people's hands, held them in our arms, wept with them, rubbed their backs, laid our hands on their arms or shoulders, and whispered prayers over them. Time passed without notice, and I cannot think of this day without a maelstrom of emotions. This shrine to suffering nestled in shaded serenity not far from our camp is forever seared into the souls of those who stood inside and outside the church that day. This experience demonstrated to me how profoundly humans are devastated by the ravages of war and trauma. Inhumanity to one another inures us to violence and perpetuates even greater inhumanity.

Our laughter-filled stroll had ended in tears and anguish, and we returned to the camp in silence, forever changed.

I was washing dishes one afternoon when Madame Rose one of my new "aunts" approached me.

"You have been wearing the same worn-out shoes since the day I met you, Clementine. A young girl should not have to dress in worn, mismatched clothing. Although your clothes are always clean and in good repair, you deserve better, my dear."

I wasn't sure what to think—first because I had no choice about what I wore. I wanted to dress in nice clothes, or at least clothes that were comfortable. But I'd long ago decided to be grateful for the few clothes I had. I had no funds or even the means to acquire newer clothes. I certainly did not have the luxury of walking to a store and purchasing a new skirt or dress, since I did not have access to a store or money.

Embarrassed, I looked at the floor. Like every young woman, I wanted to be pretty. But I knew better than to waste time or emotions wishing for things I could not have. I knew Madame Rose would never mean to shame me, but I had little to no choice about my appearance.

Just then, Madame Rose reached into a large woven bag hanging from her arm. She pulled out a pair of green shoes and held them out to me.

As I struggled for words, my other aunt, Madame Jeanne, walked up and handed me a red jean jacket, lotion, and a stylish headband.

"We do not want you to wear the same old shoes and sweater every day, Clementine. As much as it is within our power, we want to help you feel like the dignified young woman you are," Madame Jeanne told me softly. "It's important for your healing and restoration." Then my two aunties hugged me, slipped away, and left me speechless. Their words touched a dry place in my soul, and I fought the urge to cry.

I went to our room and slipped into my new garments. John, the merchant from my previous camp, had given me a new shirt, which completed my outfit. For the first time in a long time, I felt pretty and confident about my appearance. Since the war had started, I'd wondered if I could ever feel that way again, and I was enormously grateful.

Later that morning, I thanked my "aunties" for their gifts, which had come at a sacrifice to them. I was awed by such a personal blessing. They cared for me as if I was their own child. Each of them had providentially escaped with good clothes, shoes, shirts, lotions, and other luxuries practically nonexistent in survivors' camps, and they'd shared the little they had so I could feel confident, secure, and pretty. I was moved by their generosity. Most young women I knew longed to indulge in rituals and wearing clothes that helped them feel pretty, but I had long since abandoned such desires. God abundantly tended to my sister's and my care through the love and generosity of our two "aunties," even though it would have been selfish to focus on my own personal, extraneous wishes.

Our little family group established a routine. We cooked rice, green bananas, cabbage, carrots, and beans, among other delicacies every evening and ate together as a family. At times I felt like I was enjoying life at home, and this outlook helped me survive. We also spent social time with other family groups.

Since my aunties were in their early thirties, it seemed likely that they might remarry. I assumed that my younger sister would be incorporated into my family when I eventually got married, but I was not focusing on marriage because I was still working to survive. I was still mourning my family and my losses and needed time to heal and create plans.

And I also needed to find a way to locate my little sister Honorine, who was allegedly alive, and find a way for us to be united.

My dream for finding Honorine seemed impossible, but I refused to stop asking God to fulfill it. I continued to ask newcomers in the camp about my sister and sought answers from anyone who would listen to me.

Eventually, I realized that my job was not to figure out a plan but to trust God, who had a plan far better than mine.

CHAPTER 17

THE SEARCH

I sustain myself with the love of family.

—Maya Angelou

During my time in the Anglican Church camp, I had no idea that thousands of miles away in the USA, my older brother, Zacharie, was intently following news about Rwanda. He had become an international student at a midwestern university after traveling to the United States several years before the war had broken out.

I was certain Zacharie could not help me because I had no way of contacting him, and he had no idea where I was or if I was alive. The obstacles seemed insurmountable, and I was convinced that I would never see him again. I knew Zacharie was alive, but I had no hope of ever seeing him again. The chaos that had ensued during the war made it impossible for him to ever track me down. Of course, I was looking at circumstances from my limited, human perspective and did not consider that God might have a plan.

Thousands of miles away in Iowa, Zacharie was uncertain about our family's circumstances and had no reason to believe any of us had survived. He later told me, he felt tormented. When news broke about the Hutu uprising, he watched television continually to learn anything he could about the fate of our family. Zacharie told me about the isolation he felt, alone and thousands of miles from home in a foreign country while war raged in his nation.

"As I watched the conflict raging in my homeland, I knelt and cried out to the Lord, do not leave me like one abandoned and alone, dear God. Please save at least one family member. I do not want to be left alone in this world. God, please preserve the life of at least one of my brothers or sisters."

Determined to not sit by helplessly, Zacharie searched for as much information as he could find about the plight of his family. He felt compelled to take a break from his studies to go to Rwanda and search for us. His pastor, friends, and members of his church in Iowa advised him against the trip, warning him of the dangers. But undaunted, Zacharie began his journey in June of 1994.

Killings still raged in pockets of Rwanda, although most of the country was safely in the hands of the Tutsi military. With only a few family photographs in his pockets, Zacharie began searching northern Rwandan survivors' camps, showing pictures to survivors and asking if they had seen anyone in the photos. He told them he was looking for a brother or sister because he was almost certain our parents had been killed.

Person after person shook their heads no, as Zacharie passed through camp after camp. He tried not to think about the impossibility of his task. With each day, his odds narrowed, and still he pressed on.

But he remained undaunted. Something in Zacharie's spirit told him to persist—that he was not the only remaining member of his family. And he would not stop looking until he had searched every camp in Rwanda and beyond.

I awoke and prepared breakfast as I did every morning. I was preoccupied as I pondered how I would take care of Mirelle if my aunties Madame Jeanne and Madame Rose remarried. How would I manage life without my mother, father, and other siblings? I was beginning to fight discouragement related to the thought of not having control over any area of my life. I did not know how long I would be in this camp or whether we would be moved to another camp.

I fed Mirelle and did my camp chores, then sat down to visit with another resident. As we sat on the grass chatting, I glanced toward the entrance gate a short distance away. A white car was entering, and I concluded that a guest was coming to visit someone, since the vehicle was not military and probably belonged to a private citizen.

The car headed in our direction, then stopped and parked near the playground. Camp residents stopped talking as two military men with automatic rifles got out of the car. A dark-skinned, tall man in his late forties or early fifties followed them.

Behind him, a tall, light-skinned young man in his early twenties exited the vehicle.

I shaded my eyes with my hand and squinted my eyes.

The older man resembles Pastor Kamana, my father's best friend . . . but it can't possibly be Pastor Kamana. He lives nowhere near here.

I squinted my eyes and looked more intently.

The tall young man resembled Zacharie, but my brother had been living in the United States for several years. It would be impossible for him to leave America, much less find his way to our camp. But a spark ignited in my heart.

The four men walked confidently toward where I was sitting with my friends. The determination and pace of their stride told me they were hoping to talk to us. The younger man's stride resembled Zacharie, but I could not allow my mind to trick me. It could not be him when I knew he was thousands of miles from me, attending his classes.

I stared at the older man, and he returned my gaze with a smile. Suddenly, I became faint, and I felt myself begin to shake. There was no doubt. My blood stopped flowing in my veins, my vision narrowed to a dark tunnel and then widened again. I slowly rose to my feet, as if lifted by an unseen hand.

It is Pastor Kamana! He has found Mirelle and me and has come to get us!

The idea seemed surreal. I smiled timidly at him, still uncertain.

As the men neared, I could see their features more clearly. My brain shifted into slow motion as my eyes froze on the face of the tall young man.

Zacharie! Zacharie! He found Mirelle and me! How is this possible? Am I hallucinating?

Two Tutsi military men from our camp approached Pastor Kamana and Zacharie. The four men stopped in the middle of the playground and conversed briefly. I could not hear what they said, and I continued to stare, dazed and unable to move.

Suddenly, my mind snapped back to reality. I ran full speed toward Zacharie and Pastor Kamana, hugging him first to give my heart time to prepare for the miracle of sinking into my brother's arms. As I hugged Zacharie, I allowed myself to think the words that had been unthinkable.

My brother has come for us!

Zacharie embraced me fiercely, and his hug told me all I needed to know. We were both fighting to believe we had found each other and were too shocked for words, but we did not need them. Mirelle and I were safe, and we were found. The words pounded in my head. We were found.

I took a deep breath and pulled away from my brother.

"I am not here alone, Zacharie. God has given us another miracle. I turned and raced toward the play area to find Mirelle. Her eyes grew wide as she saw me running toward her, and panic flickered across her face.

"It is all right, sister. Zacharie has come for us!" I grabbed her by the hand and pulled her toward our room. "We must hurry!" I urged her.

Something deep inside me feared that Zacharie might disappear before we returned. The feeling persisted as we hastily gathered our meager belongings, hugged our beloved "aunties," and said quick goodbyes to friends. I barely had time to think about how much I would miss our two beloved aunties. How could I ever thank them?

My mind tried to absorb how quickly my life had just changed. God had obviously directed my brother to us, yet my mind was a jumble of gratitude, joy, and fear that Zacharie might be gone when we returned.

But he and Pastor Kamana were standing exactly where I left them. Mirelle leaped into Zacharie's arms, and he spun her around. Pastor Kamana gave us a few minutes to bask in our joy while he spoke to camp personnel. Then Zacharie explained his plan.

Within a few minutes we were driving out the gate as our camp family waved goodbye to us in the distance. We drove to Kigali, where Pastor Kamana had been staying when Zacharie found him.

As our vehicle passed through the countryside, we observed the devastation of war: displaced people carrying their possessions, military trucks, destroyed homes, and cows roaming freely.

When we arrived in Kigali, we were welcomed into the home of one of Pastor Kamana's friends, who had also survived the killings. The family was warm and hospitable. My brother and Pastor Kamana would leave early in the morning to look for our sister Honorine, and check on the rumors that she was still alive.

Mirelle and I awoke the next day unable to focus on anything but Zacharie and Pastor Kamana's return. We sat in the front yard staring at the gate and praying for a white car to appear in the distance.

I was unable to eat all day, and evening was beginning to fall. Every muscle in my body had grown taut with worry. As the sun slipped low on the horizon, a white vehicle approached in the distance.

I prayed for it to continue in our direction. Moments later, it stopped in front of the house where we were staying.

I felt dizzy as Zacharie stepped out, then turned and gently assisted a tall, beautiful girl from the vehicle.

I could barely keep from dancing as my eyes swept her face.

My beautiful sister Honorine!

Person by person, God was restoring our family. My brother had asked for one brother or sister and had been given three. We were now a family of four. I had feared I would never see even one of my family members again, and God had reunited me with a brother and two sisters. Yes, my losses were immeasurable, but my gifts were also without measure. I wondered how Mirelle and Honorine were dealing with their enormous losses and how I could better help them heal. Now that Zacharie had found us, perhaps together we could create a plan for helping our sisters.

Family—just thinking the word made me weep with gratitude.

Our reunion in those next few hours was precious—joyous, yet tragic and heartrending.

Zacharie, Mirelle, Honorine, and I remained in Kigali for a few days to inquire about the fate of other family members. One man we spoke with sadly told us that our other sister, Vestine, had definitely been killed in his house, along with his sisters. We looked for her anyway, along with our two other brothers, Dave and Josiah, even though we knew his words were true. Something inside us would not let us stop looking until we had exhausted every possibility. We owed this to every member of our family, and our search gave us time together to process the news we'd heard. This was precious to me.

We visited another friend who had closely followed news about our family members. She confirmed the grim reports regarding other missing family members (two brothers, our parents, our sister, God sister, and many extended family members). With this information, it became clear that our search for our family had ended, and the time had come to begin making decisions about our future.

Zacharie felt he should help us come to the United States where he was studying, and we could begin our lives together. Although the plan sounded ambitious, we believed the God who had reunited us could work out the details. So we dubbed America our "promised land" and looked toward the future.

But I had no knowledge of the process, especially since any governmental normalcy in Rwanda had been thrown into disorder. I would need to rely on Zacharie regarding the needed steps to immigrate to the United States. In the back of my mind, questions nagged regarding how and where I would find employment that would support my sisters and me until we could get there. But I had seen doors supernaturally open for me repeatedly on this journey, so I pushed my reservations aside. I would not stop trusting now.

Unaware of the obstacles before us, my siblings and I stepped out in confidence, believing our responsibility was to trust God for one step at a time. My sisters, my brother, and I had been miraculously reunited, but our journey back to life together had just begun.

The moment I caught sight of Zacharie walking toward me in the camp is forever seared in my memory: the shock of knowing it was him and the terror of risking the devastating blow of being wrong. My hope was too fragile for me to risk— hope was my lifeline, solace, and motivation.

But that day, as other days, taught me that hope is only as secure as its object. My hope the day Zacharie found us was that God would take care of us, no matter the devastation around us.

Though tears and tragedy marked my path and the path of my family members, each agony and heartache I lived through was pierced by the thread of God's purpose and stitched to His own healing heart.

CHAPTER 18

LEFT BEHIND

Patience is not simply the ability to wait—
it's how we behave while we're waiting.

—Joyce Meyer

We were now a family of four grieving those we had lost, yet grateful we had each other.

Despite my brother's deep sadness, he assumed a positive tone as he announced his plan to bring us to the United States. The first step was for us to journey to Kampala, Uganda.

We were about to embark on an arduous trip through foreign lands to travel to a new country where no family or friends would await us. Zacharie's plan sounded daunting to me, and I was certain it must have terrified my younger sisters. I squeezed their hands in reassurance as our brother spoke.

"Uganda is the best place to process the necessary paperwork to secure visas for all of you to come to the United States. I will make sure you are situated before I go."

Zacharie's expression told me he sensed our concern.

On a bright Saturday morning, we boarded a taxi at a crowded station in Kigali and traveled north toward Uganda to meet Pauline, the angelic woman who offered to host our family. Her generosity reminded me of my mother, and I tried to compartmentalize those feelings.

Although Uganda was unfamiliar to me, my brother seemed confident about our whereabouts. I trusted him and began to relax. I was excited to have the opportunity to explore this new country. A crushing weight had been lifted. We were safe. I did not have to worry. We were with Zacharie.

It became increasingly obvious that Zacharie could not stay with us indefinitely. He needed to work from the United States to begin the process of bringing us to live in America on a family reunification plan. I tried to push away my rising feelings of anxiety. I wept in secret, fearing our impending separation.

He assured us he would not leave us alone and comforted us with the same Bible verses about the exodus and journey to the promised land that I had been thinking about. These Scriptures gave us hope that our needs would be met, that God would lead us, and that we, too, would arrive in our own promised land. He added that, like the children of Israel, we would all soon be living in a land of milk and honey. He used these examples to support what he believed was the wisdom of leaving us to go back to the United States, finding a home for us there, completing the required paperwork, and then returning to take us there, after he finished making the needed arrangements.

I would be fully dependent upon Pauline and hated feeling dependent, but at the same time I was grateful for her generosity. I fought paralyzing anxiety as the days counted down to Zacharie's departure and prayed continually.

God, I believe. Help my unbelief.

Someone was shaking me, and I was shivering with cold. I rolled over, my head in a fog, to see if my sister was trying to waken me.

Every muscle in my body ached in protest as I tried to move. My body was drenched in sweat, and my head was throbbing. The slightest movement agitated my nauseous stomach.

I was now fully awake and aware that I was violently ill. My symptoms were familiar. I had malaria, and Zacharie was leaving to return to the United States in three days.

I moaned, and my youngest sister answered.

"Get Zacharie," I whispered to her. "I am sick and need medicine. I am sure I have malaria."

My brother immediately recognized that he had to get me to a clinic for medication so my condition would not worsen.

"We must pray we can find a clinic that is open on a weekend," he spoke as he helped me stand. "I cannot leave if you are this ill."

I leaned heavily against my brother as he tried to help me walk to the nearest taxi station. I was too weak to walk unassisted and too heavy to carry. I told myself not to moan as I forced my legs to move.

But the distance to a taxi station was farther than we anticipated. Each step sent pain shooting through my body, but

I refused to complain. Eventually, we came to an abandoned marketplace where food had once been sold.

"I am exhausted, brother. I must sit," I panted.

We stopped, and Zacharie eased me onto a wooden crate so I could gather my strength.

I can barely walk, God. How am I going to survive and take care of my sisters after Zacharie leaves? I feel helpless, and I am afraid.

People stared at me as they passed. I felt embarrassed and ashamed to appear so ill and feeble in public.

We soon rose to continue, and I struggled to keep even a slow pace. It took nearly an hour to walk from Pauline's home to the taxi station.

We quickly boarded a taxi and desperately looked for a clinic that was open. I needed to get well quickly so Zacharie could return to the United States. I prayed as we drove up and down streets in search of a medical facility.

After nearly half an hour, Zacharie spotted a clinic and half carried me inside. A harried-looking nurse curtly told Zacharie that I would need an injection, but they had run out of new needles.

No new needles?

We quickly turned and left. I told myself not to cry and to be strong as I leaned on Zacharie's shoulder and trudged slowly back to the taxi.

We arrived home totally exhausted. When Pauline heard what had happened, she immediately left to find a pharmacy and purchase over-the-counter medicine—large white pills that

I took for the coming week. Because of God's mercy, I made a full recovery, and Zacharie left for the United States.

We made new friends and socialized with neighbors, who quickly accepted us and made us feel like family. Some were from Rwanda and spoke our language. Every Sunday someone picked us up in a taxi and took us to their church. But as soon as we began to gain stability, our circumstances changed. Our hostess, Pauline, decided to travel to Rwanda for a time. So Pastor Paul asked a woman from the church named Josephine to watch over us.

Josephine was a devout Christian who spent much time praying and did not eat often. She fasted a great deal as part of her regular spiritual discipline.

I was tired of waiting to resume my life. I thought I should be in school or working instead of chatting, fetching water, and worrying about the future. I spent many days at the United States Embassy in Kampala filling out papers and waiting for our visas to be processed. Getting to the embassy required walking a challenging distance. Repeating this task day after day exhausted my body and spirit. Several months elapsed. I became numb with worry about what would happen to my sisters and me.

One of the biggest challenges of waiting is the inability to see what is on the other side or when or if the wait will end. Of course, my sisters and I were yearning for a reunion with Zacharie in the United States, but we had no evidence that the process was moving forward. In difficult times, our inner sources of strength and resilience are our most powerful sources of endurance. I was motivated primarily by faith and family. I had sisters to care for and a brother who was waiting for us in America. I also trusted that God had a plan for us, and our time of waiting would soon come to an end.

Ironically, during the challenge of waiting, I discovered my gift of listening and offering others comfort. I often visited and prayed with people. Since I was essentially doing nothing, I wanted to use my time to serve others. I learned that when struggling people feel heard, they sense hope. As men and women confided in me and unburdened their problems, I set aside my pain to minister. Others had ministered to me, and now it was my turn to listen, encourage, and pray. I was blessed as people talked about their pain and problems, and I could offer comfort, encouragement, and prayer. Reaching out to the hurting helped us both as we lifted up one another.

Sometimes I struggled to believe because I did not see outcomes that made sense to me. Solutions and timelines that seemed to be obvious answers to problems were hidden from my earthly eyes, and I became impatient with God. Our waiting in Uganda and in other circumstances, ultimately taught me that I *can* trust God, who is working in ways I do not see, and on a timeline that is not mine.

One morning I woke up early. Because of rain, a tent had been set up for a Christian crusade. I put on my red dress and wrapped myself in my traditional African cloth. I decided to attend the event alone and walked to the tent, then sat down in the grass and began to sing *What a Friend We Have in Jesus*. As

I sang, I claimed the words that tell us to bring Jesus our heavy burdens and not to bear needless pain. I asked the Lord to take away my burden about traveling to the USA.

I longed to talk to God about my exasperation regarding our prolonged wait for our visas and my self-loathing for feeling unproductive. Each day of the conference God met my need— through comfort from a stranger, a timely Scripture, or a message delivered to my heart.

I'm with you, Clementine. I have provided for you thus far, brought your brother and sisters to you, and I will complete what I began. I direct and protect you every day.

Wait . . . just a little longer.

Do not fear. I go before you.

Do not be ashamed. I see you.

Do not fear that you are not working hard enough. Help others while you wait on Me.

At the end of the conference my circumstances had not changed, but *I* had changed. Hope stirred inside me, a gift from the Spirit of God. He had answered my request.

My siblings and I now faced the last steps of our journey, and I looked ahead with new confidence. Our heavenly Father would not fail us now.

CHAPTER 19

GIFT OF HOSPITALITY

No one has ever become poor by giving.

—Anne Frank

hen Zacharie called to check on us, I was forced to tell him the sad truth. I was tired of being unproductive, unable to work in this foreign land, and tired of feeling like a failure. The energy drained from my spirit as I tried to explain our dire circumstances without complaining.

"Our only purpose for enduring life in Uganda is to see the consulate," I pleaded into the phone, praying he could understand. "Day after day we sit in a stuffy room, endlessly waiting to talk to someone who can help us. Nothing ever happens. What should we do?"

But Zacharie was convinced that our visa applications needed to be processed in Uganda. He believed that quitting would be unwise, since a ray of hope had appeared. "You have been granted an appointment to talk with the United States

Consulate in Uganda about your visas, sister. Your waiting has not been in vain."

Despite my frustration, I agreed to remain hopeful that we soon would see progress.

The day of my long-awaited appointment finally arrived, and once again I made the long walk to the consulate building and the familiar bench in the waiting area. As the moments ticked by, agitation rose in my chest, and I prayed, asking God to calm my fears.

When my name was called, I drew a deep breath as I rose from the bench.

At that moment I heard a clapping sound and jerked, startled. As I glanced around, I saw that the weary refugees crowded into the reception area were clapping for me. We had sat together for many days and weeks. One of us being called into the office spoke hope for all who remained behind.

I rose, walked through a doorway, and entered a room where a woman stood waiting to greet me. I believed she was the United States Consulate, but I was not sure. She lifted her eyes from her paperwork and smiled ruefully at me.

"I'm very sorry to tell you that you have been wasting your time in Uganda. You will not be able to obtain visas here."

I felt as if she had slapped me. I stood in shock as her words sank in. We had *wasted* our time in Uganda? I wanted to cry but would not allow myself the indignity.

She went on to say that the Joint Voluntary Agency (JVA) in Nairobi, Kenya, operates a United States refugee resettlement program, and this is where our case would be processed.

I was confused. What did this mean? Did we need to travel to Nairobi and begin the grueling process of waiting again? How could the girls and I *possibly endure* another wait?

Disappointment and sadness flowed through me, but I could not allow my emotions to control me. My sisters would look to me for leadership, and I needed to remain focused and positive. My task was to concentrate on the next step—how to get my sisters and myself to Nairobi.

The day after the interview, Zacharie called.

"You will need to travel to Kenya."

"How will we get there?" I asked.

"By bus." I heard the apprehension in his voice.

"Can we leave on Monday?" I pleaded. "Then we can go to church and say goodbye to our friends."

"You need to leave as soon as possible."

I understood my brother's concern. Our separation caused him great anxiety, and bringing us to the United States had become far more complicated than any of us had predicted.

I needed to talk with Josephine, who could offer me wisdom. When I went to speak to her, she graciously offered to accompany us to Nairobi. This gave me great peace of mind. I packed our belongings into the brown suitcase I'd purchased: gospel music tapes, shoes, clothing, Bible, songbook, lotions, photograph album, prayer mat, and a traditional worship drum.

We woke up early to depart from the Kampala bus station. We crowded into the bus, found seats, and rode for many hours. Each time the bus stopped, I asked Josephine if we had reached Nairobi. I must have sounded like a petulant child with my incessant inquiries. Each time I asked, she patiently explained that the journey was long, and we might not arrive in Nairobi until early the next morning.

Eventually, we reached the Ugandan/Kenyan border. Police boarded the bus to check passports, and I immediately began to tremble. When they approached us, Josephine and I handed them our documents. One of the officers inspected my passport, looked at me, then began yelling as he gestured for us to get off the bus. Josephine, obviously as surprised as I was, politely asked him what was wrong. Angrily, the officer told us we did not have visas to enter Kenya. We had been told our pastor friend would meet us at the bus station and pay our visa fees when we arrived in Kenya.

We explained this to the policeman, but he would not accept our answer. Instead, officers escorted us off the bus as they continued yelling about our violation. Josephine tried to negotiate on our behalf, but the officers refused to listen. The bus driver kindly waited, thinking we would pay the fee and get back on the bus. When the officers discovered we did not have the necessary funds, they curtly told us to retrieve our baggage. The bus driver found our luggage, set our suitcases on the side of the road, then closed the luggage compartment and drove away.

My heart was pounding. It was night and we were several hours from Nairobi. I pulled my sisters close. Were they frightened? What on earth were they thinking?

It became clear we were being abandoned at the side of the road in the dead of night. In a state of shock, Josephine and I stumbled through a discussion about our limited options. We were trapped at the border at night in a strange environment, surrounded by people we did not know. I suggested we make a pay-phone call to Pastor Kanyange. Josephine agreed and directed me to a nearby phone. I was relieved when Pastor Kanyange answered. But moments later the call disconnected before I could explain what had happened. Pastor Kanyange and I had spent too much time greeting each other, as was our custom, and I'd not put sufficient change in the phone.

I quickly called him back, skipping polite greetings, and hastily told him we were stranded at the Ugandan/Kenyan border and needed to pay for our visas. He responded with great concern, assuring me that everything would be okay. He told us to remain calm and that he would come as soon as possible and pick us up. He directed us to stay where we were and avoid walking around.

Since Josephine had traveled to Nairobi before, she knew it would be some time before Pastor Kanyange would arrive, so she suggested we find a place to sleep. This was not a comforting thought. The darkness was impenetrable, and we were all fighting fear.

I suggested we try to locate a house and plead with the residents. Josephine did not like the idea of knocking on a random door at night. She felt we should remain near the bus station until the pastor came in the morning. I feared that loitering around a bus station all night could be dangerous, but I complied with her suggestion. To discourage anyone from approaching, I placed our suitcase on my head and strolled the area confidently, acting as if we had a purpose for being at the bus station at night.

After a while, we felt more confident about our safety. We also became bored, so we expanded the distance of our walk. As we strolled to the east, we passed bars and people milling about. As we walked, we passed a young woman in her mid-twenties who appeared to be Rwandan. I suggested to Josephine that this might be a safe person, and perhaps she could offer us advice about where to stay. I assumed she lived in the area.

I set my suitcase down, and Josephine and I introduced ourselves. The woman was pleasant and lived nearby. I told her what had happened to us and expressed our concern about being near the border through the night.

"You can stay with me," she offered, adding that she lived in a humble, one-room house.

I was surprised at her generosity and immediately accepted her offer. Josephine, however, hesitated. She was concerned that the woman's home might not be close enough to the bus station to allow us to easily connect with Pastor Kanyange when he arrived. But safety was our highest priority, and we accepted her generous offer.

Our new hostess led us along a path overhung by banana trees. Wind rustled the leaves and mingled with the sound of our footfalls brushing through fallen leaves. I cringed at the sound of the noise that triggered memories of fear-filled days and nights when I was fleeing for my life. The slightest sound triggered the fears I'd experienced in hiding. While darkness terrified me, it also helped me feel secure. I was grateful that Josephine was with me.

I took long, hasty steps to reach the woman's home as quickly as possible. Josephine and our host talked casually as they strolled behind me at a comfortable pace, obviously not afraid. The walk felt like an eternity to me. We finally arrived at her home: a small oval house made of grass with a thatch roof. Our hostess invited us to enter the single room, which was lit with a kerosene lamp.

The woman told us her name was Valentine and instructed us to make ourselves comfortable while she prepared a meal for us. She served us hot tea as she prepared a meal of sliced plantains, sautéed meat, and vegetables.

That night we slept comfortably on the floor on a woven mat. Our hostess also provided us with blankets. I felt honored and pampered by the simple luxury of a full stomach and a warm, safe place to sleep. I rested well—a true blessing and a gift from a stranger.

Early the next morning, Valentine prepared a breakfast of tea and bread with butter for us. We ate and thanked her for her hospitality and kindness. Then we hugged her and asked for God's blessings to be upon her.

"At times I feel like God isn't there," she said.

"We all feel that way sometimes, but feelings change," I replied. "We can depend on God because His love for us does not change. Even when we do not feel Him, He is close to us as our provider, protector, healer, and Father. Even when we feel like God isn't there, He feels our every grief and pain because He never leaves us."

We had no way of sufficiently thanking our hostess, but as a small gesture of our gratitude, I gave Valentine new shirts from our suitcase. I can still remember the gratitude that filled my heart for the opportunity to be able to give back to someone else.

Valentine walked with us to the bus station.

By midmorning, Pastor Kanyange and his son arrived at the bus station in a fancy red car. They hugged us and apologized for the wait, thinking we had been waiting at the station all night. When I told them how God had cared for our needs, Pastor Kanyange took money from his pocket and gave it to Josephine. He also gave her money to give to the angelic girl at the border who graciously hosted us overnight.

I cried as I hugged Josephine and said goodbye. This beloved new friend had selflessly taken care of us in an unfamiliar land. Transition requires separation and sorrow, and this pain marked our journey again and again as we pressed forward to our promised land. We held on to the hope that America would hold new friends, but we also knew we would face new obstacles, joy, and tears.

In the days ahead we would discover that God often provides for the needs of His children through people who are unaware that they are participating in heavenly miracles. Simple kindness can evoke power that ripples through generations into lives yet unseen.

CHAPTER 20

NAIROBI

We must let go of the life we have planned,
so as to accept the one that is waiting for us.

—Joseph Campbell

"Sister, you must wake up, we have arrived in Nairobi."
I bolted awake. My youngest sister, Mirelle, stared back at me.

"You have been sleeping for hours. You missed seeing the countryside."

I shook my head to clear the fog. Our car was parked in front of a gated guesthouse that belonged to the Methodist church. A uniformed security guard stood at the gate. My sisters and I would be safe here.

Pastor Kanyange escorted us to the sleek, modern reception area, where a pleasant middle-aged woman behind a large, curved desk handed me a set of keys. Pastor and his son assisted with our luggage as we walked across the polished, brightly colored tiled floors to our new room, which boasted two white twin-sized beds with cheerful yellow bed covers. Pastor Kanyange gave us his telephone number and reassured us that he was available if we needed help. Then he and his son departed, and my sisters and I unpacked.

But as I moved my clothes from my suitcase to our shared dresser, familiar fears echoed in my mind.

We are alone again, and I'm responsible for my sisters in a new country and a new city. What will we do while we wait? The girls need to be in school! How long will we be here?

I set out to explore the facility and discovered a glimmering swimming pool, pristine landscaping, and a large dining room that served breakfast, lunch, and dinner. I did not roam beyond the fence because Zacharie had advised us not to wander around the neighborhood or explore further.

The guesthouse was in a beautiful, quiet Nairobi suburb. A sweet cleaning lady took out our trash each day, replenished the soap, and cleaned the showers. We now enjoyed the luxury of daily showers and eating meals in the cafeteria with the other guests. The food was beautifully prepared, and the facilities were immaculate. All our basic needs were met.

After dining, we walked back to our rooms and enjoyed the beauty of the landscaped grounds. None of us had experienced the luxury of time or safety that were necessary to the appreciation of beauty since the war began. So flowers, birds, and green expanses of grass now held a captivating charm for us. We were now living in a sensual paradise, but our hearts were still preoccupied with loss.

We soon began to make friends. One of our first friends was Furaha, the woman who cleaned our room. She noticed that none of us attended school, and we were always in our room. We didn't have books or activities to distract us, so we soon became bored. Mirelle was interested in learning to swim, but I had concerns. Neither Honorine nor I could swim, so we couldn't help Mirelle if she struggled in the water. So I decided, my sisters could watch people swim but never get into the water.

Furaha came to work one day with a swimming suit in her purse. Wanting to honor her kindness, I thanked her for her generosity and accepted the suit. Mirelle eagerly put it on and ran to the pool as I followed close behind. As she entered the shallow end, a young lifeguard observed my sister's enthusiasm and my concern and walked over. He asked about her swimming skills, then offered to teach her how to swim when the pool was less crowded.

While Mirelle received her swimming lessons, I kept my eye on my other sister and talked with the older man, Ed, who guarded the gate. He appeared to be in his late fifties, which made him old enough to be my father. Perhaps this is one reason my heart was drawn to him. His frequent smile revealed a large gap in his front teeth, and he often wore a red suit coat with dress pants. His job didn't offer him much to do, and I hoped that our getting to know one another might provide mutual friendship and comfort. Before long, Ed asked if he could take us to his church. We were delighted.

Time passed slowly. We did not have jobs or books to read. Pastor Kanyange and his family visited when we needed them and helped with translation needs and visa processing procedures.

I felt it was my duty to keep my sisters' spirits hopeful. But as days dragged on, I began to feel discouraged. I told myself that feelings could not accommodate God's transcendent plans. But my emotions were tied to my limited understanding and our frustrating circumstances, which is common in life.

I looked at this time as an opportunity to teach my sisters. I chose a positive attitude each day and gratitude for delicious, abundant food and our beautiful surroundings. The girls and I explored the massive grounds and found the best locations for outdoor chats, observing other guests, watching swimmers at the pool, and watching new guests check in. I also talked to them about the lessons we could gain from waiting, such as learning to depend on God, growing in patience and prayer, getting to know each other better, and looking for ways to serve others.

We were safe in Kenya, surrounded by beauty and abundant food, but we lacked work or studies to engage our minds, and we were still waiting to be reunited with Zacharie. My sisters were longing to go back to school. I'd learned that during national disasters, schools become disrupted. Feeling useless, I looked for ways to serve others. Nevertheless, I was haunted with guilt about being unemployed, even though it was vital for me to care for my sisters.

Many people had heard about our plight, but knew little about us. We were a curiosity to people at the guesthouse—three young sisters who ate by themselves, did not go to school, and seemed to have no parents. We were together constantly, did not participate in recreational activities, owned no books, and seldom relaxed by the pool like other guests.

Sensing my boredom and desire to be productive, Zacharie called and suggested an idea. He offered to hire me to translate Swahili proverbs into Kinyarwanda. Swahili was one the languages I knew at that point. He explained that America offered many opportunities, and translating a Swahili/Kinyarwanda book would look good on a résumé. This could lead to employment opportunities because my work would show intelligence and initiative.

The idea excited me, and I accepted his job offer and promised to do excellent work.

I hung up encouraged. I finally had a job! I'd never done translation before, and I knew it would be a challenge, but I created a plan for organizing my work and dove in.

Engaging in a mental task was exhilarating, and I believe Zacharie knew I needed this when he suggested the project. He knew my love for study and realized the "work" would reinvigorate my spirit.

I worked diligently each day. When I struggled with the meaning of certain passages or words, I asked for assistance from people I knew and trusted: our cleaning lady, the watchman, the receptionist, the lifeguard, and fellow worshippers at our church. By engaging in this work, I learned that meaningful compensation comes in using our gifts, engaging with people, growing, and learning.

After months of waiting, we were informed that our visa problem was coming to a resolution. As we waited, we leaned on one another and tried to remain positive. To help us prepare for immigration, we were instructed to take English classes offered by the International Organization of Migration (IOM). I was encouraged, thinking that we would finally have something purposeful to do.

A kind, petite Kenyan lady with caramel-colored skin and short hair taught the classes. Refugees from various African countries attended, and we were all waiting to go to America.

Lectures included concepts about life in the United States. My sisters and I alternated taking notes during class.

We were given a book that included tips for how to adjust to American culture. One cultural concept introduced garage sales. People had told me Americans had a lot of cars, so I assumed a garage sale was a place to buy cars. I was surprised when our teacher explained that people bought and sold used items at inexpensive prices at garage sales.

I was confused. Why would people sell their possessions in a garage? But I was excited about the possibility of purchasing merchandise inexpensively.

Our teacher also told us about snowy parts of the US. If we relocated to a frigid part of the country, we would need to wear hats and gloves to protect our heads and hands from the cold. Some of my classmates—especially older members—became worried when they heard about snow and cold weather. They muttered in their native languages about strange and dangerous weather that possibly awaited them. Younger people, especially boys, stood, cheered, and shouted that they were ready to take on snow and cold. The idea of living in a place where I would need to cover my head and hands sounded harsh to me, but I told myself I was ready for snow and cold. My brother Zacharie had adapted to living in the cold climate, and I knew that adaptability was necessary to succeeding in a new environment.

One afternoon as I sat in our room translating, a knock came at the door. I opened it to find a young man standing with my two sisters. All three of them were smiling broadly. My heart stopped. Somehow, impossibly, my dear friend Jacob—one of the young men who had guided me safely to the French peacekeepers—was standing in the doorway with my sisters.

We joyfully embraced as my sisters blurted out how he had found us. Jacob had made his way to Kenya via the Congo and was living in Nairobi with his two brothers, Joshua and Matthew.

I grew even more astonished. I had never expected I would ever see my friend again, and now he was standing in front of me! His smile and warm embrace were gifts from God.

The hours that followed were a precious reunion. He told me how he had prayed that he and his family would eventually learn my fate. I had also prayed to learn what had happened to him and his family. He showed me a picture of everyone, and I was flooded with warm memories. We prayed together, told our stories, and he thanked God for keeping us all safe.

I'd trusted Jacob before, and I trusted him again, in Nairobi. Assuring us we would be safe, he soon took us to Uhuru Park to attend faith-based crusades with singing and preaching, which allowed us to leave the guesthouse for brief periods. On another occasion, he accompanied us to the marketplace, where we saw the Masai people in their beautiful red clothing.

We enjoyed these excursions immensely, but I always worried about missing a call from my brother and having to explain our absence. Our time in Nairobi was another challenging period of waiting. We relied on God as the object of our trust as we waited in Nairobi.

And waited.

Waiting. The word defines, to a great degree, my struggle to survive the genocide and to immigrate to the United States. One period of waiting followed by another and another and another. Sometimes in closets. Alone beneath the sky on a rooftop above my pursuers. In abandoned houses, survivors' camps, and foreign lands. Waiting for God to open the next door . . . and the next . . . and the next.

But in the waiting, I learned to relinquish more of myself to the limitless safety and rest found only in Him. And I learned that waiting is a time of learning and listening, a time to store up wisdom for times ahead when it will be needed.

For wisdom in waiting will always be needed.

CHAPTER 21

MANY HANDS, MANY HEARTS

*Standing as a witness in all things means being
kind in all things, being the first to say hello,
being the first to smile, being the first to make
the stranger feel a part of things, being helpful,
thinking of others' feelings, being inclusive.*

—Margaret D. Nadauld

The call came as I sat on my bed pondering a future I felt was beyond my reach. The door that had been closed to us for so long had finally opened. My sisters and I had been granted permission to travel to our promised land, the United States of America. I was overjoyed.

Along with Zacharie, strangers in Iowa had been diligently working on our behalf during our time in Uganda and Kenya. Many Africans had vouched for my sisters and me, and Americans stepped in beside them, working tirelessly for three young women they had never met. This further reinforced my belief that the world is filled with compassionate humans.

Only good can overcome evil. The power to fight evil with good comes as a by-product of living out the love God gives us. Our family was torn apart by one tribe's hatred for another. Yet other people across the globe fought evil with good by rallying around three orphans, without concern for color, tribe, affiliation, or belief. Higher powers would equip me to battle evil with good, but first, I would fight battles of cultural acclimation, language acquisition, educational success, and making America my home.

The following narrative is based on the journal notes of Dorcas and Dan, who assisted in a collaborative effort to bring my sisters and me to the United States.

During 1994 and 1995, my husband, Dan, and I became involved in the emigration and settlement of three sisters who survived the Rwandan genocide. In May of 1994, news of Rwandan events shifted to beyond horrifying, and I felt the heart cry of a parent who watches their child run into the streets in the path of an oncoming truck. The crisis was personal to my husband and me. Around this same time, our Rwandan friend, Zacharie, told us he received a call from a cousin that cast grave doubt on whether any of Zacharie's family members had survived the killings.

This news horrified us. Zacharie had become like family to us.

In the fall of 1993, a friend had introduced us to a "special international student" who was studying at the University of Northern Iowa.

"Just call me Zack," he'd told us.

Zack visited our home often, and we were intrigued by his exceptional mind. He could capture detailed historical events like a camera. One day he held us spellbound as he passionately traced the history of the African language from the southern regions of the continent to the north. Zack loved life, and we loved being with him. He soon became family.

It was during this time that we received news about the Rwandan genocide. Reports were so ghastly that we could barely absorb the horror. Entire Rwandan neighborhoods had been slaughtered, and within six weeks, over three-quarters of a million murdered men, women, and children had been dumped into streets, swamps, and rivers.

At the news of the killings, Zacharie called a cousin who told him that his father, mother, and all his siblings had been killed.

Zacharie's family was ruthlessly torn from him in an instant.

But despite his cousin's report, Zack felt a deep certainty that all his family had not been killed. He determined to fly to Rwanda and find them, asking God to spare just one sibling or parent so he would not be alone in the world.

We were terrified for his safety and begged him not to go. He had just entered his early twenties, and his plan seemed impossible, as well as dangerous.

"Tutsi forces may be in control now, but both Hutu and Tutsi are still killing one another. Military forces and militants may not trust you. It is too dangerous! You cannot go alone, you will be killed! Please!"

But Zacharie had "set his face like a flint" to find his family. Our job was to pray for him and support him. He quickly purchased tickets to Africa and set out, while we waited and prayed.

We alerted our church, our family, and friends in other churches. Reports about the situation in Rwanda were not reassuring. Sporadic killings were still occurring all over the country, as well as in neighboring countries where refugees had fled.

After several agonizing weeks, Zacharie called. He had miraculously found three of his sisters and settled them in Uganda, where they could live safely until they could travel to Kenya and then to America.

But how could all these steps be accomplished? His sisters had no visas. Their identification and documentation had been lost in Rwanda. But that was not all. How could he get three girls from Uganda to Kenya, then from Kenya through the US State Department's Kenyan embassy and the United Nations High Commission on Refugees (UNHCR) to America? Would the girls qualify as refugees? And what kind of support would they require while they waited for approval?

The process seemed beyond daunting, but Zacharie was relentlessly committed. Our church and faith community pledged our support. We found family sponsors who would be officially responsible for the girls. The two families lived across the street from one another. Senator Charles Grassley, who was a member of our church, was extremely helpful with logistics, such as how to interact with immigration services and what was required to obtain visas. We learned, for example, that Kenya was the launching spot, and so the first step became to get the girls from Uganda to Kenya. But without passports, this would be risky business. We were told about a couple from Rwanda, Pastor Kanyange and his wife, Beata, who could assist the girls.

We spent long days, weeks, and months trying to negotiate travel. Dan stayed up until midnight several nights a week so that he could be first in line at the UNHCR office in Nairobi when they opened each morning. Each time he made contact, he was told the girls needed to gather one more item of information or complete one more step. Dan called at least twenty times and sent many faxes. Zacharie, of course, was doing everything he could, but much of the work had to be done through the citizens who would host the girls.

After a painful wait, we finally received three photographs—three young women who would change our lives. Emotions surged as we looked into the faces of Zacharie's sisters: Clementine, Honorine, and Mirelle.

Responses quickly came from seven other churches that wanted to help. Every act of preparation increased our joy as we anticipated the girls' arrival and observed peoples' enthusiasm. Our community had caught the vision to bring the girls to Iowa, and we were claiming our community as their new home.

Our family put all our communal skills to work. Dan and I wrote, organized and telephoned, and our daughter Rebecca worked graciously with many people while bringing her bright spirit to our task. She made phone calls, prayed, and took care of home chores while we were on phone calls or writing letters. Our other children gave us emotional and prayer support.

We bombarded Senator Grassley's office for advice and contacts, then made weekly progress reports to our church. Still, the process seemed interminably slow.

One day out of exasperation, Senator Grassley called the State Department.

"This is Senator Charles Grassley. Every week someone gets up in our church to report on the progress of bringing three Rwandan refugees to the United States. Each week I hear, 'And Senator Grassley is working on it.'

"I would like to know—if Senator Grassley is working on it, why is nothing being done?"

Apparently, Senator Grassley's straightforward query stirred waters in the State Department. Soon after, we received word that paperwork had been approved and a date had been set for the girls to be brought to their new home!

What would become their new families and friends, plus reporters from local news sources gathered to meet the tiny plane that landed at our small airport in Waterloo, Iowa. With a whir of propellers, a clanking of doors, and a fluttering of waiting hearts, three sisters stepped out of the plane.

For the first time, we saw the faces our new family members.

I look back on that day knowing that the coming years in Iowa would test my resiliency and fortitude in new ways. The waiting, loss, separation, and fear that I experienced during the genocide had prepared me for new forms of despondency and despair that would be part of my cultural rerooting in a new nation. America would prove to be my promised land, but it would also test my character, faith, and tenacity in ways I'd never experienced.

My sisters and I were exhausted from waiting day after day for the same response: no progress. We did not know about the efforts on our behalf in the United States. We did not know that an American senator heard reports every Sunday about our efforts to get to the United States. We were grateful when we learned that Senator Grassley had called the State Department to expedite our transition to the US.

I will never forget the day we heard that we had been granted passage to the United States. After the first wave of excitement passed, my thoughts turned to the many people who had made this miracle possible for us.

How could I begin to thank everyone who had helped us, comforted us, and had given to us when they had so little? And how could I thank people in America who determinedly worked on our behalf when they did not know us? As a gesture of gratitude, I purchased unique African crafts as gifts and T-shirts that read "Safari" to represent our journey.

I also wanted to give gifts to the kind people in Kenya who had befriended us during our agonizing waiting period. They had tended our spirits and given us hope. I decided to give most of our clothes and shoes to the wife of Ed, the watchman. When

I asked him for directions to his house, he led me to a small grass hut not far from the guesthouse, and I suddenly realized he and his wife lived in extreme poverty.

The doorway to the watchman's home was low, and I stooped to enter as his wife graciously greeted me. After we chatted, I gave her the clothing and shoes we had acquired while in Uganda. She expressed her deep gratitude. She could not understand how displaced orphans could give her such wealth. She cried as she expressed disbelief that we could joyfully give to others after the losses we had endured.

She and her husband laid their hands on my head and asked God to bless us, praying that He would guide us safely to our new home. When she told me she would fast for us, I was humbled—that a woman in poverty would bless us through the sacrifice of fasting.

The time to depart for the Nairobi airport was nearing, and I was growing nervous. We made one final stop by Pastor Kanyange's house, and they offered us a lovely dinner, prayers, and well wishes for our journey. His would be the last African home we would enter before departing for America.

When we arrived at the Nairobi airport, the crowd was chaotic. I speculated that if the Nairobi airport was busy, the Iowa airport would be much worse. I tried to calm my fears with the thought that we would see Zacharie when we landed, and all would be well.

We were flying with refugees from other African countries. Each of us carried a white plastic bag with the IOM logo printed on it. Our bags held brown envelopes that contained our photographs, signed by an official.

We boarded the plane and settled into our seats. I'd never flown before. A refugee from Sudan, who apparently had flying experience, explained how to buckle the seat belt, lift our eating tables, and use the headphones. Everything seemed complicated, but I pushed through.

As we flew across the immense Atlantic Ocean, I experienced conflicting emotions—confusion, excitement, curiosity, and concern about how I would adapt to life in a new land. I'd already been overwhelmed by new experiences in the airport and airplane, and I wondered how many unfamiliar situations would bombard me when I stepped onto American soil. It would have been difficult for me to understand that *everything* would be different when I stepped out of the plane in Waterloo, Iowa—the fragrances of people's perfumes, their clothing styles and colors, endlessly paved streets and sidewalks, green grass surrounding homes and businesses, unfamiliar hairstyles and colors, unfamiliar language, many cars in the streets, strange-tasting food and beverages, the many items called "appliances," animals freely wandering inside homes, and many, many other things.

Our first stop was in Amsterdam. Old friends greeted us when we landed, including my childhood friend Mila. After we visited briefly, my friends guided us to our next gate. This airplane took us to New York City.

We arrived in New York in the evening. After deplaning, I became fascinated by the sight of automatic doors. I'd never encountered this technological marvel. Everything captivated me: clothing styles, strange food, and the many things that engrossed people's attention, such as telephones, computers, newspapers, magazines, books, and more books.

We were transported to a nearby hotel where we were given food and a comfortable place to sleep. We were served sandwiches and fries from a plastic container. My sisters and I nibbled at our unfamiliar food, and I wished for a familiar plate of rice and vegetables.

The following morning, we boarded a plane to St. Louis, Missouri, where we climbed aboard a small aircraft that flew us to Waterloo, Iowa.

As I settled into my seat, deep sadness clouded my heart. I was leaving my deceased family members behind. Of course, this was necessary, but the reality struck me like lightning, and profound grief surged through me. Would I ever return to visit their graves? Were we leaving a surviving loved one behind? Would our enemies enjoy the fruits of all our family's hard work? What would the future of our nation look like?

And what would happen to the many friends I was leaving behind—displaced, homeless, orphaned and without surviving brothers or sisters? Would those who had perpetrated horror upon one another ever experience remorse? Or would the hatred that propelled their actions take deeper root in their hearts?

My mind shifted to *my* future in an unknown land. Would I be able to learn a new language and thrive in my new country? Would I make new friends, fall in love, and have a family of my own? How would I care for my sisters? What would be their future?

My thoughts circled back to gratitude to God for reuniting me with my siblings, for a new beginning, and for the opportunity to begin a new life where my sisters and I would be welcomed by people who reached out to us and cared for us before they ever knew us.

One thought made our departure bearable. I knew what my parents would have said to me as we left Rwanda: "Make a new life, Mukeshimana. Work hard. Be kind and care for others. Trust God."

Our plane cut through the air toward our new home in Iowa. Life in Rwanda and the places where we'd temporarily lived seemed a world away. As clouds scudded past, I silently grieved the loss of my "home"—the feeling that washed over me when I embraced family members, laughed with them, or as we ate together.

Perhaps it would be a feeling that would wash over me again as I met my "new family" in America, or down the road when I met my husband—if I could open my heart and wait for it.

CHAPTER 22

A SMILE IN ALL LANGUAGES

Where we love is home—home that our feet
may leave, but not our hearts.

—Oliver Wendell Holmes Sr.

A s our plane jolted onto the landing strip and taxied toward the tiny airport in Waterloo, Iowa, my mind focused on only one thought—my brother.

Zacharie, I missed you so much these past months, sometimes I felt I would never make it here. You were so far away, my heart hurt. What a joy it will be to have you in my life again! Do you still look the same, my brother? Will we still feel the same closeness after such a long and painful separation?

For a moment fear gripped me. Could our experiences have changed us, and the relationship that we always shared be different now?

Zacharie was in Iowa, but he was a sophomore in college who was struggling with the stresses of being a college student while finding his way to adulthood and stability. On top of that, he was facing challenges from losing his parents and siblings, who'd been on the other side of the globe during a war when information was nonexistent. He'd put his life and academic opportunities at risk when he took time off from school to come find us. We owed him so much.

My sisters and I stepped out of the plane and walked down the narrow stairs toward the tiny terminal. As we hurried through the sea of smiling faces and hearty embraces, I came to a startling realization. My sisters and I would need to work our way through new layers of adjustment, new phases of grieving, and find our way to a new understanding of *family* and *belonging*.

As we passed through glass doors and entered the airport, we were welcomed by people from local churches, the community, and our host families—with smiles and embraces that comforted—yet jolted our weary hearts. People who'd followed our story in the media had come to greet us, as well as local news teams. Bright camera flashes startled and temporarily blinded me. I was bewildered. I had no preparation or context for the abrupt attention and questions from reporters, and the experience unsettled me.

When my vision cleared, I searched the crowd until I spotted Zacharie pushing his way toward us through the throng. He gathered the three of us into an embrace, and peace rushed over me like a tsunami hitting shore. I did not want to let him go. For the first time since I'd left my home and family that horrific day in April, I felt as if I could breathe. The ache that I had felt in my heart for months melted away.

I knew Zacharie was not the answer to my grief and loneliness, but he was an older sibling. I could lean on him, and he shared the culture and memories I hoped to preserve for my sisters. We had the same memories of our mother and father that the younger girls might not remember. Together, we could create new memories and find ways to heal and rebuild our lives.

I needed to live successfully in my new culture. I did not want to just live in America; my desire was to thrive in my new country and give back what had been given in this land of opportunity. And we were the answers to Zacharie's prayer that he would not be left alone without family. We had much to be grateful for.

I rode with my brother as we drove from the airport to the town of Cedar Falls, just minutes away. I was certain he had to be fighting deep emotions to finally have us with him, and I wanted to be at his side. Zacharie commented on our surroundings as he drove, showing me things he thought I would enjoy hearing about.

I marveled at the golden cornfields that stretched as far as I could see. I'd never seen so much corn! I noticed unfamiliar varieties of trees and massive amounts of grass growing everywhere. Surprisingly, patches of short, lush grass surrounded every house, which was an unfamiliar sight. But the lush foliage reminded me of Rwanda and gave me a sense of home. Natural beauty always spoke to me of God's love and presence. And everything Zacharie said was positive and affirming, to encourage me.

I was eager to see my new home—the place where we would be starting our new life. I didn't know what to expect, other than to know it would be different. We would no longer live in limbo, questioning the unknown and longing for our brother. I could finally dream again about a future for my sisters and myself—a return to school and longed-for study. Planning seemed daring and even a bit frightening after living day-to-day for so long on daily portions of hope.

From the moment I knew we were going to America, I wondered about the American mother and father who were willing to take African siblings into their home without the ability to see into the future. What courage they had to welcome people from a culture unknown, although my mother and father had always welcomed strangers into our home, including people from foreign countries. Hosting strangers was part of the way I was raised.

Did our American families have fears about hosting us? What factors had gone into their decisions to accept us? My sisters and I certainly wanted to be gracious and polite while we were discovering how things "worked" in our new homes and culture. I did not know when it was appropriate to ask questions, which was awkward, and I certainly did not want to appear rude.

There were so many things to learn, so many things I did not know. I felt a great burden to honor our parents by respecting our new families and not being an inconvenience. But how could this work when we needed to learn the culture and did not know what we did not know?

When we pulled up in front of our new home, I wasn't sure what to think. Our family had lived in a single-level home in Rwanda that had wrapped us in love, laughter, and irreplaceable memories. My new family's house was a large, stately blue and white historic home with an enormous lawn and a driveway big enough to accommodate several cars. It was in a neighborhood of similar "historic" homes in Cedar Falls.

When we went inside my new house, I discovered unfamiliar home appliances. I was told they were a washing machine, dryer, enormous refrigerator, and a vacuum, among other conveniences. For the first month or so, I felt disoriented in a space so unfamiliar from anything I had known. The size, the shape, the furnishings, the scent, *the dog*, the essence of the house—these things were all foreign, which made sense and which I welcomed—but at the same time made me feel orphaned in a new way.

Even though I knew I had nothing to fear, unfamiliar surroundings were stirring anxiety. I didn't understand that I was being overloaded with the unfamiliar. Nothing looked, smelled, or sounded like anything I'd experienced before. Even small details in our upstairs bedroom felt overwhelming. I was experiencing culture shock.

I didn't want anyone to know I felt awkward. It was important to show appreciation and gratitude for my new family's generosity. To admit I felt overwhelmed would make me appear ignorant or ungrateful. So, to compensate, I tried to ignore my fears and, instead, focused on our new family's kindness, generosity, hospitality, support, hugs, and smiles. I also focused on how I could be helpful. As I thought about these things, I noted that compassion and connection are the same, regardless of culture. At our core, people are the same. This awareness seemed to calm me, and my anxiety dissipated.

The strategy worked so well, that I used it over and over. Focusing on positives became a survival mechanism over the course of my life. Our parents had taught us the importance of expressing gratitude in good times and in difficulties, so focusing on the positive came easily to me.

Yet, I also learned from the negatives in Rwanda and from all the places I had lived. Positive and negative experience are borderless. Negative experiences forced me to rely on God and increased my faith. They also placed me in circumstances where unexpected people sacrificed and took risks on my behalf, and where I became the recipient of God-directed nurture and care. The tragedy and suffering I experienced permanently magnified my empathy and compassion, and I will never see the world in the same way. Difficult experiences are not only opportunities to learn about our environment, but also to assess the way we respond to our environment.

Later in my life, I came across a plaque that read, "A smile is the same in all languages." Those words encapsulated my first days in America. I was comforted by the kindness of new families that were empathetic, generous, and caring, and I naively assumed that all other Americans would respond to me in the same way. I was young, trusting, and guileless. But I would soon learn that I'd been wrong to generalize.

Food is one of life's greatest comforts. It represents love, security, family, celebration, reassurance, heritage, culture, and so much more. To be unrooted in a foreign land without the consolation of familiar food—and one's favorite home dishes—is a loss that is difficult to describe. One of the most important things to me when I began to settle in America was learning to duplicate my mother's dishes and experience the joy of eating her food.

Acclimating to American food was as much a matter of the heart as it was a matter of the palate. My favorite foods initially were chicken, pastas, vegetables, and fruits. However, it took me a bit of time to adjust to some new flavors, which is understandable. Adapting to new cuisine is a universal process. How we respond is an individual choice. It can be easier starting with foods that taste familiar and that agree with your palate, then introducing new foods from there. Learning to enjoy American food was a priority to me. Food was also much more than nourishment and flavors to me. It was a celebration of friendship, fellowship, support, and welcome around a table—as my family had always done.

Each morning, our new family ate breakfast together—often cereal with milk, which was new to me. I was always grateful for the food set before me and willing to try new things. I often longed for my mother's sorghum porridge, but I quickly developed a strong liking for American grapes.

So many things were different about America that I felt overwhelmed. But the simple truth was that I needed to acclimate—to everything from stairs to breakfast cereal to winter weather to a big dog to a thousand things I had yet to discover.

One of the things I immediately discovered was our new family's loving and accommodating nature. Our new mom had placed signs on the walls all over the house that spelled out English words along with their Kinyarwanda translations. This helped us feel welcomed, understood, and appreciated. We immediately knew that she had spent a great deal of time and effort to help us make immediate connections to both our new home and our new language. Human connection is an important aspect of respect, acceptance, and establishing a sense of safety. Our new family thoughtfully created ways to accomplish these things for us.

The new dad was humorous and kind—qualities that translate across cultures. He made us laugh by lightly touching us on a shoulder to prompt us to chase him around the house. Later, I learned he was initiating a game called *tag*, and I believe he did this to help us feel like part of the family and was grateful.

I later transitioned into a new home where, again, I was welcomed with open arms. The father of the home was a University of Northern Iowa administrator, and I often rode with him back and forth to campus, which gave me time to get to know him.

The mother of the home was a stay-at-home mom who cared for her home and children and drove them to their various activities. One of my most treasured memories is of her teaching me my first American "job," lawn care. I distinctly remember her showing me how to push the lawn mower—something totally new to me. We cooked together, washed dishes, grocery shopped, and sat together on the porch sharing prayer requests and praying. Each of these moments bonded us in a special mentoring relationship.

I will never forget the day, after I'd been in America about six months and was struggling to become independent, when I was overtaken with grief, and she held me in her arms as I cried. Her love and support gave me the inner strength I needed.

In this new home, I was given my own beautiful bedroom with a bed having a green and gold bedspread along with a study desk. This would be the home where I would learn to be independent, claim my identity in a new land, accept the reality that I was motherless and fatherless, and would soon venture into the world as a woman. A family legacy rested upon my shoulders, and I felt the weight.

A large box with a drawing of a cat had been placed on the floor on one side of the room. When I opened the box and reached in, I found it filled with thick, heavy sweaters that people at church had collected for me to wear when the seasons changed.

However, the weather outside was hot at the time I first opened the box, and I was puzzled. Why would anyone need so many sweaters? While I felt grateful for the gift, I was certain I would never need such heavy clothing. I couldn't envision any possible use for them. I closed the box and forgot about the sweaters for several months.

During our training with the IOM, we had been forewarned that some emigrants would be placed in cold weather states. I convinced myself that other refugees (not us, of course) would be banished to suffer in inclement weather. But when my sisters and I arrived in Iowa in June, we found it warm and sunny. I was comfortable wearing sandals, skirts, and even shorts, which were new to me. I banished the thought of the cold that awaited me in a few short months.

My new family had four children. Although I loved all four, I enjoyed playing with their two youngest kids, who made me feel like a big sister. However, the boys also found ways to draw me into their playful pranks and schemes. One night I was unwinding and preparing to go to bed. I took my shower and put on my pajamas, then headed to my room to get in bed. But when I pulled down my covers, I jumped back with a scream. A black snake was coiled in my bed.

As I struggled to catch my breath, I heard the boys laughing behind my bedroom door.

The snake wasn't real, and they knew they'd "gotten me."

I immediately saw the humor and laughed with them. I recognized that these shared experiences draw family members together. For a long time, the boys talked about their prank with great pride, and I always laughed with them. They were treating me like a sister, and this was their form of teasing me. Learning to bond with them through shared humor was an important element of becoming a "member of the family." It was important for me to become comfortable laughing at myself and understand that their prank was a form of affection, not disrespect.

Our first Fourth of July celebration was memorable and especially significant to me. I'd fought long and hard to come to America and join my brother. I felt especially blessed to be here.

The family drove as a group to a farm where our hosts' friends raised pigs on an immense acreage. I held baby pigs, rode on a tractor, and shucked corn. This was an exciting introduction to America's heartland. On the surface, it was simply a mishmash of shared events. But it was a true learning experience for me— an initiation into some of the nuts and bolts of American farm life. I felt like I'd walked into an encyclopedia.

I also attended church with my host family. The people at our church were warm, loving, and welcoming. The pastor was an engaging speaker and caring minister, but my English skills were still developing, and I had trouble understanding everything he and church attendees said to me. Since Scripture was written in English, I didn't understand Bible passages.

Even songs were a struggle. I often recognized melodies but not words. Still, the songs lifted me up, and familiar melodies helped me reconnect with my faith and my culture. But at the same time, I felt alienated and cut off from those around me. Eventually, I came to understand most of the Bible readings, but I still struggled with sermons and illustrations. I did recognize that speakers often used humorous stories to illustrate their point.

One day I missed the humor of what the pastor was saying, despite my best efforts to understand. As he delivered the punch line of his story, the congregation burst into laughter. I decided to laugh with them to show my appreciation for his humor.

But by the time I joined the laughter, the moment had ended, and the pastor had moved on to a serious point.

I looked ridiculous, and the joke was on me. Some people stared, since I'd seemingly laughed for an unknown reason. I was embarrassed and unsure how to respond.

Later, I shared my experience with friends. They found it humorous and enjoyed a huge laugh. I joined in again, understanding that I needed to learn to laugh at myself and not take life too seriously. This simple choice to leverage humor and be willing to laugh at myself made it possible for me to turn awkward moments into bonding moments.

As I continued to acclimate to my new culture, I also chose to evaluate my circumstances from the perspectives of those around me, rather than to choose offense. This discipline often turned awkward moments into bonding moments.

My first few months in Iowa were filled with new challenges, new friends, and a growing sense of family, healing, and community. My American family introduced me to new experiences, embraced me, and facilitated a welcoming, nurturing, and healing summer. Our new families were caring and accommodated our obvious language difficulties. My honeymoon period lasted until the end of my first summer. My life began to change, and for the next four years I would feel like I was running down a hill, a split second away from a life-altering fall with every step.

The education I'd longed for was about to begin. But the future we envision and the reality we experience are often separated by realities that require determination, commitment, support, and discipline. I'd soon discover that the education I'd expected and the education I would experience would be separated by circumstances that would send me into a battle of a new nature.

CHAPTER 23

THE ROAD TO SELF-SUFFICIENCY

There are no secrets to success. It is the result of
preparation, hard work, and learning from failure.

—Colin Powell

B rilliant sunshine poured through my upstairs bedroom
window. No longer was I easily deceived and assumed
that blinding sunshine meant warmth. I shuddered at the
cold as I threw back my blankets, slipped into the thick robe
always waiting at the foot of my bed, and slid my feet into furry
slippers.

I pulled my pillow from my bed and placed it on the floor.
Then I knelt on the pillow, folded my hands, and placed my head
on my arms as I did each morning as I humbled my heart.

Dear God, only You know how overwhelmed I feel. We are
finally in America, and the relief I hoped I would find has simply
melted into new concerns. I must find a job to pay for the many
things I need, but I've learned that my language is not yet good

enough to find a job. And my classes are much harder than I thought they would be.

Everything is harder than I thought it would be. And I am always cold, God. It is so hard to concentrate on anything when my body is freezing and in pain.

Dear God, You know I am not afraid of work. I do not like being dependent on others for rides, clothes, meals, pencils, and paper—especially things too personal to mention to others.

God, please help me. I know I must go through this. Give me strength for the challenge. I need new mercies every day and fresh courage to push through the struggles that lie ahead. But You go before me, and You never leave me. Thank You for giving me all that I need today and every day.

The education I'd longed for had begun at the University of Northern Iowa (UNI). I was already discovering that the education I'd anticipated and the educational journey I would undergo would send me into unanticipated battles.

First, accomplishing even the smallest task in my new homeland felt like it required three to four times the emotional, mental, and physical energy I'd expended in Rwanda. Language was my greatest barrier and created obstacles to accomplishing everyday tasks like grocery shopping, filling out documents, and learning new skills.

I had always been a good student, but I was not prepared for how difficult it would be to learn English. I was about to hit my first colossal academic learning curve—the preparatory classes required for all incoming foreign students who did not test at the required level of English proficiency in reading, speaking, writing, and listening. Most incoming students from cultures and educational systems where English is not a high priority often find themselves placed in similar prerequisite intensive programs.

At UNI, these classes are part of the Cultural and Intensive English Program (CIEP), along with a cultural and social introduction to the United States. When I arrived at UNI, I took an English competency test and was placed in reading, speaking, writing, and listening classes. However, with naive overconfidence, I attempted to simultaneously enroll in regular university classes.

Life had taught me that obstacles do not predict defeat. And my parents had taught me that challenges require creativity, courage, persistence, and collaboration. I was determined to learn as quickly as possible. So why not forge ahead with courage and persistence?

I was ecstatic to finally be a university student, so while I waited to be granted full admission to UNI, I investigated classes at a community college that was located on the opposite side of town. If I enrolled, I'd need a car, which meant I'd need miraculous gifts, driving skills, and driving-related English language, or I would have to go to classes by city bus.

Since I didn't see signs of those miracles, I opted for riding the bus. The only catch was that I'd never ridden a bus in America before and did not know how the process worked, but I pushed my fear aside, and confidently secured community college admission. Assuming that riding a bus couldn't be that different from one country to another, I never gave the matter a second thought. This is a good place to mention that newcomers to a new land or culture should never base decisions on assumptions. Always investigate by asking questions of someone native to their newly adopted country. What is a bus ride like? What should I expect, and how can I prepare?

Early my first morning of class, I walked to the bus station to get a ride to the junior college. When a bus stopped, I climbed aboard and found a seat. Only a few silent people sat scattered throughout the vehicle. I assumed the bus would come to the community college, stop, and the driver would announce the location and let me out. How hard could this be?

I looked out the window to watch for the campus to make sure I got off at the right place. As we drove, the bus passed areas of the community I'd never seen before, and I assumed we'd reach the school soon. But after we had driven for quite some time, and I began to get anxious. It didn't seem possible that the college could be this far away, but I remained in my seat, hopeful that I would see the campus soon. When I checked my watch, I realized my class was already halfway finished, and my heart dropped. How could I have missed my very first class? What would I possibly say to my professor—that I hadn't known where to exit the bus?

Soon the last passenger got off, and I was alone with the driver. He said nothing to me and continued driving. A few minutes later, he pulled into a parking area, turned off the engine, then slipped out of his seat and walked toward me as I struggled to think of what to say. The simple truth was my only defense.

"Where are you going? This is the end of the line."

"To the community college."

"Didn't you see it? We passed it several times."

I was embarrassed. I had been waiting for him to announce the location so I would know where to get off. And I had not seen a sign for the college anywhere along the route, so I'd spent nearly three hours riding in circles. The driver had completed his day's route and pulled back into the station with me, a lost sheep.

Ashamed, I called a friend who came and rescued me in midafternoon. But I felt exposed, like a child who forgot their lines in a pageant. Asking for help to maintain your life can feel burdensome and strip you of your privacy. People asking for help are often asked questions like "Why?" "Is this necessary?" "How long will it take?" And we can never be certain how the person on the asking end is responding inside. Are they truly happy to help, or are they saying *yes* to be polite? Are they annoyed but afraid to show it? Do they wish that we'd ask someone else? To help maintain our dignity and self-respect, we must find ways to reciprocate grace. Givers should also be willing to receive.

Transportation is a basic essential for quality of life, safety, community, and well-being.

That day on the bus I learned that some refugees, immigrants, and newcomers to communities don't know what they don't know about their new culture. Because this is true, we're constantly caught off guard by surprising, embarrassing, or uncomfortable situations. I expected the bus driver, as the "authority" on the bus route, to call out the stops along the way, rather than to assume that riders knew the location of each stop. And because I was still acquiring language skills, I was reluctant to ask him. What I thought would be a simple ride to my class turned out to be an important learning experience about the public bus system.

After the bus debacle, I decided that if I was going to get a college degree, I needed to attend the University of Northern Iowa (UNI), which was closer, and where I was already enrolled in CIEP courses. Closed doors are not always bad. Sometimes they force us in a direction that takes us to our destiny. It seemed clear that UNI would be a better fit for me. Looking back, I would advise other people in my position to take an orientation bus ride with someone familiar with the transit system *before* a first class or a job interview or medical appointment. Or call the transportation department and ask for details about riding the bus.

Determined to prevail, I set up a meeting with the admissions officer at UNI, who granted me partial admission that limited me to two university courses while I completed the English training program.

When I opened and read my UNI acceptance letter, I thought my legs might give out. My persistence had paid off. My feet were finally on the path to my university education! I immediately thought of my parents and how proud they would be. I was enormously, tearfully grateful. My childhood dream was coming true!

And I was also unspeakably afraid. The task of earning my college degree loomed larger than anything I'd faced since escaping the Interahamwe. Thankfully, I was beginning with just two classes.

Little did I know how overwhelming those first two classes would be.

While I was fighting to survive academically, I was also under pressure from multiple directions. I was looking for a job to me help pay for expenses like books, lunches, clothes, and incidentals. And although my international CIEP friends and I were all at school learning English, I felt different from the other students. Most visited their parents during holidays and took trips to places like Chicago, New York, and Daytona Beach. I did not have a parent or grandparent, so I didn't leave school for vacations.

Most students also talked about what their parents and brothers and sisters were doing, and those conversations triggered grief for me. I persistently felt awkward, different, left out, and lonely, but I chose a positive mindset and used vacation breaks to focus on my studies. I worked very hard not to compare my life with the lives of people around me. Still, the sting of loneliness and "otherness" haunted me.

I'd been told about Iowa's freezing winters but didn't believe the reports could be true because the summer had been so hot. And how can someone possibly envision something they've never experienced or seen?

When fall arrived, temperatures started to drop. Suddenly, the box of sweaters I discovered in my room became meaningful, and long before other people appeared wearing winter clothes, I was frighteningly cold and bundled up.

On the first day of class at the end of summer, most students showed up in shorts and sandals, but I wore my heavy brown coat, gloves, and hat. My teacher and classmates burst into laughter when they saw me in full winter gear. But this was the first frigid weather I'd ever experienced and the coldest my body had ever been. The thought that temperatures would soon plummet below zero was truly frightening. How was I going to survive midwestern subzero temperatures? I knew I needed to set my mind to endure it, but the thought still seemed impossible.

As days went by, the cold grew bitter, and life became even less bearable. I asked God to help me withstand the frigid weather and assist my body in fighting the cold. I couldn't fathom how people could have fun, laugh, and carry on with their lives, unperturbed by the icy temperatures.

I found it difficult to express these feelings to American friends because the extreme cold was a fact of life many of them had lived with since they were born. I did not want to appear like a "wimp" who was whining about something as mundane as the weather, but the painful cold stalked me everywhere I went, no matter what I was doing. I was cold even when I was inside my classroom or our house and continually wanted to crawl into bed under the covers.

Then one morning as Christmas approached, my host mom called out and woke me.

"Clem, look out the window! It's snowing!"

I jumped from my bed, peered through the window, and observed that the ground was blanketed in glittering white. The beauty did not fool me. I knew that once I stepped outside, the pristine white powder would become my enemy.

My host mom instructed me to dress in layers of sweaters, stockings, and pants before venturing outside. I piled on socks, sweaters, and put on my long coat, then went outdoors with the family. I felt peculiar and stiff, stuffed into so many layers of clothing.

Gingerly, I attempted to walk. Members of my family told me to be extra careful on ice, but that walking on snow shouldn't be difficult.

I wasn't sure what they meant by watching out for *ice*. I could only see snow, and it was threatening enough to my safety. Was *ice* an even more diabolical hazard? I did not need an additional enemy in my war against Iowa's life-threatening cold.

My host dad called out this time and told me the ice was slippery, and I could fall if I wasn't careful.

This thing called "snow" was apparently more dangerous than I thought. But what was ice? How could it be even more dangerous than snow, and what did it look like?

Fortunately, it snowed very little that first day. The precipitation that did fall melted quickly, and I did not see any dreaded ice. At least I didn't think so. And surprisingly, I felt comfortable walking on the powdery white blanket.

However, a few days later a much bigger storm occurred. Mounds of snow were heaped everywhere. I ventured out, taking baby steps to keep from falling. Despite my improved snow-walking skills, I was tense about the huge mounds and ubiquitous cold. It was January, which was deep into Iowa's snow season, and my anxiety increased with each new day of darkness and cold.

One day following a snowfall, I was walking from the library toward another campus building. I was trying to avoid the big, brown-crusted snow piles that had been frosted by sand that was spread to help control icing. I chose a path across a shiny area, assuming it would be the safest route.

With my first step onto the glistening surface, I fell and bounced like a toppled banana tree. I lay stunned for a moment in the dirty snow and sand. The foul mixture covered my neck, nose, and mouth.

I tried to get up, only to fall again as my feet slid out of control.

I tried again. Slowly and unsteadily, I pulled myself to my feet and inched away from what I assumed was "ice" and onto snow again.

In pain and shock, I continued walking, my eyes scanning the path before me for shiny glare. I was miserable and aching, but now I knew why my host family had warned me about the dangers of ice. Somehow, I survived with my bones and dignity intact. For a reason unknown to me at the time, the struggle with the ice made me sad.

A unique sense of loneliness exists among those who leave their homes, families, culture, and foreign tongue, to travel to new lands. The sense of alienation—of being cut off from anything familiar—is overwhelming. The taste of your favorite food. The scent of your home. The contours of your land. The music and language of your childhood.

All is stripped away, and you live in an exhausting world of unrelenting struggle: to be understood, to be respected, to hear, enjoy, taste, and touch the simple things that everyone else knows so inherently that they do not even *know* what they know. The constant pull of these intangible things can be overwhelming. To find a friend who can name and acknowledge the pain of these struggles with you is a treasure.

To be repeatedly humiliated by the indifference of weather often feels demeaning, emotionally exhausting, and depression inducing—especially, weather you have never experienced. You fall. You become wet. You can become injured. You're delayed. Your body hurts. You're inconvenienced. Citizens of your new land stare at you, and you're embarrassed. You sometimes see pity and recoil. The emotional toll defies description.

Several days later, I was walking from the CIEP office toward the library. As I exited a classroom building, a gust of wind caught me, threw me to the ground, and knocked the wind out of me. I lay for a time trying to catch my breath, then slowly rose to my knees and stood. Within seconds, a second gust flattened me again. This time, I stayed down, nursing my pain. In resignation, I wiped away the tears that had sprung to my eyes and cried out to God.

You saved me from machetes. You protected me at border crossings. You shielded me as I walked among killers. Did you protect me from all those dangers for me to die now in snow, wind, and ice in America?

My back hurts, and my head is throbbing. My feet and toes are so cold I cannot feel them. My skin is cracked and bleeding, and my mouth burns from the wind. My ears are pounding in pain, and my hands are numb. What other torture is coming, God? Is this how You care for me after saving me from the machetes of the Interahamwe?

I thought back to my class discussions with other students as we talked about living in new climates. But no discussions or educational films or *any* classroom experience could have prepared me for the emotional and psychological battles that came with unexpected challenges in my new country. I did not know that wind chills could reach as cold as thirty below, and temperatures often hovered near zero. I wanted to weep, but my tears would have frozen to my face. As I cried out in pain, God gently reminded me how He brought the children of Israel out of slavery. On their way to Canaan, they lamented about the difficulties they'd encountered. He reminded them to not complain against Him (Numbers 14: 26-27). My painful journey out of Rwanda taught me that God uses suffering to teach me that He is faithful and to equip me for my future.

As I lay crying in the cold outside the classroom building, God spoke to me. He had not left me. He'd given me the desires of my heart and brought me to America, but the road in my new homeland would be hard. The weather would be just one battle of many that waited ahead.

Moments later, He gave me the strength to securely stand and take small, steady steps. With God's help, I found my way home that night through the first of many storms. And His strong right arm held me firm in the days ahead.

CHAPTER 24

HUMILITY'S GIFT
OF INTERDEPENDENCE

Compassion is the keen awareness
of the interdependence of all things.

—Thomas Merton

One truth my parents engrained in me is that life is not to be expended upon the pursuit of self. Because we are created in the image of God, our lives have purpose and meaning. Thomas Merton, American author and Trappist monk, states this thought succinctly in the quote above. When we understand the universal interdependence of people and relationships, we are compelled to respond with compassion for others.

My life has repeatedly demonstrated this truth—within my family, during my escape from Rwanda, in my time in many camps, as well as living with others in their homes or the open air or temporary shelters, and throughout my education.

One of the first places I experienced the benefits and blessings of interdependence was during my years at the University of Northern Iowa.

Because of our affinities and shared studies as foreign students, CIEP students spent most of our time together. Simple things bonded us—hanging out together in the cafeteria, library, study areas, or outside. Or the connection we felt hugging each other and hearing our varied accents and broken English. We always found simple ways to encourage one another in our goals. And if one of us found a kind, empathic friend, the rest of us secretly hoped we might eventually find compassion and assistance from that person too.

I spent a lot of time with Nina, who was from Spain and who always made me laugh. One day, Nina and I were studying for a writing test in the lobby of the education building and worked straight through the morning until lunchtime. We were both hungry, didn't have food, and didn't have time to go back to our dorm (or house) to eat.

In desperation, we searched the pockets of our clothes and then every pouch and pocket, nook and cranny of our purses searching for dimes and nickels and pennies and that one last urgently needed quarter. I can remember the waves of panic and the feeling of desperation as I turned out each pocket, only to find used candy wrappers, sticky pennies, and a used, wrinkled tissue.

That was the feeling in the pit of my stomach the afternoon Nina and I searched for a combined amount of $2.70—which would be enough combined resources to purchase one doughnut and one drink from a vending machine. Our plan was to each eat half of the doughnut and share the drink. But I first needed to find my half of the funds—about $1.35 in change, which would be every nickel and dime I could scrape up.

When I was done searching the deepest recesses of every pocket of my purse, I'd miraculously found *exactly* the change I needed.

Not a cent more or less.

Slowly, I inserted my coins in the machine as I counted each coin and selected a doughnut.

But it didn't drop from the slot.

I felt a familiar tightening in my chest. I didn't know what to do. I had no more monetary resources on that day. So Nina inserted her dollar and made a second attempt to buy a doughnut, knowing we could still drink from a water fountain.

To our horror, the vending machine took Nina's dollar, too, and gave us nothing. We now were penniless and had no options for getting food. My parents had taught me to be self-reliant, and I did not consider it respectful to ask people for resources to solve my problems.

It's difficult to explain how humbling and conflicting it is to be an adult and be constantly dependent on family, friends, or community for the simplest needs in life—toothpaste, shampoo, toiletries, food, clothing, books, study materials, and incidental funds.

How much is too much? How many times is the limit for asking too often? Should you always request the least expensive version of an item? What if the fit isn't right—does it sound ungrateful to ask to exchange it? What if the item you need is seen as unnecessary? Do you try to explain *why* it is needed or go without? How do you ask such questions without feeling shame? No matter how kind that person may be, anxiety is natural. Every need becomes a point of tension as you try to show genuine gratitude for what you have while continually questioning how to express your genuine need, whether it be for a ride, a tutoring session, or a tube of toothpaste. More than anything, I wanted to be known as a grateful, gracious, and responsible person.

Undaunted, Nina devised a plan to retrieve our doughnut. She had a confident personality and was pretty, energetic, and outgoing. I was the quieter and more reserved of the two of us and more reluctant about the plan. Nina didn't seem at all bothered about the thought of hitting the vending machine. She instructed me to watch for people who might look our way, then beat and kicked the vending machine like a prizefighter. Part of me was terrified, and another part of me was proud of her.

I knew I should stop her, but my stomach was rumbling. We would be taking our test within an hour, and we needed nourishment. But the machine did not care that our stomachs were grumbling, and we were penniless. Both our money and doughnut remained imprisoned. Nina asked me to assist her with a second plan to free the doughnut we had now paid for twice. Confidently, she instructed me to step closer and whispered her plan in my ear. We were to tilt the machine forward, then rock it back and forth until the doughnut fell. Determined, together we shook the machine as hard as we could. Looking back, I still cannot believe I did this.

Nothing fell. A flood of shame washed over me for my hunger-induced assault, but I was also disappointed. My stomach was churning, and I knew I could not possibly do well on the test.

The challenge of communicating expectations is always difficult in cross-cultural situations. No matter whether you are a newcomer to a culture or welcoming new people into your culture, you will often feel awkward about how and when to ask question and how to do so respectfully. We often are unaware of the subtle dos and don'ts of other people groups—how to greet one another, off-limits conversation topics, to touch or not to touch, degrees of formality, body language, and the list goes on and on.

I want to clarify that my immediate, extended family members, as well as friends made a genuine effort to anticipate most of my needs and provide support when asked. They were generous beyond my expectations, but I often did not tell them what I needed for fear of seeming too needy, ungrateful, or unwilling to contribute my part.

Not far from us, a man noticed the havoc we were causing and graciously approached us as we were concluding our assault on the vending machine. I will never forget the compassion on his face—an Ethiopian doctoral student named Abel. Mortified, we blurted out our story. He wisely and gently advised us that hitting and shaking the contraption would not work—primarily because it was not functional.

Smiling, Abel asked us what we wanted to drink. I told him we enjoyed hot chocolate. He purchased a cup and muffin for each of us from a machine in a different location. We gratefully thanked him, then laughed as we went to enjoy our bounty. He had the insight to "see" us and ask us what we preferred to drink, a small but vital gift.

Nina and I took our tests and scored well, but this experience also cemented our knowledge that it always our responsibility to prepare for the exigencies of our day. For me, this also required self-advocacy and interdependence as I navigated an uncomfortable conversation with my friends discussing a subject that was "invisible" to them because they did not share my perspective, experience, or culture. These vital conversations can be one of the most important aspects of achieving cross-cultural understanding. We cannot relate to tension, shame, isolation, frustration, and sadness until we recognize their roots and remove them. I later discovered that internal cultural and self-imposed barriers can block us from achieving the interdependence we and others need and long for.

CIEP classes did help me learn how to read, write, speak, and listen in English. But despite my diligent study, I frequently felt stressed. Learning English was not about mastering content, which came easily for me. The language was complex and nuanced, and because of its unique challenges, I often wanted to quit. But, of course, I would never do that. I had a goal, and I would not be deterred.

Late one Sunday, I was agonizing over a difficult paragraph in a textbook. After studying the entire weekend, I still didn't understand the passage. I'd used a dictionary to look up the meaning of unfamiliar words, but this had taken an enormous amount of time and energy and helped little. I'd expended my study strategies, and it was time to throw the net to my community and ask for help. The more I involved myself in the lives of others, the more I learned valuable lessons about interdependency—the structure that had been the foundation of my home.

Later that night at the student union building, I saw an American friend sitting at a table with another international student. Barbara waved me over to sit with them. She was a charming, beautiful girl who helped international students with English. We chatted about our studies, and Barbara turned to me as I sipped my tea.

"Clementine, do you need help with English?"

I put my cup down.

Need help with English? Had she read the look of distress on my face? Or sensed my anxiety?

"I've spent all day studying one paragraph, and I still cannot understand what it is saying. If you could help me with this one passage, I'd be immensely grateful."

A few minutes later her friend left, and I pulled out my book. Barbara read the paragraph slowly, pausing at the end of each phrase to allow me time to absorb the meaning. Then at the end of the paragraph, she carefully explained the content. But before she got to the end of her explanation, I'd grasped the essence of the paragraph.

Her inflection, pauses, and pace gave my brain the required clues to make connections in meaning. Suddenly, something I'd worked so hard to understand became clear! She'd helped me *hear* how to read as clusters of meaning, rather than individual words and concepts. I suddenly felt understood, as if a pressure valve had released in my chest.

I hugged her as relief flooded through me. Perhaps she could teach me to see groups of words as units of thought, the way she'd read to me. We set up a time to meet, and Barbara and I became study partners—but more than that—dear friends. As she taught me, I taught her in a natural rhythm of friendship.

Barbara made me feel comfortable, and I could talk to her easily about anything. We shared our faith, as well as our common struggles with studies and college life. We celebrated each other's accomplishments, went to social events together, prayed, and did laundry together. She taught me how to cook and bake American food, like upside-down pineapple cake and chili, and introduced me to Panera bread. She also helped me understand puzzling aspects of American culture. Our friendship was interdependent, as we looked for ways to contribute to one another's lives. I felt joy in positively influencing her life, and I know she felt the same way about me. Interdependency takes on a natural ebb and flow that becomes a natural, life-enhancing part of life for both individuals.

In return for reading assistance, I taught Barbara how to make African foods, such as beef and chicken stews, rice, beans, and tea. I enjoyed helping her with her laundry, cooking for her, keeping her company when she needed a friend, and listening to her as she worked through life challenges. Although she was a committed Catholic and I am Protestant, we found common ground in our faith in many other areas and talked about our faith as easily as we talked about campus life.

My conversation partner Monique, who friends in my circle called the "Mother of International Students," also helped me practice speaking and listening in English. I was drawn to her outgoing nature, and in winter she wore a striking pink coat and white hat that reflected her vivacious nature. Spending time with her not only fed my mind, but it also enriched my spirit.

Monique often read my papers and corrected my English, making sure I applied correct rules of punctuation. She also helped me learn how to do research and spent a lot of time with me in the library—so much, in fact, that some people thought Monique was my mother. But she also stepped beyond my studies to help me understand American culture.

For instance, Monique helped me understand that statements about weight and size in America are considered offensive. This was a valuable lesson to me. Unfortunately, I learned it *after* making several cultural blunders. She was willing to take a risk. I could have taken offense at her correction, but I knew she was offering insight to guide me away from social blunders. Every culture has different societal expectations, and I *wanted* to learn how to act and respond.

Monique also noticed that when I introduced myself to people, I asked their age, then noted whether I was older or younger. She gently told me that I should not make comparative references to age. I'm enormously grateful for her willingness to share these insights and others about social aspects of American culture. I tried to return the favor. She and I often talked about

Africa, and she frequently mentioned that she would like to go there someday and see where her ancestors had originated. I told her about my life, my family, and the culture she could expect.

Barbara, Monique, and others opened their lives to me. I felt safe, accepted, affirmed, respected, and loved by them. Shared areas of life drew us together as friends and as women. When we discovered cultural differences, we explored them so that we could better understand one another. The process of exploration built trust and drew us into deeper relationships bound by respect, affirmation, acceptance, kindness, and compassion. The strength of relationships like this created intercultural bonds of understanding and interdependence. These women were the mortar that cemented my college success because of the strength of our relationships.

I eventually graduated from CIEP. I received a certificate of completion. Our graduation ceremony was a huge milestone for me. I'd accomplished a challenging academic goal and was moving toward earning bachelor's and graduate degrees, fulfilling my childhood dream, and honoring my parents' sacrifices for me. Enriched by the wonderful memories and skills I gained from my CIEP years, I enrolled in regular academic courses at UNI.

Despite obstacles, I gained full admission to the University of Northern Iowa. I knew a battle lay ahead of me, but I chose a positive attitude. I could not control whether my college professors would be difficult to work with or encouraging and affirming.

However, I was certain of one thing. Choosing a positive attitude and engaging my committed work ethic would create rich soil that would nourish my success. And interdependency and committed relationships would tend that soil and nurture the positive seeds I had already planted along the way.

CHAPTER 25

CULTURAL MINEFIELDS

Courage doesn't always roar. Sometimes courage
is the little voice at the end of the day that says,
"I'll try again tomorrow."

—Mary Anne Radmacher

One fascinating aspect of living in a new culture is how easily "minefields" can throw your day, week, month, or attitude off course—*if* you give them the power to do so. Living in a new culture includes becoming a member of a new family, transitioning from city life to country life or moving from part of the country to another, going to work at a new job—or a myriad of other examples that don't involve immigration. Even getting married involves cultural adjustments on the part of both spouses. Not being prepared for these kinds of adjustments can send people's emotions reeling.

As soon as the school year started, I was bombarded with both written and unstated dorm expectations as well as unfamiliar cultural minefields of American campus life. I refer to these cultural expectations as minefields because I didn't know they existed until I stepped into one, and an unexpected consequence detonated.

I was also trying to corral academic requirements that—to me—felt like I'd chosen to ride a runaway horse. I had enjoyed my courses in health promotion and appreciated my great relationship with my academic adviser. However, when the academic office told me I was still required to complete several general education courses to graduate, I was instantly discouraged.

Just as I thought I was hitting my educational stride, I was knocked off my path. These required classes were challenging, but I dutifully enrolled in compulsory courses in humanities, music, and culture.

I was discouraged when I discovered I was required to purchase *several* textbooks for my first humanities course. I'd never known of a class that required that many textbooks. I wanted to cry at the thought of trying to master the content of several books for one class. But I remembered my mother's words: "When you hear whispers of defeat, God will give you strength to fight your way through."

My friend Louise had told me that general education courses were fun and easy. Her words had comforted me until I realized she held a distinctively different idea of what "fun" and "easy" meant. As a US-born student, she came to studies of music, art, and humanities with ingrained American cultural, historical, and experiential knowledge that I lacked.

The director of student services reached out to help me. She found that my textbooks were filled with historical names and places and technical terms from sciences and other areas of learning that defied my abilities to interpret because of my lack of American cultural background. By the time I completed my first book of required reading, my class had moved on to the second and third. What they could absorb in one week took me three weeks. For every assignment I was required to complete, I *first* needed to learn enormous amounts of historical, technical, and cultural background and context to comprehend the reading. Of course, most students already knew this information by virtue of their cultural upbringing.

The director began teaching me reading skills such as skimming, locating supporting concepts, and using headings and other graphic organizers to find core concepts and main ideas. She also summarized main ideas in words I could easily understand. Her strategy of teaching targeted reading skills increased my speaking, listening, and reading comprehension immensely. More importantly, the strategies she taught me increased my understanding in *all* my classes. But beyond that, she modeled how significantly a teacher's efforts could positively influence a student's learning and could show them they were intelligent, capable, and able to excel.

But even with the director's gracious assistance, my stress level still soared. I'd never encountered academic pressure of this type and magnitude. A high percentage of the instructional content in humanities courses is rooted in Western culture. Implications, associations, contexts, nuances, references, humor, sarcasm, examples, historical references, and events—they all eluded me. And all of these types of thinking skills required a mastery of language and more. I lived in constant terror of failure and not achieving my dream of completing my education. Pursuing education had been my parents' cherished goal for me, and it became *my* goal so I could honor them in their deaths.

Failure became unimaginable. So, it came as no surprise when I developed persistent body aches, pain in my shoulders, and began to have difficulty sleeping.

I registered for my music class, assuming it would be easy. I thought we would memorize songs and sing them, and since I had good recall skills, I wasn't concerned.

To my dismay, however, students were expected to master in-depth knowledge of composers like Mozart and Beethoven, including the ability to identify their compositions by ear. This presented an enormous problem for me—once again related to culture.

Many of my classmates had taken music lessons, participated in bands or choirs, played instruments, and "read music." Some even played multiple instruments. Music was also an enormous part of American culture, and many of my classmates had radios or other electronic devices that played their favorite music. Music was played in stores and car radios wherever I went, and it permeated American culture.

This, however, was not my childhood experience in Rwanda. Although music was part of our culture, I'd never taken music lessons or played in a band. I'd learned traditional Rwandan songs and church hymns by ear. My mind had been trained to recognize *vocal* music, not instruments, except for an occasional background guitar or drum.

Most Rwandans at that time were not surrounded by music that was broadcast from electronic devices. Nor did we hear the latest popular hits flowing from speakers in our local stores. My ears had not acclimated to the melodies, harmonies, and musical structures of songs in the Western world. I was musically illiterate in American music, just as every student in my class was musically illiterate in Rwandan music and would need education to understand the structure and context of our melodies and harmonies.

Our class was required to listen to compositions and identify the composers and instruments used in each musical piece. But I could not discriminate among the notes, much less identify which instruments were being played. I did not have the auditory/ neurological foundation that was a cultural prerequisite for this music class. My brain could not recognize patterns, tones, and harmonies that were easily identified by native-born Americans. In essence, I was being asked to interpret a language I'd never been taught. How could I possibly succeed and pass?

Frustrated and lost, I sought out the director again and explained my struggle. She listened patiently, then suggested a possible solution. She advised me to buy a compact disc player, then, immediately after each class, bring the player and the disk of music used for that class to her office. She would point out the nuances of the music and help me identify the distinctive sounds. Hopefully, with practice, my ears and brain would begin to make connections.

I was immensely grateful for the director's help, but, in practice, this teaching-learning method was enormously complicated. I sometimes felt as if I might lose my mind trying to discriminate between the many unfamiliar sounds. However, the director diligently devised new creative strategies to help me learn, and slowly but steadily, I improved.

Both her words and nonverbal communication demonstrated ongoing support. She knew how and when to implement compassion, patience, and grace and knew these components of empathy would positively influence my academic future.

Even with my director's help, I studied late each night. I cried a lot, but I also prayed continually.

When it was time to take an anthropology course, my friend and prayer partner Louise and I enrolled in the class together. By the time the course began, my ability to speak and comprehend English had significantly improved. With newfound confidence, I sat in the front of the classroom the first day, choosing a seat where I could capture every word the teacher spoke.

I never skipped a single day. I was punctual and prepared. I listened attentively. I diligently completed assignments. Nevertheless, I still struggled to understand the professor when he spoke fast, which seemed to be often. But I comforted myself with the thought that if I missed the lecture content occasionally, I could still read the textbook and learn what I needed. I told myself that this approach, combined with Louise's tutoring, would give me the tools I needed to pass the class.

And then, a new minefield.

Around midsemester, the professor told our class we would be watching a series of videos. Other students were elated, but this was not good news for me. My listening skills were not as strong as my reading skills. I was certain that trying to learn by watching videos was a surefire way for me to fail. Fighting discouragement, I gave myself a pep talk, telling myself I had overcome more difficult learning obstacles and that understanding the videos wouldn't be a problem. I only needed to pay attention and focus.

True to his word, the professor showed a video in our next class. I listened as best as I could and tried to make sense of what I heard and saw, but I had no idea what was going on during the first part of the film.

Moments later the scene shifted, and my anxiety eased. People in the video were sitting around a fire pit peeling and eating yams. I was familiar with yams! Confidence washed over me, and I rapidly began taking notes.

When I asked the professor to check the notes, I discovered I'd missed the point entirely and interpreted the scene from a Rwandan context. From then on, I studied for his class with a friend and asked questions that helped me understand cultural elements that I often missed or misinterpreted. American friends helped me interpret what I was seeing and hearing through an appropriate cultural lens. My persistence paid off, and my final grade reflected my efforts.

In further efforts to learn about my new home country and push toward independence, I also worked and volunteered. I chose activities with intentionality. For instance, I never went on vacations, shopping trips, or went to movies. Instead, I focused on my education, friends, and feeding my spiritual life by attending faith-based meetings on campus. Every activity I chose was a goal-based investment of my time. I could afford nothing less.

"It's important for me to do well in this class." I spoke softly to Louise as we sat across from each other in the noisy cafeteria. "It's a graduation requirement, and I *cannot* fail."

I clasped my hands on the table as I spoke. Louise knew my story and part of what I'd overcome. I sensed she knew that assisting me would cheer me on toward my dream.

"Of course, Clementine," she smiled back at me. "I'm happy to help you as much as I can."

Before we began study sessions together, Louise had already devised a system for helping me communicate in writing. I would tell her what I wanted to express, then she helped me communicate my thoughts in English. Unfortunately, the transition from oral to written wasn't always smooth. We often laughed when we identified the differences between what I *wanted to express* and what *actually came out* in writing. I quickly learned that laughing at my errors and learning from them was critical to a good attitude and, therefore, my success.

I was relentless, never gave up, complained, or said the work was too hard. I always tried to do what Louise asked of me, no matter what. My positive attitude provided incentive for her to keep coaching me, even though I needed a great deal of help. In return, Louis consistently blessed me with a positive attitude and grace that not only gave me a solid foundation for learning, but also fed my willingness to learn and adapt.

Later that year, Louise and I were working together when the yearbook photographer stopped by to take a picture of me to accompany a story about my experiences as a new student in America. The photographer, a young female student, also snapped a few candid shots as we worked, and the yearbook later published a picture of us giggling together—Louise with her hands over her face because she was laughing so hard. The picture summarized my relationship with her—memories colored by laughter.

I sometimes invited Louise to pray with me at a local church. Leaders had given me keys so I could pray there whenever I felt the need. Louise would seat herself next to me at a table, but soon she would hear my voice coming from the floor. I often dropped to my knees as I prayed with passion and vigor. Her partnership in prayer meant more than I could express.

I introduced Louise to African food. She loved curries, chapatis, fish, and mangos. She had never tasted African food and was grateful for an opportunity to try new, exotic dishes. I enjoyed offering hospitality. My parents had taught me to open my home to those in need, and this was part of my nature.

Louise also tagged along with me to gatherings with other African students, where she was welcomed as a friend. She was often the only white face, but she was grateful for the opportunity to be making new friends and to be immersed in another language and culture, even though she was geographically in "her own backyard," so to speak.

By the time we took a world religions class together, I was nearing graduation. I didn't need Louise's help anymore, but we still sat near each other because it just felt right. Once I graduated, I was able to begin working on my master's degree. The pressure I'd felt in my academic studies was beginning to ease. Iowa was beginning to feel like home. I was seeing the positive rewards that were the results of my hard work. Most of all, I was grateful for good friends who had embraced me, believed in me, and stood beside me to help pull me through.

Cultural minefields were only occasional surprises, and when they detonated, I found ways to navigate them with grace on my own.

My mentors—lifelong, precious friends—had taught me well.

CHAPTER 26

EYES OF EMPATHY

*The friend who can be silent with us in a moment of
despair or confusion, who can stay with us in an hour of
grief and bereavement, who can tolerate not knowing . . .
not healing, not curing . . . that is a friend who cares.*

—Henri Nouwen

"Clementine! Clementine! You must come quickly!"

I bolted upright in bed. Someone was pounding on my dorm room door. I glanced at my bedside clock. It was nearly midnight. I got up and quickly wrapped myself in a swath of red and white African fabric and threw open the door. A friend was standing in the hallway, a troubled look on her face, and I was immediately concerned.

"Sophia needs, you, Clementine," she blurted out. Vicki, a petite blonde, was Sophia's best friend from El Paso and spoke with a buttery accent I had slowly come to understand.

I prepared myself for bad news. Sophia's mother was elderly, and my first thought was that perhaps she had passed away. My mind raced as I tried to envision ways I could offer Sophia comfort in her grief if her mother had died. I knew the inconsolable anguish of suddenly losing a mother without the opportunity to say goodbye.

I silently prayed and prepared words of comfort as Vicki and I ran down the hallway to Sophia's room. As we entered, I saw tears pouring down my friend's face as she sat on her bed.

"It's terrible. Sophia's pet fish has died," Vicki announced in a solemn voice. "We need to help her prepare a funeral."

I blinked as I watched Sophia's face. Yes, her tears were genuine. Vicki was not playing a joke on me. I'd learned that Americans often develop close relationships with their pets, such as cats, dogs, and horses, but I had no context whatsoever for how to grieve the loss of a pet fish.

Or even *why* to grieve the loss of a fish.

But I stood silently and observed as I struggled to understand.

Is this some kind of college ritual?

No. Tears are pouring from Sophia's eyes. Her grief is real, and she's obviously finding comfort in Vicki's rather strange show of support.

Although I did not understand grief for a pet fish, I *did* have a context for honoring grief and honoring friends. The greatest gift we can offer those in pain is assurance that we care, that we are ready to listen, and that we will stand beside them. I needed to respect this situation with appropriate and respectful responses. I glanced around for clues on how to react, since I did not instinctively know what to do.

Sophia's eyes were red and swollen. She was obviously miserable and needed comfort. I was one of her closest friends, so comforting her was not only my responsibility, but my privilege. I took a seat next to her on the bed and placed my arm around her shoulder.

While I remained perplexed about the thought of a fish funeral, I was overwhelmingly relieved and grateful that Sophia's mother had not died. As I looked at my friend's tears, I understood that grief transcends culture. I quietly told her how sorry I was that her fish had died as I squeezed her shoulder.

Vicki suggested that we wake up two of Sophia's other friends. One was a young man from South Korea and the other was a student from Iowa. Both lived in another dormitory. I offered to stay and comfort Sophia while Vicki went to wake up the other two friends and bring them back to Sophia's room to offer their support.

As Vicki left, I asked a weeping Sophia what had happened to her fish.

"I changed the water in the tank," she sobbed, "but I forgot to close the lid. My fish must have jumped out because I found it dead on the floor . . . staring toward my bed."

Tears of regret and guilt poured from her eyes. I comforted her as best I could and offered to go with her to Walmart the next day to purchase a new fish. The idea seemed to lift her spirits, and I was grateful.

Vicki soon returned with Sophia's friends, and Sophia told the story of cleaning the tank again, with additional sobs. When she was finished, Vicki quietly announced that it was time for the funeral and to say goodbye to the fish. I was secretly a bit nervous, since I had no idea what the funeral would look like or what might be expected of me. I hoped I wouldn't be asked to speak, since I had no idea what I would say except that I was sad that a pet that Sophia cared about so much had died. But I knew that the greatest gift we can offer those in pain is the assurance that we care, that we are ready to listen, and we are standing beside them.

Vicki took the fish as I wrapped my arm around Sophia's waist. Together, we all walked to the women's restroom in our nightclothes, where Vicki flushed the fish down the toilet. Once again, I wasn't sure how to react. A beloved pet had just been flushed down a public toilet. Perhaps someone could explain this anomaly to me later. I looked to Vicki for cues to guide my instincts, as I did not know what to do.

Sophia cried even more as the echo of the swirling water bounced off the bathroom walls. We all hugged her and offered words of comfort. The next day, I took her to Walmart, and she bought several brightly colored fish to replace the one that had died. Somehow, I felt as if doing this helped her, although I didn't really understand why.

While a funeral for a pet fish confused me, I understood that the loss caused my friend grief, which made the fish funeral important to me. I would not minimize or devalue a friend's suffering. Pain is pain.

Everyone needs the comfort of friends in times of grief. The gift of compassion does not require understanding, but an open heart willing to listen. Compassion and empathy do not require a common language or culture, but only a willingness to enter into someone else's story. We grow as we learn to speak the language of compassion, and in so doing, strengthen the tapestry of the human spirit, no matter our race or culture.

CHAPTER 27

TENACITY WINS

Through perseverance many people win success
out of what seemed destined to be certain failure.

—Benjamin Disraeli

One of the most traumatic aspects of the Rwandan genocide and any war is the instantaneous and utter paradigm shift that comes with the rationalized and celebrated debasement of human dignity. In the Rwandan war, the world saw the dark side of the human heart on display as two warring powers fought for domination. And in that struggle, people like me survived by sheer tenacity, resilience, and the grace of God. Without tenacity, I would have laid in the mud and given up. Without resilience, I would have resigned to injustice and grief and refused to push past my pain.

Elizabeth Edwards stated that "Resilience is accepting your new reality, even if it's less good than the one you had before. You can fight it, you can do nothing but scream about what you've lost, or you can accept it and try to put together something that's good." This was my constant plight—facing new realities of loss—the loss of parents, loss of siblings, loss of home, loss of friends, loss of culture, loss of comfort of the familiar, loss of safety, loss of connection with my childhood memories, and so much more.

My weight of grief was so great that for months after I set foot in the US, I struggled to know how to grieve while trying to move forward toward the future. Without tenacity and resilience, I would have curled up and given up. Every day, I forced myself to take the next step toward my goal, even if that single step was minuscule. I refused to stop moving forward, knowing I would never start again.

Although some people may have seen it as a minor need, one of my biggest frustrations was my lack of any form of transportation. I understand that not owning a vehicle isn't a problem in cities with well-developed transportations systems and millions of people live comfortably without cars in large urban areas.

However, my new city did not have a highly developed city bus or transit system, and I did not know how to ride a bicycle, which would not have even provided a transportation option for me in winter. Without a car, my personal, work, and academic lives were significantly hindered every day. I was responsible to show up for classes and my on-campus job. I also belonged to both university and community organizations.

So, I asked for rides from my host family, friends, fellow students, church members, and even my professors. For years, I prayed, worked, and saved for a vehicle.

In preparation for becoming a car owner, I optimistically took a driving course. My classmates were teenagers, which I found embarrassing because I was older. Even more embarrassing was that most of them were experienced drivers.

Even though I signed up for a driving class, I had little time to practice and lacked access to a vehicle. I occasionally rented a car for a day, then searched for a friend to help me practice.

Every time I got stuck walking in a downpour confirmed my need for a car. I was tired of arriving at classes with sodden books and dripping clothing. Not to mention squishing around my classes in soaked shoes all day. Umbrellas only kept *some* of the water off my head. My legs and feet were often saturated, and on rainy days my shoes made embarrassing squeaky sounds that some students found quite amusing.

I didn't mind walking to my classes and to work, but I longed for independence. I wanted to take responsibility for myself. I disliked asking other people—no matter how kind they were—for the favor of a ride. I felt constantly indebted to people I could not repay. My need for transportation was a limitless daily need and intensely personal. And simultaneously felt as whimsical as the desire for a strawberry shake at midnight and as vital as a visit to a sick or crisis-stricken friend. A vehicle meant freedom—to go where I wanted or needed to go when I felt justified in going, without having to present a rationale or defense to anyone for my choice. This is a basic freedom and rite of passage for an adult. A car represented adulthood, autonomy, independence, and the power to choose.

One day after work and classes I walked home, my energy drained. Before I reached the edge of campus, desperation and exhaustion had overwhelmed me, and all I could think about was getting home, taking a shower, and changing out of my soggy clothes. I'd barely gone a block when I collapsed in exhaustion under a tree. In frustration, I cried out to God:

I am tired of being tired, God. I work as hard as I can and never rest. I try to be a diligent student and good employee, but I'm so tired all the time that sometimes I feel I can't go on. I'm doing everything I can. Please help me, God.

I was in agony, and tears flowed down my face. I did not know how to manage the tension, stress, and pain that wracked my body day and night.

I'm fighting a no-win war, God. I can never do enough. I'm dependent upon others to take me everywhere because I can't earn sufficient income fast enough to buy a car. I don't understand so many things about American culture, and I still struggle with English. And I've barely had time to grieve the deaths of my family and friends. It's too much! I don't even have the strength to walk home.

I sat beneath the tree as a gentle breeze stirred. My thoughts drifted, and my heart calmed as a waft brushed my face again.

Knowing that God moved the wind that refreshed me, stirred my tenacity. I stood and took one weary step, then another. I pushed away my fatigue by visualizing the day when I would own a car, finish school, and be able to help other weary souls. Thinking about my final goal always invigorated me.

So many people are tired and lonely. People are without hope and cannot see beyond their exhaustion, trials, struggles, and heartaches. May I be able to offer them hope and come to their aid, Lord. More than anything, they need You, our Great Provider.

Over the next months, I accumulated a modest amount in my bank account toward buying a reliable car. A friend had bought an older car for $400, and it ran well. He told me if I could save enough, he and his buddies would help me find and purchase a dependable car.

I was overjoyed since I'd already saved more than $400. My friend believed I could find a good vehicle at a car auction. He connected me with another friend who had experience purchasing cars, spoke English well, and was familiar with negotiating car prices. From my perspective, this was a perfect opportunity for me.

The following Saturday, my friends drove me to the auction lot, which was a field filled with rows of cars. A few minutes after we arrived, a man in a cowboy hat began the auction. He spoke so fast that I could not understand what he was saying or what participants were supposed to do. The auctioneer held up bidding amounts and moved them from lower figures to higher amounts as people bid. Once a car was bought, he moved on to another vehicle.

A black sedan with shiny tires had caught my eye. It was attractive, the right size for me, had leather seats, and was totally undamaged. My friend started the bidding at $600, and a thrill ran through me.

He's bidding on a car for me! I'll never have to walk in the rain again.

As the bidding progressed, I became mesmerized by the car's beauty and forgot that I had a bid in play. A few moments later the auctioneer announced that the car was sold, and it was mine!

My prayers had been answered, and I was finally a car owner!

I was overcome with joy. I would no longer have to rely on other people to take me places or walk again in the rain or snow. I could bless other people with rides when they needed it. I felt giddy. I would finally be independent and could contribute to the lives of people like me, who were learning and growing and becoming and moving forward.

"Miss Clementine?"

A man wearing jeans and a blue Henley shirt with the auction company name embroidered in red was standing to my left.

"If you could just follow me to the office, we can sign the purchase papers, and I can give you the keys to your new car."

My heart thrilled at the words. *My new car.* Visions of me sitting behind the wheel and driving to UNI filled my head as I followed him to the office and signed.

When I exited the office building, my friends gave me high fives to congratulate me, then insisted that I pose for a photograph sitting in the driver's seat. I beamed with pride.

I silently praised God for answering my prayer. He knew how desperately I needed this source of transportation that would grant me a new level of independence. I could not wait to get to school to begin giving my friends rides to repay the rides they'd given me.

We decided one friend would drive the car home with me, and other friends would follow us. Everything went well until we reached Highway 57 and crossed the bridge over the Cedar River. I suddenly heard engine noises. The car shuddered, and I began to feel sick. I knew something was clearly wrong with the engine.

Recognizing the problem, my friend nervously began offering suggestions.

"Pull over!"

"Turn around and go back!"

"Look for a gas station!"

"Let me drive, you're not doing it right!"

But I resolutely soldiered on until the car convulsed and died in the middle of traffic, refusing to start again. When I saw the look on my friend's face, I knew my beautiful car—my hope for freedom—had succumbed. My sweet victory had been short-lived.

Our helpers stopped behind us when we stopped, and they and my friend pushed the car to the side of the road. Tears dripped from my chin as I watched. The funds I'd worked so long to save was gone. I'd spent it on a defective car. I'd learned that Americans would call my car a "lemon." I was devastated.

Once the car was safely off the road, my friends did their best to comfort me. Someone suggested that when I saved more funds, I could get a better car. I'm sure the person who said it did not understand that his words were far from comforting. He had no idea how long and hard I had worked to pay for a car I would never drive. Once again, I'd have to depend on others for transportation, or walk to work and classes, no matter how bad the weather or how tired I was. This car had not been a luxury. I'd bought it to lift a burden, not only from my shoulders, but from those who had so graciously helped me with transportation for so long.

Now my savings was mostly gone, and my beautiful car sat at the side of the road, worthless. I was back where I'd started, except I was more exhausted, and my fund was nearly gone.

We found someone to tow the car, which took a significant portion of my precious few remaining dollars. But what was I supposed to do with a dead car? I had insufficient resources to fix it. The junkyard could use it for parts or possibly sell it for me.

This seemed like a reasonable idea. Friends took me to the junkyard to offer my car for sale, but I was hugely disappointed again when I was offered a mere $50. Then a friend who was also a mechanic told me he'd buy the car if he could pay me in small installments over time. The idea seemed reasonable, so I thanked him and accepted his offer. We towed the car to his garage, and he started working on repairs.

One month passed, then another, with no word from my mechanic friend.

When I called, he told me he'd been in the hospital and had been unable to work. He assured me he was aware of our financial arrangement and promised he'd pay me as soon as he could. He added that he'd done me a favor by taking the car off my hands. His perspective seemed understandable. It took him nearly a year to pay me half of what I'd paid for the car. Determined to be gracious, I thanked him for the payment and told him how much I appreciated him.

God does bless us through answered prayer. He also blesses us with object lessons, rather than objects, to teach us the importance of tenacity and trust. Unfortunately, some newcomers often turn to one another when they seek counsel because they do not know anyone else or how to ask. My well-intentioned friends were not well educated about assessing used car mechanics and navigating American car auctions. This experience taught me important lessons that I could later pass along to others.

I also learned important lessons in resilience. Life often knocks us down. When it does, we must get back up again and use the wisdom we gain from our defeat to move forward. No matter how discouraged I felt, I needed to press on and try again. I could not allow my mistake to stop me.

Life may have knocked me down, but tenacity, resilience, and hope, won the day. I was blessed to have parents that taught their children from the time that we were very small that failure and disappointment are part of life and part of learning process. Because of their consistent instruction and encouragement, I was soon passing along free rides, a bit of wisdom about car auctions, and advice about humility and the value of learning from our mistakes.

CHAPTER 28

FINDING LOVE IN A NEW LAND

Unless the LORD builds the house,

those who build it labor in vain.

—Psalm 127:1

When I was young, like many girls, I dreamed about the man I hoped to marry—a man I described as a gentleman. In my eyes, a gentleman protected his family, was levelheaded, loving, wise, respectful, mature, and gentle. My parents had taught me that I did not have to be wealthy to be happy—that true joy comes from our relationship with God, our family, and showing His peace and kindness to others.

While I agreed with them, I also believed that prosperity could save people from certain kinds of pain in life—for instance, by providing access to medical care and educational opportunities. So over the years, I began praying that God would bring a man into my life who shared not only my parents' values, but also desired to provide a comfortable life for his family.

I also dreamed of one day having a large wedding with many guests, but for many years after the genocide, I could not allow myself to think about marriage. I was too busy surviving, adapting to a new culture, and finishing my education to indulge in wedding dreams.

However, being engrossed in my studies couldn't halt the relentless ticking of the clock. No longer a child awaiting parental guidance. I found myself orphaned but mature enough to yearn for a castle of my own, a family to love and care for, and longing for a life partner to share the journey in sickness and health, prosperity and scarcity. I knew it was time for serious contemplation, mostly in solitude.

In this decisive moment, a myriad of emotions and questions flooded my mind, often keeping me awake as I pondered endlessly. My thoughts swarmed like a hive of bees: Who would be the suitable husband for me? How tall, how wealthy, how old, and what language would he speak? What kind of family would he come from? Would he be a fellow Rwandese or a fellow American? Yet, I couldn't ignore the issue of my own readiness for such a commitment. Was I capable of being a good wife, and did I have enough time to prepare myself for the sacred bond of marriage? How about the details of the wedding? Will I be able to enjoy a series of traditional customs in my homeland, such as *gufata irembo* (courtship), *gusaba* (bride price negotiation), the introduction ceremony, *gukwa* (dowry ceremony), *gusezerana* (exchanging of vows), or *gutwikurura* (seclusion ceremony) without the presence of my parents? Or will I remain in my new land and celebrate with my siblings and American village? There were too many questions, but at the end of it all, marriage is not for one person. It is between two people and their families and friends, after all; first things first.

On several occasions during formal and informal "meet and greet" or "meet and talk" events at the University of Northern Iowa as a graduate student, I connected with a young man from Tanzania whose name is Israel. Modestly, but with sincere curiosity, we began talking and discovered mutual interests— important mutual interests, in my opinion, like core cultural and faith values.

Over the next few weeks, Israel and I spent time getting to know one another. We studied, talked, took long walks, visited parks, and sat alongside a nearby river and lake, as well as strolled around campus. I learned that he was just a few years older than me and a man of few words. When he wasn't studying, running, or playing soccer, he enjoyed campus-based Christian groups and activities.

It wasn't long before Israel asked me to attend church with him. His invitation seemed like a possible "next step" in introducing me to his friends, as well as worshipping with him. After his friends picked him up at his apartment, they would pick me up to join them.

When the car pulled up on Sunday, Israel's friends were sitting in the front seat, and

Israel was sitting in the back. Like a perfect gentleman, he opened the door for me and helped me into the back seat.

"*Umependeza, karibu,*" he said quietly in Swahili, which means, "You look beautiful. Come in." I shyly told him "Thank you" in Swahili. I'd carefully chosen a pretty, modest dress and was carrying a small black purse. I'd also taken extra time with my hair. Israel did not say much as we drove, but I could tell he was happy to be with me. His friends in the front seat chatted as we drove.

"May I look at your Bible and hymnal?" he finally asked. I was pleased that he took the initiative to speak first. I showed him my Kinyarwanda Bible and the hymnal that I always carried to church. He flipped through the hymnal looking for familiar songs, then through the books of the Bible to see which verses I'd underlined in ink.

He's checking me out, I told myself.

I asked him to show me his Swahili Bible and paged through it looking for the verses *he* had underlined. He didn't have a hymnal, but I'd already learned that Israel loved music—especially hymns and gospel songs.

After we arrived at church, we sat together, and I noticed that Israel knew a lot of hymns we were singing by heart. I decided it was my turn to ask a question.

"How do you know so many hymns?" I asked.

Israel smiled. "I grew up in a Lutheran church, and I learned all the hymns there. I also sing in a youth choir."

I like these things about him, but I'm not going to tell him. Instead, I whispered that I had attended a Presbyterian church, and many of our hymns were the same.

I sang quietly, and he sang enthusiastically during our first service together. Later I would discover that the man who was winning my heart played the guitar and relished music. He also never complained and was content whatever his circumstances.

After the service concluded, our conversation flowed naturally, and we gently smiled on our way home as we rode next to each other in the back seat of the car.

One of our favorite places soon became an area at Prairie Lake Park, not far from the UNI campus. We would drive there and sit in the grass along the shore and watch the geese that fed on the far side of the lake. We often took our lunch and shared fresh fruit, vegetables, and sandwiches while we enjoyed one another's company. It soon became clear that we had much in common. Israel had grown up on a farm, loved to cook, and helped raise his younger siblings. Family was a top priority for him. He loved to laugh, and I loved to listen to the sound of him expressing joy.

Israel and I had grown up eating different foods, but we enjoyed cooking for one another and trying each other's cuisine. One of his favorite foods was Japanese sweet potatoes, and we looked a long time before we found them at an ethnic grocery store in our community. He also loved to visit the Amish community near us in the town of Hazleton and purchase their fresh bread, apples, vegetables, eggs, chicken, and meat.

In those simple moments, our compatibility, mutual respect, and affection for one another grew. As I observed his character and as he examined mine, slowly, we grew closer. Almost a year into our friendship, Israel invited me for walk in our favorite park. Only a few people passed us as we walked next to each other. Suddenly, Israel turned, told me he loved me and wanted to spend more time with me.

I was thrilled! I had already started to open my heart, and before I knew it, we found ourselves fully committed to each other.

Israel proposed to me on Mother's Day a little over a year after we'd met. Of course, I accepted, as my mind spun in a rush of emotions. Saying *yes* meant that everything I had ever known and learned would change. Were we prepared to stand by each other in joys and the trials life would bring? My spirit told me that Israel had not come into my life randomly and together we pressed forward.

As I joyfully planned the details of our wedding, a treasured and poignant memory washed over me time and time again. I was in high school getting ready for church on a bright Sunday morning, and as I walked through the house, I passed by my father. He was wearing his Sunday pants and slippers standing over a bowl of water as he shaved his beard, holding a mirror in one hand and carefully guiding a razor with the other. He always wore a long black mustache, neatly trimmed on the sides. Watching my father shave always made me feel safe. He and my mother maintained the rhythms of my life, and the ebb and flow of those rhythms told me that all was well in the world. As I passed him that morning, he paused and smiled.

"One of my greatest life dreams will be achieved when I stand beside you one day, Mukeshimana, in the honored position of father of the bride, as your groom asks my permission to marry you. I anticipate that day with great joy."

My father's tender words and loving expression hung in my thoughts as I prepared for my wedding. That memory was a gift—as if my father had come back to speak a blessing on our wedding and tell me that Israel would keep me safe.

Nothing could describe my fresh grief over my parents' death. My father and mother had been cruelly murdered before they could see even one of their four daughters or three sons married. They never had the opportunity to meet the men and women we would marry or embrace their grandchildren.

I would soon marry the husband whom God brought into my life. I had prayed for him and dreamed of him. Instead of focusing on my grief, I reflected on the joy my parents would have lavished on me at my wedding. I turned my thoughts to the future. My father and mother would not be at my wedding, but I felt their love and presence with me along with their blessings and a deep gratitude for Israel, who would step into life beside me as my husband. I focused on the unfolding joy in my life and walked confidently toward my future.

My parents would want my wedding to be a time of joy, so to honor them and my beloved husband, I *chose* joy.

I allowed my mind to turn to joyful thoughts of bridal gowns, flowers, ceremony details, how I would fix my hair, the jewelry I would choose, reception food, visits from much-missed family and friends, and most of all, becoming the bride of my beloved Israel. The time leading up to the wedding passed quickly, and with each passing day, I felt my parents' love and blessings.

In the days before the wedding, Israel and I practiced walking down the aisle and saying our vows, which we'd written in both English and Swahili. Our family and friends orchestrated bridal showers, decorated the church, addressed invitations, and volunteered to serve at the reception. Their participation felt like a hug from my new family, my American family.

Wedding preparations occupied my attention until the morning of the ceremony. Around ten o'clock in the morning people began flooding into the church, and in a burst of emotion, I suddenly realized that living out my most cherished dream was moments away. I was about to enter into this covenant of marriage.

Our wedding was held on a bright, cold morning in November of 2001. We chose simple, elegant decor with white pew bows, stately candle stands, and a unity candle at the front. Brilliant fall weather outside highlighted the ambience inside the church.

Extended family did my makeup, and also that of the bridal party, and I felt indulged as friends carefully applied the products to my face. I further celebrated with my first manicure in a natural shade. The bridesmaids wore stylish neon blue dresses. I walked down the center aisle wearing a spaghetti-strap wedding dress and open-toed shoes, a necklace and bracelet, and a traditional white veil. The most important thing is that I felt beautiful for my husband, and his eyes told me that he only had eyes for me, his beautiful bride.

The church had filled quickly. People had come from around the world—Africa, Canada, Europe, and across the United States. My surviving siblings and extended family members attended, along with church members, professors, college and internship friends, and people who worked with me all came together to make the day special. My brother, Zacharie, walked me down the aisle, and I could not have been prouder walking beside him.

My bridesmaids included my biological sisters, my American sister, and my childhood friend Mila, who came from the

Netherlands. Her mother Karen (who speaks my native language of Kinyarwanda) assisted our local church pastor in officiating our wedding vows. Hearing my childhood language in my marriage ceremony touched my heart deeply. Mila expressed beautiful memories of our time in Rwanda as part of the ceremony. My little sister recited a poem. A University of Northern Iowa gospel choir sang, followed with singing by the guests. My husband and I exchanged our vows, knelt, and the pastor prayed over us. According to Rwandan custom, we each retained our names, and I added Israel's, according to Tanzanian custom. The ceremony was simple but beautiful, and a lavish reception followed the ceremony. By the end of the ceremony, I was overcome with emotion. Every aspect of our wedding was saturated in significance and love. I could almost feel my parents' smiles.

Our wedding was an expression of joy, gratitude, and love between husband and wife, as well as supportive friends who had encouraged and mentored us. Nevertheless, Israel and I were still students who could not take time away from our responsibilities. I was a newlywed who had a thesis to write, and Israel needed to complete his school examinations. I spent much of our honeymoon studying and writing in my old library chair. We chose to be content in our situation and not compare our circumstances to those of people around us. Instead, we chose contentment in each other and the many simple gifts we possessed.

Our wedding was one of the most meaningful and joy-filled events of my life, but I could not help but grieve for my parents and late siblings. Journeying through dating and engagement without the counsel and encouragement of my parents had saddened me deeply. Not having my mother near to help pick out my wedding dress, talk about shoe styles and jewelry, or discuss details about the reception was an emotional void. I missed her hugs, handholds, and gentle words of wisdom. I missed her love and comfort. She would never be able to sit with me privately and teach me how to be a good wife, how to handle marriage challenges, how to raise children. She would never be a grandmother, and that was what it was. I ached for her presence many days. I yearned for my father's sweet, loving smile, assurance, a rock to lean on. I would never take my kids to see my parents! "*Ngiye iwacu*," meaning, "I am going to my parents' house" would no longer be part of my vocabulary. Nonetheless, my husband, family members, and friends surrounded us. I was embraced by many people and felt blessed.

I often looked back with joy on my wedding day. But doing so always sparks grief for the loss of my parents and siblings, who I still miss every day. Looking back at my wedding day also shows me how extremely loved I had become in America— and still am. The dearest people in my life—people of all colors and ethnicities—came to celebrate with Israel and me that day, people he and I hold in our hearts as family. We both continue to be blessed with precious friends not only near us, but around the world.

My wedding stirred new gratitude for the precious friendships I possessed and the many things in my life that the Rwandan genocide did *not* take from me. No matter the atrocities I witnessed and the suffering I endured in Rwanda, God has allowed me to seed kindness and beauty into the world and to be a catalyst for a message of resilience—even through our wedding. I feel honored and blessed that our marriage—

one between a man and a woman from two different nations, surrounded by loved ones of diverse colors and cultures from around the world—overcame the forces that defeated my nation, through the power of kindness, unity, and love.

Our wedding was my threshold for stepping into a new stage of life. I would not be defined by my losses and pain, but rather, by my faith, resilience, strength, and commitment to coming alongside those who need courage and hope. Each day held opportunity for infusing life into the world around me, and I was ready to begin.

CHAPTER 29

PAYING IT FORWARD

*Keep away from small people who try to belittle
your ambitions. Small people always do that,
but the really great make you feel that you, too,
can become great.*

—Mark Twain

I stood in my tiny kitchen drying dishes with my favorite bright red towel. I placed the forks and spoons in the drawer in front of me and slid my glasses into the upper cabinet to the left of my kitchen sink. Beside me, Mary, my dear friend dried my yellow Dollar Store plates and set them in the cupboard on her side of the sink. We'd enjoyed a lovely lunch of sandwiches, crunchy vegetables, fresh peaches, and catching up on loved ones and life. Since I'd graduated with my bachelor's degree, we hadn't had much time for visits.

With the final plates in the cupboard, we took our glasses of iced tea and headed to the comfy chairs in my tiny living room.

"I'm excited to hear about your public health seminar at Johns Hopkins after graduation and your trips to Israel and China, Clementine. Those are all huge accomplishments." Mary smiled warmly, and I glowed inside. Her friendship always fed my spirit.

"The Johns Hopkins seminar was wonderful, of course, but there were challenges," I confessed. I could be honest with Mary. She would see right through me if I wasn't. "Most of the people invited were far more qualified than I and had multiple advanced degrees and prestigious positions at well-known institutions. At first, I was intimidated." I twinged at the memory. "Then I realized it was a privilege to sit with the brilliant, experienced, and well-known people gathered there. I was among those with firsthand knowledge about world public health issues. I'd lived and worked beside people who struggled with these issues. I was also highly qualified to discuss the scenarios they were teaching about from the perspective of real-life situations and with intimate knowledge of the contexts their research was impacting." I took a sip of my tea. "Unfortunately or fortunately, life has given me experiences and insights that cannot be taught in a classroom." I put my cup down on the table beside me.

Mary nodded. "Clementine, your words are true. You were wise to attend, regardless your feelings of inadequacy. You cannot grow if you don't challenge yourself. So, who did you meet while you were there?"

I reached for one of my favorite peanut butter cookies on a plate on the table between us. Mary had always loved eating with me. "Staff from the Center for Disease Control (CDC), Johns Hopkins University's School of Public Health faculty, staff from the Red Cross's International Committee, members of the Geneva

Convention of Human Rights, as well as other organizations. At first, I was intimidated by everyone else's credentials until I recognized that I, too, possessed valuable perspectives that others could learn from. I, too, have something to share, otherwise, I would not be there."

Again, Mary nodded as she pushed the cookie plate closer toward me.

"I think you have so much to share with others, Clementine, from what you've told us in various conversations when you shared your testimony. When your dad visited the sick in the regional hospital near your home on weekends, he took you with him to carry his Bible and pray, right?"

Pictures flooded my mind as a lump formed in my throat. "Yes." My voice came out in a near whisper. "That was one of my favorite times in the week. I would hold the children's hands or help soothe them as my father prayed for them. I glanced around my apartment as I finished my cookie.

Mary set her glass on the brown garage-sale table I'd proudly purchased for my living room and smoothed her khaki skirt. "I can't stay much longer. I have a dentist appointment with Dr. Trunnell at 1:30, but I do want to hear about your overseas travels. Did you enjoy them?"

Again, her question touched me.

I swallowed against rising tears. "Mary, the word *enjoy* is not adequate. Being given the opportunity to travel to China to present at the World Federation of Public Health allowed me to contribute my ideas to the global community. This was a gift from God I will never forget. I am still humbled when I think about it."

She reached over and squeezed my hand. "And Tiberius?"

I paused a moment. "I worked with their Department of Social Work, addressing the needs of children and families through health education and promotion. My work there brought me deep satisfaction because I saw my efforts being appreciated. I learned a lot too."

As Mary hugged me goodbye, the scope of all I'd accomplished struck me. More times than my eyes could see, more purposefully than my mind could comprehend, God had spared my life and brought me to far places and opportunity I'd never dared to envision.

What could possibly be next?

I turned back to my apartment and chair, dropped to my knees, and began to pray.

I stared at the long-awaited envelope in my shaking hand. The contents would determine the course of my professional career. I could I hardly believe I was touching it. After so many years, so much sacrifice, so much effort, so many thousands of miles, so many tears, and so much loss—to be holding the hope of my future in my hand terrified me. But it also struck a chord deep in my soul.

Clementine, you were called to this, equipped to do this, created by Me to do this. Be confident, and point people to Me through the gifts I've given you.

The return address was artistically printed *New Voices Fellowship*. I took a deep breath before tearing open the envelope as I sat at our scarred kitchen table in Cedar Falls, Iowa.

With my master's degree finally completed and the new Mrs. Msengi happily settling into married life, the time seemed right to step into full-time professional employment. A colleague suggested that I apply for a fellowship, which was a new concept to me, but after investigating, I forged ahead. A fellowship could provide opportunities for me to serve refugees and newcomers to my community. My mind went back to the little girl who accompanied her father to the hospital and carried his Bible. A fellowship would mean I could finally fulfill the childhood vision planted in my heart while at my father's side.

Among the fellowships I'd discovered was the New Voices Fellowship, funded by the Ford Foundation and offered through the Academy for Educational Leadership in Washington, DC. Approximately fifteen fellowships were offered each year, so the odds of earning one was extremely small. But winning the fellowship would allow me to remain at the University of Northern Iowa, where Israel had started a doctoral program, and pioneer a human rights project.

I plunged in, submitting a proposal that targeted enhancing the health and well-being of refugees in Iowa. I was holding the response in my hand.

I slowly tore open the flap, unfolded the letter, and scanned the words.

". . . are happy to inform you . . ." I read the sentence twice, then raced into the living room to tell Israel.

The fellowship involved mentorship and training by the New Voices staff, as well as a position as the head of a refugee and immigrant outreach project at UNI. Both the recognition and the experience would be invaluable, and I had been selected among many applicants from across the United States. The realization nearly brought me to tears.

For the next two years, I worked and spoke representing refugees' needs, challenges, and unique concerns. This allowed me the privilege of listening to their stories and assuring them they were heard and understood, which required enormous time and emotional energy. Although my work came with emotional exhaustion, the people I served needed an advocate who could connect to their needs—something that came naturally for me.

On another spectrum of my job, I constantly spoke to the public about policies, procedures, budgets, and research-based presentations that were key to implementing needed community change. I felt the burden of these responsibilities, as well as vital grant writing and research.

One of my most memorable accomplishments involved co-developing a refugee and immigrant health section (RIM) within the Iowa Public Health Association. This was a memorable pioneering effort that addressed public health concerns I had observed in my childhood community and felt an emotional connection to address. I also assisted with creating booklets about issues that frequently and often dramatically impacted the quality of refugees' and immigrants' health. I also engaged in statewide research on Iowa refugee public health assessments.

This work deepened my experience in public health and opened the opportunity to give back to my community and assist people in need. I'd achieved my goal of being part of strengthening the lives and futures of people in my community and beyond. I'd grown into a community leader. I was ecstatic about the changes in the quality of lives we were seeing in refugee and immigrant populations.

I talked with refugees and immigrants and listened to their concerns about acclimating to their new community. These conversations, coupled with my experiences in these same areas, helped me create a collaborative environment where refugees, immigrants, local residents, businesses, and services could come together to address refugee and immigrant health and social needs as they attempted to assimilate into their new community.

We worked with youth and women and matched them with mentors who helped them learn activities or skills that would be most helpful to them. For instance, some were taught how to drive or how to navigate local grocery stores. Other mentees asked to learn how to use the public transit system or to set up accounts at local banks. Others needed help applying for scholarships or enrolling themselves or their children in school. As a non-English-speaking newcomer to a new community, having a local resident come alongside you and help you learn these practical skills is *immeasurably* helpful.

Our assistance was as diverse as the volunteers who offered their time and skills and the requests for teaching from our newcomers: sewing, writing résumés, shopping for winter clothes, learning to swim, enrolling children in school, learning how the American school system worked, going to the doctor, navigating American holidays and the details of their celebration, understanding the local community, and knowing what to expect at a dental or medical appointment.

In my new role, I was considered an expert in the field of refugee integration. Loaded with a new arsenal of expertise, I set out to create a uniquely hands-on organization that inspired others to similar efforts. I realized that establishing a self-sustaining organization would be a large undertaking, but I was driven by my passion to create a one-of-a-kind outreach where newcomers could learn how to integrate into a new community while receiving practical help learning to master tasks that local residents would consider routine or mundane.

I had already been assisting international students in a similar way from my apartment. For instance, I offered a cup of tea and a listening ear, encouragement, and group opportunities to laugh, share experiences, and lift spirits. However, my vision had been to launch a nonprofit that would provide more diverse, formalized, educational opportunities, as well as mentoring, to the larger community of incoming refugees, as well as individuals and families enrolled in and ESL classes.

With my New Voices Fellowship grant, my dream became a reality, and my nonprofit was born.

I balanced my computer on my lap as I sat on our living room couch. For the past several weeks I'd been conducting Internet searches on "seed money" for developing my dream organization. It was 2003, the New Voices Fellowship had ended, and I was envisioning my next goal on the horizon.

I scanned website information for a second time. A foundation called "Echoing Green" was offering funding similar to what I was seeking. The website read, "We are looking for people with ideas who want to make a change." I believed I had a great idea, and I wanted to make a difference in people's lives. My grant concept was a perfect fit for Echoing Green.

I read further. The problem, once again, was that competition for the funds was extremely fierce. Undaunted, I downloaded the grant application and quickly filled it out.

Whenever I have felt a burning passion for a cause that could bring positive changes to others, I have tenaciously forged ahead. Reaching my goal would not be easy. I was attempting to create an organization unlike any I'd ever seen. Bringing my dream to fruition would require enormous sacrifice from me, as well as my family, but developing this nonprofit would be my way of thanking my community for all they'd done for me.

For a second time, I sent off a grant application. And for a second time, I waited.

I waited through three phases of this application process. Following that, I flew to New York for a face-to-face interview. And I waited again in agony for the decision that could change my career.

Then suddenly, with the ring of the telephone, my waiting was over. I'd been awarded the fellowship to start the organization of my dreams! I was thrilled to discover that the United States recognized true visionaries and was willing to invest in untested leaders. How different the world would be if no one had dared to believe in trailblazers with new ideas or those from modest backgrounds like me. In my case, two life-changing, career-shaping fellowships directed me to leadership roles that pushed me toward my purpose.

With support from the Echoing Green Foundation, I established a board, created a development program, and managed the day-to-day operations of our new community organization. Our nonprofit mentored immigrants, hosted community-based activities, and provided a long and varied list of services. I even taught immigrants how to create their own nonprofit organizations. I was and am proud that my hard work and tenacity allowed me the privilege of becoming a role model and inspiration to others.

One of the greatest hurdles and impediments to success faced by immigrants in a new land is isolation. Enormous strength and support are required to overcome the incessant battles and seclusion created by lack of language and knowledge of a new culture. Seemingly simple tasks like learning how to shop, finding safe and comfortable housing, and accessing health care and education for children can be overwhelming—especially because *all* of these tasks, and so many more, are *critical* priorities. The purpose of my nonprofit was to help immigrants and refugees integrate into their new community, reduce their isolation, and offer them vital information and assistance for navigating daily life.

Managing the organization presented expected challenges, but I maintained a positive attitude and pressed forward. I believed I possessed valuable knowledge and experience that my fellow humans could glean from to successfully transition to their new land.

This was a time I had to muster tenacity to transition from a woman people in my community identified as a refugee, to someone recognized as a leader with the capacity to impact change. It can be difficult to alter the perceptions of those accustomed to viewing someone as an underdog, learner, or newcomer. This requires a paradigm shift and a commensurate transition in thinking. To make this change, we need clear communication, a commitment of support by community members, and mutual grace.

During this same period, I also published a cookbook titled *Everyone Is at the Table*. This book symbolized my vision for the organization: bringing people together to solve everyday problems. Our organization valued everyone, and I am proud of the legacy I was able to endow in people in my community.

After I'd invested several years in this work, my husband accepted a position as an assistant professor in Texas. In preparation for our departure, I organized volunteer appreciation luncheons, and my clients hosted a dinner. As a founder, I felt validated to see growth in my fellow new Americans as they organized the dinner. I was both humbled and grateful for the various recognitions of my work.

The organization had mentored university students by training them as interns with community professionals, which opened doors of opportunity. Our organization also promoted connection among diverse people in our area, creating relationships these students would likely never have had opportunities to make. The motto of the organization was "Bringing Cultures Together to Grow One Community," and we successfully accomplished our mission.

While achieving my goals and finding fulfillment serving my community, I discovered that innovative endeavors often come with risks, serving as seeds for lifelong lessons. Throughout this journey, I was reaffirmed by my faith and my family, all the while striving to balance my zeal for my work with the need to care for my health.

Taking moments to step back, reassess, and reflect has been crucial Self-reflection opens new opportunities for growth that may be missed when we simply do what we have done before. Thankfully, I have learned to look inward to see how my attitudes, behaviors, habits, and internal dialogue influence my interactions with the world. Was I making the changes I want to see in me? Humility? Grace? Love?

Evaluating my heart, attitudes, and choices, rather than scrutinizing my circumstances and others, has allowed me to focus on God's vision for my life in the world and has equipped me to move more confidently into my future.

The time had come for transition, as it always does. But to what, and how would I know the next right step?

CHAPTER 30

TRANSITIONS

*If you want to be relevant only in your household, then
you only need to know the things that are important
in your house, and if you want to be relevant in your
neighborhood, you need to know what's important in
your neighborhood . . . and if you want to be relevant
to the entire world, program that computer known
as your brain with all kinds of information from
everywhere in order to prepare yourself.*

—Dr. Ben Carson

During my struggle to escape Rwanda and find refuge, my life
was battered with transitions. Many came unannounced,
with gunfire, machetes, and life-threatening urgency. We
were fleeing for our lives—and if we survived—we would likely
never return.

Other transitions came slowly in the survivors' camps, as we sought solace in our shared suffering and crushing grief, in the comfort of those who had also lost what could not be replaced. We forged new bonds—not to replace the lost, but to sustain our hope through the living.

But God—the one who offers hope beyond the veil of darkness—sustained me.

Months and even years later, Iowa's leaves flamed crimson and yellow, and thoughts of winter swirled in my head. My husband, Israel, had accepted a job as an assistant professor in in Texas, which meant I would soon say goodbye to my friends and extended family in Iowa.

I turned to my dear eighty-year-old friend Marilyn for wisdom about making this enormous life transition. Marilyn was my walking partner at the local mall, and she encouraged me with her positivity, enthusiasm, and perpetual smile. When I was with her, I often thought about what life would have been like if my mother was still living. Marilyn offered to me what felt like motherly wisdom. I never felt a "generation gap" between us. Our conversations were easy, and our friendship had deepened to a level of enriching comfort and trust. She was and still is one of my dearest friends.

Over the challenging months of transition from Iowa to Texas, Marilyn often discerned my concerns before I found words for them. She offered me wisdom, encouragement, comfort, and companionship when I felt discouraged. Sometimes she cooked with me, and when she did, I felt like I'd been given a special gift.

Marilyn and I met at a mall and walked as we chatted for about forty-five minutes. But when we needed breaks, we sat on benches and indulged in deeper conversation. My friend and I never lacked for topics to explore. School responsibilities, children, and managing the nonprofit filled my life, and I valued opportunities to slow down and spend time with a friend. We shared values regarding family, faith, friendship, hard work, and integrity. I always left Marilyn encouraged and strengthened.

My dear friend didn't always tell me what I wanted to hear. Instead, she offered wisdom about the challenges and the learning curve of adapting to a new community culture. But she also lifted my spirits with reassurance and wise counsel. I felt safe talking to Marilyn about my problems and struggles because she freely spoke about her own challenges and missteps. Our spirits fed one another, and I was enriched by deep joy whenever I was with her. Marilyn's wisdom and companionship were precious gifts that eased an important transition in my life and helped me more easily reach out to others.

In the mid-2000s, Israel and I were expecting our newest addition to the family. I was elated that the Lord had blessed us with a new baby, but I knew I'd face nine months of severe morning sickness and nausea. In addition, I needed to prepare our home to be put on the market, organize for moving, and support my husband as he completed his dissertation. As a busy graduate student, father, and husband of a pregnant wife, Israel did not get much rest. We were both working hard to conquer one day at a time.

It comforted me to know that Marilyn had experienced many years of marriage and knew how it felt to be overextended and exhausted. No matter how tired I was, she always drew my focus back to the vital priorities and many blessings in my life.

The time to sell our family home neared. With the help of our new realtor, we listed our home on a Monday and had an offer by the following Wednesday. In less than a week we sold our house. We were ecstatic!

Israel was ready to begin his new job, but I didn't have much insight about how the cultures of Iowa and Texas might compare.

I'd missed east Africa's warm climate, so I was happy I'd no longer have to deal with hazardous ice, winter clothing, or blizzards. Nevertheless, I felt sad to leave the city where I'd been welcomed as a refugee, received my education, met my husband, and started married life that had blossomed to a family with four children. I knew I'd make new friends in Texas, but I also realized that making friends would take time and effort. I'd been blessed with friends who "fit" me, like a hand slipping into a glove, and I was excited to expand my network of friends in Texas to help me acclimate to the community.

But the next weeks of our transition to Texas proved to be more than challenging for this mom who was chasing three small kids and packing for a move while in her third trimester of pregnancy.

Israel flew to Texas during that summer to search for a house while I remained at home with the children. His teaching responsibilities would begin that fall at the same time that our oldest children would start school. I would be approaching the due date for our fourth child in late summer, so I would remain in Iowa until our newborn was strong enough to travel.

This plan discouraged me, but I needed to do my part. Israel would have his hands full making arrangements to get the children signed up for school while starting his university teaching job with a grueling schedule.

Our daughter was born in early August. I watched with a heavy heart as my husband packed suitcases for our three older children and prepared to drive to Texas. No matter how much I wanted to, I could not go with them. Our one-week-old baby needed a few more weeks to grow stronger before we could undertake a trip and join the rest of the family. The day Israel and the three older children pulled out of the driveway, I cried while our baby girl slept, concerned that my emotions might upset her.

I cried the next day . . . and the next. I wanted to be with my family and move into our new home together, but this was my reality and I needed to accept it. I prayed as I nursed the baby that day. Israel had always helped me care for the children, and this was the first time I had taken care of a newborn without him. From the moment our children were born, he was a supportive, hands-on father. My heart was torn and ached to be with them.

I focused on the baby and our special time bonding together. We cuddled, sang, and rocked, but she cried often. I bathed her twice a day, fed her, sang to her, rubbed lotion into her soft skin and combed her soft, curly black hair. Israel would talk to her when I called him to talk about her changes. I'd talk to the other children or hear them running around the house as they waited for our moving truck to arrive.

A few weeks later as I sat nursing the baby, the phone rang. Israel told me he was packing up the family for a hurricane evacuation. They were heeding warnings to leave early, and he assured me they would be fine and were heading north on the interstate.

I'd learned about tornadoes in Iowa, but hurricanes were a new weather phenomenon to me. Israel did not sound alarmed, so I assured him I would pray, and we hung up. Taking my cue from him, I assumed that hurricanes did not warrant concern. I'm glad that I did not know much about them, or I would certainly have worried much more.

The baby had grown stronger, and the time had come for us to head to Texas. I would not be driving to Texas alone, or even driving at all. My friend Marilyn's son Rich graciously offered to drive us to Texas, and I was extremely grateful. I'm sure he was encouraged by his mother, who wanted to support us during this time of transition. I was deeply touched by Marilyn's concern for me. The thought of driving across the country by myself with a newborn baby had exceeded my sense of adventure and common sense. I found it difficult to find words to express my thanks to Rich for his generous gift.

Rich drove while the baby and I rode in the back seat as we set out on our two-day journey to Texas. This allowed me to care for the baby and enjoy the changing terrain as we made our way southwest.

Rich and I enjoyed great conversation. Sometimes the baby would cry, and we would stop, get out of the car, and swing her in our arms to calm her. We eventually arrived in Corsicana, Texas, which is where my family had evacuated, due to the hurricane. A rush of joy flowed through me as we hugged one another and talked about their adventure over the past days. The hurricane had passed, so our family thanked Rich for his kindness, and we headed back to our new city and our new home.

I had barely unpacked when two weeks later another hurricane hit, and we evacuated again. This time we searched for hotels and motels where we could find refuge, but other evacuees had left before us, and everything was booked. The roads were jammed, making the evacuation process daunting with small children and an infant to care for. To make matters worse, our car battery died while we were in bumper-to-bumper traffic.

Recognizing our dire circumstances, we called the police and asked for help, but the chaos of the evacuation made it impossible for them to respond. Tension rose by the minute as car after car passed us and ignored Israel's pleas for assistance. Finally, a compassionate gentleman pulled his car to the side and offered a jump start.

We all possess the ability to help during chaos, but we must *choose* to act. The best of the human spirit shines most brightly in the darkness. Audacious souls are stirred to action by the plight of others. *They cannot pass by and not act.* We thanked our hero profusely, then continued north in our search to find a place to stay for the night.

Our oldest child was showing labored breathing. She had been fine before we left, but her breathing had suddenly changed, and traffic congestion made it impossible for us to get her to help. With no options, we continued driving and watched her closely.

We finally found a room in a Sheraton on the border of Texas and Arkansas in a town called Texarkana. We rushed our daughter to a hospital where she was immediately hospitalized and released after treatment. After this arduous ordeal, we drove home to Beaumont and collapsed in exhaustion.

As we drove home, I thought about the abrupt changes in our life. I was extremely thankful for the servant-hearted people God had placed in our path, as well as those God had allowed us to help. In a short span of time, we had welcomed a new baby, Israel had started a new job, we had moved to Texas, evaded two hurricanes, and our daughter had been treated for pneumonia. Several people had selflessly walked beside us—Marilyn, Rich, and the stranger who had come to our aid. We never walk through life alone, and God had given us precious opportunities to walk alongside both friends and strangers.

Change inevitably comes, and it can bring blessings or hardships. As we establish ourselves in new communities, friendships help us navigate the waters of change. Israel and I needed to move out of our comfort zones to make new friends and establish new connections in Texas. We needed to search for communities where we could contribute and find the kind of affirmation and respect I had known with Marilyn, and where we could offer that affirmation, respect, and support to others. These things would come slowly, but they would come. In times of transition, we often face both the stress of the new and the unknown, as well as opportunities to develop our strengths and rely upon our support networks.

As I leaned back in my seat, I prayed we would soon experience calm, serenity, and the reassuring rhythms of routine. I prayed that God would send me another "Marilyn" to minister to the needs of my soul, and that I could serve as "Marilyn" to someone else.

CHAPTER 31

VALENTINE AND CHOPPED PECAN MYSTERIES

*Sometimes it feels like life has buried us
in the dirt, when in reality we've been planted
with an opportunity to grow.*

—Tina Hallis

We soon settled into our new routine in Texas. Our eldest daughter's first day of school, I felt a special glow of mother's pride as I helped her get ready. She'd finished breakfast and dressed in carefully chosen blue jeans and a green sweater. My job was to fix her hair to put the final touches on her "look."

As I pulled her long, soft, curly Afro into a ponytail, I noted the curve of her cheek, the shape of her nose, the subtle smile on her lips. How much she resembled my mother! A flood of memories flooded through me—talking to my mother as she helped me get ready for school, conversations as I helped her cook, her gentle direction as she taught me how to tend the garden, and her healing touch when I was sick. Her presence had been an ever-present part of the flow of my childhood, and I knew she was watching as I helped her first granddaughter prepare for school that day. That knowledge was bittersweet. I longed for my children to know the rich heritage that flowed to them through the lives of their grandparents.

I swelled with joy for my daughter, then plummeted into sadness that my parents would never see their grandchildren. I gave my daughter a hug, asked her to be a good girl, and to do a good job at school, just as my parents had hugged me and told me each day before I went to school. Whether in Africa or America, certain threads of my family culture would always remain the same.

My new life was filled with delight as a mother, wife, educator, professional, friend, sister, and contributing member of society. I no longer perceived myself as a refugee with no hope or future. I still proudly possessed the rich heritage of a Rwanda-born woman, but was fully engaged in my community and supporting my family as any other responsible American.

However, engaging in my new community did not come without challenges.

Several months later after sending our eldest out the door, I finished preparing our youngest for school and finished up household duties. Then, I went about my errands for the day. This time, my new task was to find Valentine's Day cards for our daughter's class.

Valentine's Day was new to me. Our eldest child was introducing us to this tradition through her party at school. Valentine's Day celebrations were unknown to me when I was in Rwanda, so I was unaware how Valentine's Day would be celebrated in her school. I was also unaware what Valentine's Day cards for a child's school party would look like. In my mind, cards were cards, and the task would be simple. I would go to a store, head to the card department, and purchase a card for each child.

As the saying goes, "You don't know what you don't know." I was about to learn this.

I walked confidently into my local discount store in my black and green skirt and yellow shirt, carrying my African-made, green cloth bag. I found the section of the store designated for seasonal items, and I located a variety of colorful Valentine candies in multiple flavors, but I could not find cards. For thirty minutes or so I searched every shelf trying to find Valentine's Day cards.

To make this a positive learning experience for myself, I was making my best effort to find the cards on my own before I asked for assistance. I believed it was *important* for me to make an independent effort before asking someone for help. So I searched until I exhausted every option, then finally signaled a clerk.

"Excuse me, I'm looking for Valentine's Day cards for children. I've looked everywhere but can't seem to find them"

She smiled. "I'm so sorry. That's because you're on the wrong side of the store. You need to look in another aisle that will offer many more card options."

I thanked her as I turned and hurried toward the other aisle. Once again, I began my search, but this time I could only find large, expensive cards that didn't seem to be what the teacher had described.

Twenty of these cards would be pricey. This can't be right.

So, despite my fatigue, I kept looking. Eventually, I returned to the aisle where I'd seen the heart candies.

I'm buying boxes of heart candies. If they say "To" and "From" on them, that's close enough to being a card—for today anyway.

Of course, I knew candies were not cards, but at least my child would not show up empty-handed. Twenty boxes of candy would cost more than cards, but I was willing to pay the price so my child would not be embarrassed walking into the classroom with nothing. It was important to me that she feel included at her party, and I had done my best to purchase cards.

The simple truth is that those who live within their own culture do not recognize how unique and challenging even small tasks can be to those acclimating from a different culture. The friendship of another mother at this point in my life would have made an enormous difference for me—someone to ask everyday questions that can be so challenging to a newcomer.

While I was placing the candy boxes in my shopping cart, a woman who appeared to be a mother stepped into the aisle and began scanning shelves. I did not know her, but her body language made me feel comfortable, so I told her my predicament. She immediately led me to the cards I needed for my daughter.

By that time, it was nearly noon, and I was exhausted. My feet ached from searching the store. I was relieved and proud when I finally made it to the checkout counter. I'd accomplished my task!

Yet over and over as I'd worked to accomplish my goal, I'd yearned to talk to my mother and ask for advice. She had been an unshakable source of love, resilience, and strength for me. Each time I thought about quitting, the memory of her smile flashed through my mind, and I took the next step toward my goal. As the cashier rang up my purchase, I told myself to end my "pity party," leave my frustrations at the store, and move forward.

I didn't yet have friends to call to ask questions, and I frequently reminded myself to be grateful and not become weary over small things. But small things can and do frequently upset us, so we must *choose* to keep our perspective in balance. To help me do this, I often called old friends.

The following day, I set out to accomplish a task for our four-year-old preschooler's Valentine's Day party. This time, I was skeptical about how "easy" my errand would be. The students were having an ice cream party, and I'd signed up to bring nuts for topping. I wanted to be sure I brought the right kind, so I'd asked the teacher what type she wanted.

I thought this was a reasonable, simple question. My intent in asking was my hope to protect my child and myself from embarrassment if I chose a wildly inappropriate nut unbefitting a child's ice cream party. Fortunately, the teacher gave me specific instructions: find crushed pecans in the baking section.

Of course, her simple directions turned out to be deceptively misleading.

I approached two women in the grocery store bakery. "Can you tell me where I can find crushed pecans?" *Certainly, two professional bakers will know how to direct me to the pecans.*

The woman who was decorating a cake nodded and stepped forward as she pointed to the bakery aisle, where flour and cake mixes were sold. "I'm sure you'll find crushed pecans in that aisle," she smiled.

Naively, I set out, certain that my task would be easy, but, sadly, my pecan journey had just begun.

I confidently headed toward the aisle, but when I got there, I found an entire wall of nuts hanging in bags, as well as nuts stacked in cans.

Whole.

Halved.

Chopped.

Sliced.

Salted.

Unsalted.

Sea salted.

Skins.

No skins.

Shells.

No shells.

The number of choices overwhelmed me. I needed to choose the "right" nuts, but even among the pecans, the choices were staggering. Despite my desperation, I did not want to ask for help. I had already experienced the Valentine Card Rescue. Did I really need someone to show me the "right" pecans to place on ice cream?

I told myself I was an educated, independent woman—buying pecans could not possibly be too difficult for me. Again, I longed for my mother, my friend Marilyn, one of my sisters, or a friend to advise me about a simple question like this.

I took a deep breath and began reading packaging. I read *every* bag in search of pecans suitable to be sprinkled on ice cream. This took a long time, and I did not find a single label that stated: "Use these pecans on ice cream."

But once again, a shopper and a bit of initiative saved me. The Valentine Card Experience had taught me that if someone's face looks friendly, ask them what you need to know. If I needed help, I needed to put my pride away and ask.

A pregnant woman in a green shirt walked past me. Her face looked kind. I held out several bags of pecans and asked her which she would choose to sprinkle on ice cream.

"Is this for a party?"

"Yes. A school Valentine's Day party."

"Go to the snack section and look for nuts. They should come in a box."

I found a box of pecans and showed them to her, but she told me they had shells. I needed to buy pecans without shells. I thanked her and headed back to the snack section.

I chose three bags of "Hill Country Fare Pecans. All Natural. No Preservatives." I hoped these would work but couldn't understand how they could possibly be "wrong." Why were the kinds of nuts children placed on their ice cream so important?

I paid for my groceries and headed to my car. When I reached home, I unwound from the stress of shopping for nuts by eating lunch and preparing dinner for my family.

The next day I excitedly took the pecans to the preschool. I'd determinedly worked through the pecan dilemma until I found a solution. But when I showed the nuts to the teacher, she handed them back to me.

"Please go back to the store and return these. Go to the ice cream section and find pecans that are finely chopped for toppings."

Finely chopped? Was that the secret criteria for ice cream nuts? While I was disappointed, I was also grateful that I'd finally learned what kinds of nuts are used on ice cream. Her directions were clear, specific, and helpful. I soon returned with two cans: "Fisher Cold Nut Toppings."

I had finally conquered and learned one tiny aspect of American culture. I felt like I'd defeated a giant each time I learned something new. My self-confidence increased, which fed my sense of achievement and confidence. I called my eighty-one-year-old friend Marilyn in Iowa and told her about my new cultural successes. I explained that I was frustrated because I had to locate unfamiliar things I did not know how to find. But I also told her about the pride I felt when I achieved new goals. Her laughter, wise counsel, and encouragement, as always, stirred me to strengthen my resolve to continue to broaden my learning.

My family and I had been living in Beaumont about seven months when I applied to doctoral programs at two universities. Deciding to go back to school at this point in my life was extremely challenging because Israel was intensely involved in his teaching, and we were in the throes of parenting our four young children.

I'd always wanted to work in a position of leadership, but I was not sure how to make this happen. I applied to a doctoral program, with the hope that earning a higher degree would increase my chances of attaining a position at a university.

I'd felt powerless much of my life, and I wanted to attain a position where I was helping others. My voice had been silenced by war, violence, self-preservation, grief, profound loss, cultural challenges, identity challenges, and educational hurdles. I postulated that a terminal degree in public health would qualify me to lead a public health organization. Similarly, a degree in educational leadership would open doors for me to help educators.

The time had come for me to prepare for a higher level of responsibility where I could use my skills, experience, and education to make a difference, not just for my family, but as one of our nation's everyday men and women who work to make the world better.

This was my calling—the dream I had envisioned since I was a child.

CHAPTER 32

LIVING WITH PURPOSE

There is nothing in the world, I venture to say,
that would so effectively help one to survive even
the worst conditions as the knowledge that
there is a meaning in one's life.

—Viktor E. Frankl

m I truly here?

I sat in the doctoral office of Lamar University awaiting my interview for a graduate program in educational leadership. I'd dreamed of this day since I was a secondary school student in Rwanda. My heart had been set on earning a graduate degree and becoming a doctor in an area of study that would equip me to work directly with people.

I smiled. The young Clementine who first envisioned the dream did not know the journey would be so long and hard. Many people would walk beside me. Some sustained my spirit and others pulled me back to my feet when I was weary. Others cheered me on, and many carried me through the power of their prayers.

A friendly looking woman stepped into the outer office and called my name. I entered the interview room and took a seat across from the panelists. Over the next forty-five minutes they asked me a series of questions. The memory of my answers is dim—I honestly don't know if I answered well or not. But I had taken time to pray before the interview, and that simple act comforted me. Whatever the panelists' decision, I would graciously accept it and move forward.

Several days later, I received an envelope with the Lamar University seal. I tore it open and scanned it for the words I was praying to see.

I'd been accepted into the program, but a split second after the rush of exhilaration, reality thudded through my thoughts like a meteor hitting the ground. Graduate school would be a bigger challenge than the mountain I'd ascended as I'd escaped from Rwanda.

Common knowledge in academia is that nearly half of all graduate school students drop out of their doctoral programs before completion. (Statistics vary, depending on the program and the school.) This reality was more than intimidating, but once again, I determined that I would focus on positives, create a plan, and apply myself fully. The rest would be up to God.

At the same time that I applied to the doctoral program at Lamar, I also applied to a program in public health at another Texas university. I was still awaiting their decision when I received Lamar's acceptance letter. Ironically, soon after beginning Lamar's program, I also received an admission letter from the second university. Two graduate schools had selected me! I prayed about the choices and discussed them with my husband. In the end, I chose the EdD program at Lamar, which was closer to our home.

It didn't take long to discover the journey to a doctoral degree is grueling. The program required hours of intense reading, writing, editing, and rewriting. Before long, I felt the burden of my studies crushing me. I felt like a novice who was starting my education all over again and wondered if I would become another graduate school dropout statistic.

I was constantly exhausted and asked God for strength to endure each taxing requirement. Assignments heaped up quickly, in addition to thousands of pages of reading. As each day passed, I felt more overwhelmed. I came home from classes late at night, and my husband would hand me a plate of food as my four babies gathered around me and told me their daily stories. Their little hands massaged my head as they asked me if I was tired. They knew their newest little sibling was on the way and their mother was extra tired. Their concern—and my husband's—was very dear to me. Their love and encouragement helped me press on.

Our lovely daughter arrived during the final year of my program. I could not have asked for a better graduation gift! My pregnancy pushed me to work even harder so I could quickly complete my program and spend more quality time with our children.

For me to survive my graduate program and excel, I strategized. I used a variety of techniques to manage my studies, balance my family needs, and tend to my part-time job responsibilities. First, I talked to people who had been through the program to get an overview of requirements, as well as recommendations for vital organization and study strategies. Next, I prioritized and cut out time-consuming activities. The Bible states, "There is a time for everything and a season for every activity" (Ecclesiastes 3:1). I would return to these commitments after I completed my program.

I also began my assigned reading before classes began to get a head start. I focused, created a schedule, consulted my academic adviser, and conferred with Israel, who offered his experience as a doctoral graduate. I was fortunate to have a strong support system to provide valuable guidance.

The system I implemented can be applied to many life experiences. Do you have a dream? Listen to your heart, talk to people who've achieved their dream, and glean their recommendations and strategies. Prioritize and focus attention on your goal. Create a schedule and a plan. Consult an expert. Pray and commit your dream to God, and look for a support system.

In May of 2012, I stood in my bedroom, slipped into a specially selected suit, proudly slid my arms into my black and blue striped graduation gown, and placed a black mortarboard atop my curly hair. I stood for a moment and gazed at my image in the mirror. Dr. Msengi looked back at me.

"I did it," I whispered. "For you, Father. For you, Mother. And for our family and all that was lost to hatred. May I use the gift of my education to God's glory to sow kindness and peace back into the world."

Then I turned and joined my husband and our five children who were dressed in beautiful suits and dresses and armed with cameras to accompany me to receive my doctoral certificate.

My graduation ceremony took place in the Montagne Center on the campus of Lamar University. As I walked to the front row with fellow graduates, my heart flooded with gratitude that among those who earned doctoral degrees that day were students who were motherless, fatherless, refugees, orphans, poor, and vulnerable.

Once again, I was reminded of the absence of my parents and deceased siblings and the strength that I had drawn from them. My mother and father would have had difficulty containing their joy at the sight of their daughter receiving her doctoral degree, surrounded by her loving husband and children. Yet, I was certain that they were watching and weeping with joy.

I cannot begin to place God's limitless wisdom and sovereignty within the realm of human thinking. But I do know that He promises to bring good from evil, whether we see it in our lifetime and with our limited vision or not. I know I have been abundantly blessed in my life, and I don't have enough words to express my gratitude. Though I experienced extreme, life-changing, devastating loss that shaped me and scarred me, it also worked in my life for good by the grace of God.

For many years I believed being called "Doctor" was a privilege reserved only for the elite. But as I sat in my graduation gown, I realized I was evidence of the truth that everyday people *can* and *do* emerge from humble backgrounds and difficult circumstances, stronger and more resilient than they ever imagined, and accomplish their dreams.

As I pondered the significance of my graduation, I reflected on the past. I recognized afresh how much the Lord had done for me, and Psalm 68 came to mind. My life was proof of God's care for the fatherless and vulnerable. He cared for me and provided me the opportunity to earn a degree that few people have the privilege to pursue. But opportunity comes with responsibility, and responsibility requires initiative and resolve.

My journey had been long and arduous, and I faced many seemingly insurmountable obstacles. Common sense often told me to quit, lie down, or run. Despair often tempted me, "Why try?" Exhaustion often told me I did not have the strength. Yet another voice called to me—stronger, louder, persistent, and saturated in love.

"Mukeshimana, I called you for a purpose. I will give you strength for the next step."

Sometimes that strength came as food or refuge in the home of a stranger. Or an outstretched hand in the chaos. At times it was compassion and care. But often it came in renewed energy to take the next steps, to wait one more day, to give when all I had was spent, or to care for those who needed me.

My name was called, my dissertation chair and I stepped forward and we hugged. I was overwhelmed that for the fourth time I was walking across a graduation stage to receive a degree, this time my doctorate, the epitome of my educational aspirations.

Soon after graduation, I began looking for employment. I was offered a position as a tenured-track assistant professor in North Carolina. I was also offered a position as a visiting assistant professor at Lamar University. After several discussions and negotiation sessions, I recognized that Lamar University would become my next employer. Grateful, I was ready to roll up my sleeves and go to work. I accepted an untenured-tracked position as a visiting assistant professor at Lamar University.

I enthusiastically jumped into my first year of teaching as Dr. Clementine Msengi. As an assistant professor in a doctoral program, I loved every aspect of my job teaching educational leaders who are making a difference in children's lives and futures. Attaining the highest level of higher education gave me great joy. Teaching, mentoring, coaching, researching, and serving others invigorated me. Seeing my doctoral students graduate and receive doctorates of their own renewed my commitment to my passion.

Over my years of study, I drew encouragement from inspiring educators, and I continue their tradition as I join forces with influential individuals and organizations positively impacting our world. My position as a college professor allows me to inspire positive change in others, one life at time, as well as bring hope to the world through my students.

While my story may highlight the brutality and dark nature of humankind, it also demonstrates the strength, resilience, and compassion of our shared humanity. The resilience I developed grew from seeds planted by my parents and my Rwandan community. My parents encouraged my childhood dreams and stirred the passion to pursue my goals. They also helped me understand that amid heartbreak, evil, and loss, I could still find purpose. My community reinforced values of dignity, faith, and collective caring. Each breath I was given when my life was spared time and again was a gift to be used, not only for my benefit, but for the good of those in my sphere of influence.

We gain from our battles when we *find purpose in our pain* and *winnow wisdom from our wars*. From one moment to the next, the world tosses us from joy to agony, peace to chaos, goodness to evil, triumph to devastation. Resilience is learned in the presence of struggle. As we learn to overcome with courage and fortitude, we gain resilience. Then, forearmed with resilience, compassion, and a source of hope that compels us when we are weary, we help lift the fallen along our way.

But how do we accomplish this? Resilience is the product of discipline, determination, adaptability, and resolution in the face of adversity and problems. Resilience views challenge as part of life and problems as obstacles to be overcome. Resilience is a form of self-leadership that draws strength from within— strength that must be built. I was blessed with parents who taught me resilience in a culture that also positively contributed to this inner quality.

As we grow in resilience, so we must also grow in compassion and determination to protect the dignity of others. This requires a commitment to developing the art of listening and engaging in other people's stories. As we come to understand others—their past, their cultural heritage, their traumas—we are not only enriched, but we become equipped to engage—communicate, listen, understand, contribute—more effectively in our world.

Dear friends, our lives do not end and do not become hopeless when adversity impacts us. You may be dealing with stress, family conflict, abandonment, health crises, grief. Or you may have been shaken by the pandemic, natural disasters, inflation, or changes that have hit our nation and world. Perhaps you're concerned about the division or injustice that surrounds us. Our world will always be chaotic (because people are less than perfect), but it will also always be an inspiring creation.

Despite what's happening in our lives or in our world, *we have the power to make a difference.* Invest *your* strengths, assets, and influence to make the world a better place. Our world has always been in flux and always faced crisis. So we, too, must learn to embrace change and face challenging times with a spirit of resilience. This begins when you and I do our best to contribute kindness, compassion, empathy, generosity, grace, forgiveness, mercy, and gifts of time, talent, and treasure.

You matter. You're here for a purpose. Stretch your potential. Invest in yourself and others. Please join me in dismantling hate, promoting peace and reconciliation, celebrating kindness, lifting others up, and taking up the courageous mantle of leadership to bring positive change in our global society.

You have the power to be an agent of inspiration and influence.

In your family.

In your community.

In the world.

Your life, too, has been spared. How will you invest *your* influence?

AFTERWORD

I n 2024, upon the publication of this book, Rwanda marked thirty years since the ravages of genocide scarred the nation. In my mind, memories replay as if they happened yesterday.

I often reflect on the lives of almost one million people who died during a three-month killing spree that tore across Rwanda with the ferocity of a rabid animal. Visible and invisible scars of the genocide remain today. The enduring scars of the genocide, both visible and invisible, persist to this day, leaving a deep void in the lives of those affected by it.

These barbaric acts ended in July of 1994, when the RPF captured the country.

Rwanda was decimated by the sheer numbers of deaths and people left as refugees. Some leaders have apologized for the roles they played or for apathy that equaled consent. An apology letter from the Pope and an apology statement from the Presbyterian Church denomination I grew up in are included in the *Study Guide*.

Before 1994, Rwanda was known as a nation without orphanages (BBC News, 2015, see https://www.bbc.com/news/world-africa-31830220). Out of their deeply rooted commitment to care for those in need, neighbors took in other people's children as part of Rwandan culture. But the war almost instantly turned Rwanda into a nation of orphans, both figuratively and literally.

Those of us who were scattered abroad looked back at our homeland with ravaged hearts as the face of our native country shifted, even as we struggled to acclimate to new cultures. With this knowledge came choice—the choice to try to re-create the past or to move purposefully into the future.

Today, my parents' property sits vacant in Rwanda, but I am glad it is currently benefiting the neighbors, until we are able to construct a memorable structure in honor of our parents and siblings, whom we will never forget.

The ache in my heart for my father, my mother, and my deceased siblings remains. I am who I am today because of all they were and are to me. I will always grieve their loss, but their influence lives on through their legacy in me.

Although I haven't had the opportunity to visit Rwanda for nearly three decades, what I read and hear reflects a tale of remarkable resilience and optimism. Once a land covered in blood with bodies floating in rivers, it is now known among the cleanest countries in Africa. This transformation is an incredible story of the nation's resilience, marked by significant reconstruction effort that have restored hope and fostered unity, transcending the boundaries of ethnic divisions.

Today I live with a keen awareness that our every word and every act sets in motion endless effects. We have the power to give life or to destroy through the influence of our words, attitudes, and actions. I believe I was spared for a purpose—to seed life-giving hope, purpose, and vision into the lives of the weak, broken, and hopeless I meet while I am still on this planet.

May you use your strength, resilience, and the lessons learned from what you've overcome to encourage others that true strength is never given but earned. Our courage is often the strength needed by another, and in kindness, forgiveness, and service to others, we find meaning in our pain.

ACKNOWLEDGMENTS

As I reflect on my life, gratitude fills my heart. First and foremost, thanks and glory be to God, my Creator, the giver of life, and my protector. This book is my testimony of how God protected me from harm and gave me the strength to keep moving. This story would not exist without the sacrifice, support, and love of many people. I thank every person who has played a positive role in my life.

To my dearest husband, children, and siblings: I am deeply thankful for the love and support that each of you brings to my life every day.

To my beloved extended family: Our connections transcend tribal affiliations, races, ethnicities, and geographical borders, embodying the true essence of family: The in-laws, The Carlsons, the McMahons, the Robinsons, the Krumms, the Jensens, and other extended families. I am grateful for you!

I would like to express my deepest gratitude to United States Senator Chuck E. Grassley: Your critical role and support have made a significant impact on my life. Today, I am a proud to call the United States of America, my home.

To my teachers, mentors, academic advisors, and professors: You have played an important role in my personal and professional growth, making the journey of learning truly enjoyable and safe. Special appreciation goes to Samuel Musabyimana, my secondary school teacher, and to the following professors at the University of Northern Iowa: Dr. Tom Davis, Dr. Sue Mattison, Dr. Dennis Cryer, Dr. Michelle Yehieli, Dr. Karen Agee, Jackie Preston, and Dr. Susan Koch. I also extend my appreciation to the faculty at Lamar University Center for Doctoral Studies in Educational Leadership for your support during my educational journey towards earning a doctoral degree.

To my friends, classmates, and colleagues wherever you are: Thank you for your friendship and collegiality.

To the Echoing Green and Ford Foundations: Thanks for believing in me and supporting my vision.

To my faith community: May the Lord bless you for your ministries, encouragement, prayer, and fellowship. In moments of weariness, I sought solace in quiet places where I could spend peaceful time with God. Special thanks to the churches that opened their doors for me and even provided keys when I needed access. I am deeply grateful for the opportunities to have spent time in your chapels, at your altars, and in your prayer rooms to converse with God.

To my editorial team, reviewers, special counsel, and encouragers: While writing this book, there have been several individuals who encouraged me, generously shared their expertise and experiences, diligently reviewed and edited, provided valuable feedback, assisted with fact-checking, and answered my questions: Shelly Beach, Dr. Steve Murdock, Dr. Sandra Harris, Dr. Sue Mattison, Les Hewitt, Claude Munyezamu, Tess Weitzner, Dr. Dale Taylor, Dr. Carol Bunch Davis, Dr. Maria Keckler, Denise McVea, Mary Robinson, Deena Gregory, Dawn Wheat, Vijay Shah, Dave Furneaux, Stephanie Larson, Jill and Jerry Carlson, Amy Raker, Donnella Looger, Grant Faulkener, Karim Abouelnaga, Pastor Jones, Roberta Hiner, Karen Menke, Dr. Katherine Sprott, Dr. Roslin Growe, Lara Galinsky, Dr. Brenda Marina, Dr. Ezella McPherson, Dr. Grace Lartey, Helena Gawu, Linda Tait, Toni Payley, Trudi Redman, Celeste Davis, Teresa Lynne, Dorothy Featherling, Casey Ford, Dr. Robin Latimer, Robert Minix, Rebecca Deng, Pastor Haas, Laurie Stawicki, Charlotte Rady, Cynthia Ruchti, Gretchel Dixon, Linda Baer-Austin, The Hughes, and The Rathgebers. To each and every one of you, I thank you.

To my esteemed publisher, Tim Beals and the entire dedicated team: Thank you for your diligent work in bringing *Spared* into the hands of readers.

I thank everyone who has confided in me, shared your heaviest burdens with, and allowed me to serve you in different capacities. Through you, I have been able to fulfill my God-given purpose. I thank you for joining me as I live out that purpose.

Finally, I would like to convey my deepest and sincere gratitude to two extraordinary women in my life, Mary and Margaret, for the life-changing gift.

My prayer for you all is found is Numbers 6:24 (ESV): "The LORD bless you and keep you."

Made in the USA
Monee, IL
28 March 2024

55882902R00203